THE FUTURE OF GOVERNANCE

This book offers a radically different introduction to law, one that reflects the challenges and opportunities presented by the rapid technological developments of our time.

Traditionally, law has been about historic principles and rules and their application to a particular set of facts; and courts, judges, and disputes have been central to the legal enterprise. Against this approach, this book highlights four radical and revisionist ideas: by bringing modern technologies into the foreground; by presenting law as one particular mode of governance in a larger picture of governance that now includes technological modalities; by insisting that we have to think outside the traditional doctrinal box to engage with a broad range of governance questions; and by emphasising that human communities cannot flourish without good governance to which both lawyers and law are central. These four radical threads are woven into a discussion of the modern landscape of law, and together they offer a distinctly contemporary contribution to the quest for good governance. The challenge for lawyers now, the book maintains, is to contribute to thinking, both locally and globally, about how we take advantage of the opportunities presented by the newest technology, without compromising the essential conditions for human life and co-existence, and without losing what we value in law's governance.

This book is aimed at students who are studying law at university and legal academics, and others, interested in the current and future impact of technology on law.

Roger Brownsword is Professor in Law at King's College London, UK, and at Bournemouth University, UK. He is Honorary Professor at Sheffield University, UK, and Visiting Professor at City University Hong Kong.

THE FUTURE OF GOVERNANCE

A Radical Introduction to Law

Roger Brownsword

a GlassHouse Book

Designed cover image: johnason / iStock / Getty Image Plus

First published 2025
by Routledge
4 Park Square, Milton Park, Abingdon, Oxon OX14 4RN

and by Routledge
605 Third Avenue, New York, NY 10158

Routledge is an imprint of the Taylor & Francis Group, an informa business

A GlassHouse book

© 2025 Roger Brownsword

The right of Roger Brownsword to be identified as author of this work has been asserted in accordance with sections 77 and 78 of the Copyright, Designs and Patents Act 1988.

All rights reserved. No part of this book may be reprinted or reproduced or utilised in any form or by any electronic, mechanical, or other means, now known or hereafter invented, including photocopying and recording, or in any information storage or retrieval system, without permission in writing from the publishers.

Trademark notice: Product or corporate names may be trademarks or registered trademarks, and are used only for identification and explanation without intent to infringe.

British Library Cataloguing-in-Publication Data
A catalogue record for this book is available from the British Library

ISBN: 9781032831084 (hbk)
ISBN: 9781032831060 (pbk)
ISBN: 9781003507802 (ebk)

DOI: 10.4324/9781003507802

Typeset in Sabon
by Deanta Global Publishing Services, Chennai, India

CONTENTS

PREFACE

There are already many books that serve as introductions to law—as introductions for those readers who are either contemplating studying law at degree level or who have recently commenced their undergraduate law programmes, but also for readers who simply have a general interest in, and curiosity about, the law. In their own way, these books will serve their readers well; and, given the range of introductory books on offer, it might be thought that there is little or no space for another introduction to law. Indeed, in my own case, it might also be objected that, having already written one widely used introduction to law (namely, *Understanding Law*, which I co-authored through four editions, from 1992 to 2006, with my colleague John Adams), I surely do not need another bite at this cherry.

In response to these reservations, I could simply say that, in 2024, we are in a different place to where we were in the early 1990s when I co-authored the first edition of *Understanding Law*, and that we need to reflect this in our introductions to law. However, a fair question would be whether this justifies anything more than some light-touch revision and updating to existing introductions. Arguably not. When I sat down at my desk one wet Monday morning in April 1990 to draft the opening paragraphs of *Understanding Law*, the news headlines from the weekend were about poll-tax protesters clashing with the police in London and a rooftop occupation by several hundred inmates at Strangeways prison in Manchester. Although the headlines today are not about poll-tax protests in London and prison conditions in Manchester, we are still critical of the performance of the police and of the conditions in prisons; and, in the bigger picture, we still see law and its authority as being challenged. So, although 2024 is not 1990, just how different is the place that we are in today?

The reason that we are now in a very different place is not because the challenges to law's governance that were salient in the 1990s have gone away; they remain. Rather, it is because a raft of emerging technologies has created new challenges for law and, at the same time, presented new tools and new options for the provision of legal services as well as for the way that we govern. The headlines today are about our digital world, about the urgent need to ensure that online environments are safe spaces (especially for young persons) and to regulate artificial intelligence (AI) before it rips out of our control and destroys humanity. Tomorrow, the headlines might be about a biotechnological breakthrough, or about robotics, or about neurotechnologies, and so on…who knows? As these technologies sweep across the world, they present similar challenges to law's governance in all places. It follows that, although an introduction to law will have its own local reference points (in a particular legal system), its horizons need to be global.

However, as I have said, these new technologies are not only about challenges for law's governance but also about tools that can now be employed by lawyers and by those who have governance responsibilities. Traditionally, the legal enterprise has relied on rules, made by humans for humans; and, where there have been disputes, human arbitrators, juries, and judges have been called on to establish the facts and to apply the legal rules. Not surprisingly, this enterprise has its discontents. Wherever we look, law's governance is imperfect. Humans continue to break the rules; legal officials can be corrupt or captured; and, the rules themselves are often open to interpretation. To the extent that we can automate law's governance, taking imperfect humans out of the loop, should we do so? To the extent that the provision of legal services can be automated (by the use of LegalTech), should we do so? How acceptable would this be? And, to the extent that, by using technological management, we can design the places and spaces in which humans act as well as the products that they use in such a way that we no longer need rules, should we do so? But, we might wonder, would such perfect control be utopian or would it prove to be dystopian?

In 1990, these questions, which are now right in the spotlight—for students of law, for lawyers in practice, and for those who simply have an interest in law—were simply not on the agenda. That is why we are in a different place; that is why we need to think outside the traditional introductory box; and that is why, in 2024, we need a radically different introduction to law.

Roger Brownsword
Bournemouth, March 2024

1

INTRODUCING LAW

Introduction

In our multi-media age, how should an introduction to law be presented? Should it be in the form of a book, a film, a Ted Talk, a YouTube clip, or perhaps a visit to a court? And, if it is a book, how should it be produced: a hand-written manuscript belongs to another age but, in our digital world, should we perhaps ask ChatGPT to generate an introductory text for us?

To the extent that it is books that have traditionally been the medium of choice, and to the extent that the medium is the message, the choice of a book (even an e-book) might suggest a somewhat traditional introductory account. Let me nip any such thought in the bud: while the medium might be traditional, the message in this book is anything but that. This is no traditional introduction to law.

That said, I can claim to be the originator of the text; while I have used word-processing tools, I have not relied on any generative artificial intelligence (AI) tools. Even as the book is in press, this might seem very old-style. Already, in some quarters, it might be commonplace to use AI tools to generate drafts and to write portions of the text. Already, in a report from a parliamentary committee on the governance of AI (House of Commons Science, Innovation and Technology Committee, 2023), we read that one paragraph of the text was drafted by an AI tool (the committee wanting to illustrate the capability of the tool). Already, conventions are being drafted about the appropriate use of Chat GPT and about the declarations to be made where such tools have been used. At the time of writing, though, I need only repeat that I have not used such tools and that this book is my own work.

DOI: 10.4324/9781003507802-1

The purpose of this book, which is in six parts, is to present a radically different introduction to law—radically different in highlighting the importance of technology for law, in proposing that we think about law as just one kind of governance, in encouraging thinking that goes outside the box of traditional doctrinal legal training, and in painting law and lawyers in a much more favourable light than is customary.

Radical threads

The first part of the book, much of which is autobiographical, introduces four radical threads that are woven into this book. Each thread represents a contrast between the way we thought about law and were taught 'to think like lawyers' back in the 1960s when I was a law student and the way we should think about such matters today.

Back in the day, before embarking on my legal studies, I was warned that this would be a poor use of my undergraduate years because law and law degrees were not about becoming a civilised person; and, sure enough, I soon discovered that training young people to think like lawyers demanded that they be kept focused very firmly on the law and nothing but the law. In this way, we were trained to think inside a particular box within which we would be able to advise on the legal position in relation to some set of facts but to the exclusion of any questions arising outside the box—such as the question of whether laws actually 'worked', or whether legal institutions were fit for purpose, or what precisely law's governance might contribute to civilised life, and whether a justifiable case could be made for respecting the law. Furthermore, although this did not strike me as odd at the time, technology was simply not on our legal radar: law was one thing and technology was something quite different, neither relevant nor significant for lawyers.

In counterpoint to these characteristics, this introduction brings modern technologies into the foreground; it presents law as one particular mode of governance in a larger picture of governance that now includes technological modalities; it insists that we have to think outside the traditional doctrinal box to engage with a broad range of governance questions; and, perhaps above all, it emphasises that human communities cannot flourish without good governance and that both lawyers and law are central to this civilising enterprise.

The landscape of law

In the second part of the book, we walk through the landscape of law, pausing at traditional sites such as the interpretation of statutes, the handling of precedents, and the development of the case-law, but viewing it all through a radical lens. One of the central points is that we now have to appreciate that there are three dimensions to thinking like a lawyer. So, if we are asked, say, 'As a lawyer, what do you make of the Metaverse?', our initial response should be that this depends on what we mean by 'thinking like a lawyer'. If we think in a traditional legal way (in a Law 1.0 mode), then we will expect that the use of virtual environments such as the Metaverse will present a number of novel questions about the application of traditional legal principles (which were not designed for high-tech contexts). The challenge will be to make use of the flexibility of legal principles but without compromising the integrity of legal doctrine. However, as a lawyer, we might be thinking in a more regulatory way (in a Law 2.0 mode), in which case we will see the Metaverse, rather like the Internet, as a space that rapidly develops a life of its own and that might well present risks that have not been anticipated. Here, the challenge is not so much to stretch traditional legal principles in response to these risks but to articulate agile and bespoke regulatory frameworks that are fit for purpose. Until quite recently, these two modes of legal engagement would have been the only ones but, nowadays, we also have to reckon with a more technological approach to governance (Law 3.0). Like Law 2.0 thinking, Law 3.0 will engage with the Metaverse in a regulatory way but, distinctively, its focus will be on the use of new technological tools, alongside (or even in place) of rules, to do the regulatory work. So, just as those who control the Metaverse platforms will be in a position to design the virtual environment in a way that governs what is and is not possible, law's governance of the Metaverse might rely on both rules and tools to do the regulatory work; and, furthermore, those who have general governance responsibilities might treat the Metaverse as a tool that facilitates smarter technological governance in the real world.

Key concepts

The third part of the book highlights a number of key concepts. It starts with the concept of law itself, a concept that has been intensely debated in traditional jurisprudential circles. However, once we apply our radical approach to place law within the larger field of governance, we appreciate that the question of how we conceive of law is somewhat narrow. Why should we, as lawyers who now have an interest in governance in general, focus so much attention on the particular mode of governance that is represented by law? In the bigger picture of governance, it is not so much the defining features of law that matter as the contrast between modes of governance which, like law, rely on humans and rules and those which turn to technology to reduce (or even to eliminate) human involvement in governance and reliance on directions given by rules. So, as we work through the organising concepts of traditional thinking about law and legal systems, two radical thoughts recur: one is that these concepts and classifications have been disrupted by technological developments; and, the other is that the larger world of governance has moved on. In a sense, it is akin to finding that the classifications traditionally employed by bookshops have been disrupted by a stream of books about new technologies, and then to find that the world of retailing has moved on—that customers are migrating to online bookstores and that brick-and-mortar bookshops are no longer sustainable.

One of the central points in the third part of the book is that the concepts that give traditional legal principles and regulatory standards their flexibility—particularly concepts such as reasonableness and proportionality—lack a compelling anchoring point. Relative to whose or which view of reasonableness or proportionality do these concepts and principles operate? Where do we find the foundations for our conceptual frameworks, for our values and, indeed, for governance by law?

Values

In the fourth part of the book, which highlights a number of prominent values in the human enterprise of governance—not only law's governance but also in ethics—the quest for foundations for our judgments is a recurring challenge. In practice, values such as human rights and human dignity, privacy, justice, and so on are contested both within and between communities. For example, in the recent jurisprudence of the US Supreme Court, no decision has been more controversial than that in *Dobbs v Jackson Women's Health Organization* (2022) (www.supremecourt.gov/opinions/21pdf/19-1392_6j37.pdf), in which the majority held that there was no privacy-grounded constitutional right to reproductive choice and that it was for the states to set their own laws in relation to the terms and conditions for lawful abortions. While this decision provoked a furious backlash by the pro-choice lobby who see the ruling as an assault on women's rights in particular but also on human rights more generally, it assuaged the concerns of the pro-life lobby for whom human dignity demands respect for unborn human life. But, which were the right values for law to be supporting and why?

Meeting this question head-on, it is argued in this part of the book that we cannot find a compelling anchoring point for our values within our own communities; that, to find foundations for our values, we need to think beyond this box; and, that the anchoring point we are looking for is found in the conditions that make it possible for humans to exist and co-exist on planet Earth, to form their own communities with their own schemes of governance, and to develop the capacity for free and informed self-direction and moral agency. Although this is not one of the four radical threads of the introduction, it is a radical approach to a debate that tends to set dogmatic fundamentalists against out-and-out moral relativists. Whereas the former take their own beliefs, whether religious or secular, to be self-evidently right for everyone and think that there must be something wrong with humans who do not see things their way, the latter hold that, while we can have reasoned debates within our own communities relative to the fundamental values that we recognise and accept, we cannot give compelling reasons to recognise and accept those particular values as categorically binding. By contrast, the radical position staked out in the book follows the relativists in holding that we do not have compelling grounds for the values that are distinctive in our community (and, to this extent, pluralism is accepted) but it departs from relativism in holding that we can nevertheless find rationally compelling foundations in the conditions of possibility that stand outside our communities (and on which our communities stand). On the other hand, this foundationalism for humans (who cannot coherently deny the conditions for their own possible existence) is very different from the fundamentalism that finds foundations in personal faith and belief and that denies the acceptability of pluralism.

Challenges to law's imperfect governance

This takes us to the fifth part of the book in which we consider the challenges to law's imperfect governance, and then the impact of new technologies on the discontent that we might already have with law.

Long before technologies enter the picture, we can see plenty of reasons for, so to speak, good old-fashioned discontent with law's governance. First and foremost, law is a human enterprise; it might appeal to the best in humans but it leaves itself open to the worst in humans. Secondly, law's governance relies on rules which might not only be open to interpretation but also wide open to practical opportunities for non-compliance. Thirdly, as communities become more heterogeneous, what members want and expect from the law will reflect a variety of preferences, priorities, and principles such that it is simply not possible for law to satisfy everyone.

And, then, technology does enter the scene, disrupting economies and social practices and producing a churn that is immediately problematic for law. Even if law's promise is modest, simply to instate and maintain 'order', the tensions and turbulence associated with technological revolutions mean that law faces more than one challenge. In particular, there is the challenge of managing the transition from one order to another (the challenge of supporting innovation and the desired movement towards a new order without disappointing the expectations of those who have vested interests in the old order); there is the challenge of keeping governance sufficiently nimble and adaptive in the face of rapidly developing technologies (and doing this without losing the predictability and consistency of order); and there is the challenge of plurality (the challenge of instating an order that responds to those who view governance as over-regulatory and unfavourable to innovation as well as to those who view it as over-permissive and under-regulatory in exposing members to unacceptable risks).

That said, at the same time that technologies add to the challenges faced by law, they might also offer new tools for governance—whether tools for surveillance, identification, locating, profiling, risk-assessing, resource-directing, and so on—which promise to improve compliance with the rules and the detection of those who do not comply. Moreover, by automating legal processes, taking humans out of the governance loop, it might be possible to eliminate many of the failings that we find with old-fashioned law; and, it might also be possible to reduce reliance on guidance by rules if, instead, governance focuses on the architecture and design of the places and spaces in which humans act and the products and services that they use. It is one thing, for instance, to issue a rule that directs motorists to observe the speed limits but imagine governance that, in the future, does not rely on rules for human drivers but simply controls the design of vehicles in such a way that safety is guaranteed—with autonomous vehicles already on the roads, that is a future that is not so far away.

Lawyers and legal services

In the sixth part of the book, we consider the popular view of lawyers and of the services they provide. While the UK Supreme Court has some good reviews on Tripadvisor (see, www.tripadvisor.co.uk/ShowUserReviews-g186338-d1891869-r320784287-The_UK_Supreme_Court-London_England.html), we would expect the reviews of lawyers and of legal services generally to be much less positive. No doubt, lawyers could do more to improve their reputation with the public but, if this is to be really turned around, it needs to be understood that lawyers can and should make a major contribution to civilised community life.

As for improved provision of legal services, there needs to be a smart approach that thinks outside the box and makes appropriate use of new tools. Traditionally, access to legal advice and assistance, and to the courts, has been limited by cost; and, limited access to justice has been compounded by delay and procedural complexity. On the face of it, smart tools and automated processes can eliminate much of these traditional shortcomings in law's governance. However, each community needs to make its own choices about a more technological approach to the delivery of legal services. In some places, having a human in the loop might still be a priority; in other cases, communities will have no reservations about reliance on new tools. We are on a new learning curve and we all need to smarten up so that we know what works and what does not work, what is acceptable and not acceptable, and which institutional arrangements best promote governance that combines rules with tools.

In a couple of concluding chapters, the four radical threads of this introduction are revisited, and some short reflections are offered on the human quest for good governance. We have come a long way from thinking that law, as traditionally understood and practised, epitomises good governance. Today, technology is at least part of the solution to our discontent with law's governance. The challenge for lawyers now is to contribute to thinking, both locally and globally, about how we take advantage of the opportunities presented by the newest tools without compromising the essential conditions for human life and co-existence and without losing what we value in law's governance and in our own communities.

PART 1
A radical introduction

2

FOUR RADICAL THREADS

Introduction

This chapter introduces four radical threads that are woven into this text. As has already been indicated, these are threads that place law within the larger frame of governance, that highlight the relevance of technology for lawyers and for the legal enterprise, that do not de-centre the importance of thinking like a lawyer but which encourage thinking outside the traditional doctrinal box, and that advertise the potentially civilising effect of law's governance. However, before we speak to these threads, we can start with the kind of sketch of law that might open a traditional introduction to law.

The standard sketch of law

Where the sketch of law is traditional then, assuming a little prior knowledge, the standard introduction runs along the following lines. In each country, we will find a legal system and national laws. Like languages, laws and legal systems belong to 'families', primarily, the civil law and the common law families. Historically, in the civil law systems (such as the legal systems in France, Germany, Italy, and Spain), the general principles of law were (and still are) set out in Codes; by contrast, in the common law systems (such as the legal systems in the UK, Australia, Canada, and the US) the rules and principles of the law are found in the cases (the precedents).

While the judges—particularly the judges in the common law systems—have played a central role in the development of the law, nowadays, most of the laws are made by legislative assemblies—by Parliament in the UK, by Congress in the US, and by the Bundestag in Germany, and so on. In this

DOI: 10.4324/9781003507802-3

sense, the centre of gravity of law-making has moved from the judicial to the political branch.

There is more than one way of classifying the laws that are made but, broadly speaking, laws are either 'public' (concerning the relationship between the State and citizens) or 'private' (concerning the relationship between citizens). In these terms, constitutional and administrative law as well as criminal law are 'public'; and contract, tort, and property law are examples of 'private' law. Where disputes arise in relation to matters of either public or private law, legal practitioners (solicitors and barristers in the UK) will advise and assist parties, and, in some cases, represent them in court proceedings where decisions will be made by judges (occasionally with the assistance of juries). Other than mentioning that, beyond national law, there is also a body of international law that largely comprises rules and principles that have been agreed by states in treaties and conventions, the initial sketch is complete.

Given this picture of law, we might think that it does not matter too much where one starts because, by the end of the introduction, the main features of law—its rules, its institutions, its practitioners, and its practice—will have been covered. Moreover, the assumption is that, although law has a long history, its practices are *relatively* timeless. Hence, no matter how the law is introduced in the 2020s, the basic sketch will be much the same as it was in the 1960s when I was an undergraduate law student at the London School of Economics (the LSE). No matter how we approach it, the law, being relatively stable and its culture being conservative, will look much the same as it is introduced to one generation of law students after another.

Yet, nothing could be further from the truth: the law does not stand still; in times of technological disruption, it cannot stand still; and, the way in which both law students and legal practitioners go about their work today is conspicuously different to the way which they went about it back in the day (for legal practitioners, see the Legal Services Board's report on its 2022 survey of legal service providers; available at https://legalservicesboard.org.uk/wp-content/uploads/2023/06/20230425-Tech-and-Innov-survey-2022-Designed.pdf). Granted, the core of the undergraduate law curriculum in the 2020s might not be too different to that in the 1960s (other than updating the relevant legal rules and provisions) but pretty much everything else about and around the law has changed and is continuing to change.

Law through a student's eyes

To focus on the experience of law students, in my day, a key event in the induction week for new students was the tour of the Law Library. This was a 'must attend' event because, as all law students were quickly to learn, the Law Library was their laboratory. There, we students were introduced to the main sources of law—to the statutes (Acts of Parliament) and statutory instruments, and to the cases—as well as to the principal law reviews and journals in which we would find articles and commentaries on the legislation and the cases. Relative to the law school's mission, which was to train students to think and reason like lawyers, the law library was the physical 'box' in which we would undertake our studies, and the materials to which we were guided in the library formed the intellectual box that would confine and define the scope and nature of our reasoning. Thinking like lawyers, we would know where to find the law and how to apply it so that we could summarise the legal position on any given set of facts.

Without the benefit of the introductory tour of the library, finding a particular legal document, such as a statute or a case report, would have been a bit like looking for a needle in a haystack. With the benefit of the tour, students had a general sense of the geography of the library. However, to further familiarise students with the materials and their location in the library, there would often be a 'finding exercise', a kind of paperchase in the law library. For example, students might have been asked to find the case of *Donoghue v Stevenson*—which, without more, would still be a needle in a haystack—but also advised that they would find this case at '[1932] AC 562'. This would steer students towards a particular series of law reports, Appeal Cases (AC); it would tell students to look for the volume with the reports for 1932 (the reports being shelved chronologically); and then turn to page 562. Success! Sure enough, at page 562 of that volume, students would find the report of the case in question and, if they read on, they would find a legendary judgment given by Lord Atkin.

Having found the law library, and having begun to familiarise themselves with the location of the most relevant materials, law students of my time were up and running. From here on, they perhaps thought that, although they faced three years of hard work, it should all be relatively straightforward. Law is not rocket science and the materials were all there in the law library. But, no such luck: during my undergraduate years, there was a serious problem with pressure on law library resources. Both books and seats were in short supply for an expanding population of undergraduate law students.

At the LSE, as in other UK law schools of that time, law students followed a common programme of study through their first two years. For the student cohorts of that era, the most serious pressure point was in relation to accessing the prescribed law review reading for upcoming weekly tutorials. Imagine the best part of 100 students all wanting to read a couple of articles in, say, the *Criminal Law Review*. Students resorted to self-help: enterprising students were able to find what they wanted in other law libraries; similarly, students with the right connections were able to access the materials; but, the pressure on the law reviews encouraged some practices that were less than model.

In retrospect, I assume that law librarians were caught on the hop by a burgeoning population of law students whose need was for a teaching resource rather than a library set up for use by researchers and the occasional practitioner visitors. One response might have been to introduce new rules (for example, to require books to be reshelved at their correct location on the library shelves) and to increase penalties for non-compliance; but, in practice, I doubt that this would have made a great deal of difference. Another kind of response might have been to improve the practical options available to students—for example, by subscribing to more than one set of the journals that were most in demand. In other words, the response might have focused on changing the 'normative coding' (the rules, the ethics, and the etiquette governing how students ought to conduct themselves in the law library) or on smarter management of the practical options (governing what students could actually do in the law library, especially by enabling more students to read the same item simultaneously). Over time, the latter was to prove the more effective approach.

The first significant improvement came when law libraries took the teaching stock out of the main collection and put it in protected short loan collections. This eased the pressure somewhat. Law librarians, we might say, recognising that the old-school arrangements were not fit for purpose, took a more practical approach.

Thus far, technology does not figure in this story. Indeed, technology was no part of any story in the law schools of that time. Law schools and the law curriculum were largely technology-free zones. However, technology can play a key role in the management of practical options: by adding to, subtracting from, or modifying the available options; and by minimising the harm or damage that might be caused by the exercise of whatever options are available. From here on, the story in this section is about technologies that added to the practical options of law students.

An important step towards easing the pressure came with the arrival of photocopying machines. To be sure, this was far from being a complete answer. Seats in the law libraries were still in short supply, but at least students could make their own copies of the key materials which they could then read when and where it was convenient to do so. Students duly responded with gusto, copying material on an industrial scale, leading to long queues and delays at the machines. Predictably, at staff-student meetings of that time, one of the standard agenda items was the students' call for more photocopying machines. However, photocopiers were soon to be overtaken by digital technologies.

Initially, the development of electronic databases did not improve the situation; access was limited to a handful of library staff. However, with the digitisation of the stock, the world was to change. It no longer mattered how many students were trying to read the same article in the *Criminal Law Review*;

the use of materials became, as it is now fashionable to say, 'non-rivalrous'. In the end, technology was the solution—the solution to both pressure on books and pressure on library seats. To see how simple it is nowadays, just enter 'Donoghue v Stevenson 1932' in your search engine and, via BAILLI, you will get there in no time at all (www.bailii.org/uk/cases/UKHL/1932/100.html).

For today's generation of law students, there are choices about how to work, where to work, and when to work. With their laptops and other devices connecting to the materials, students are able to access their reading at any time in pretty much any place, whether on campus, in the coffee shop, or at home. Moreover, this is not the end of it. With the further development of artificial intelligence (AI) tools and virtual environments, there will almost certainly be new tools to assist law students and new places and spaces in which to interact with one's fellow students—all of which will call for some governance that specifies which uses of which technologies are permitted. Indeed, as I write this introduction, a huge debate is brewing about whether and how students should be permitted to use large language AI tools such as ChatGPT.

Technological transformation and disruption

If technologies can transform the way in which law students study, then we might wonder whether they can also transform the way that lawyers undertake their practice and, more generally, the way in which legal and regulatory functions are carried out. To which the answer is that technologies do have all manner of disruptive effects on the lives of everyone involved with the law as well as on the legal rules themselves. Sometimes these effects are positive, providing solutions to problems (such as the pressure on law library materials); sometimes they are problematic as when they challenge the capacity of law to govern them (as is the case, for example, with cybercrime). Some applications will create new job opportunities in the practice of law but, as functions (both back and front-office) are progressively automated, humans will no longer be employed as they once were. Accordingly, we should not make the mistake of thinking that law stands still. In our technological age, the pace of everything accelerates and that includes the pace of change itself.

In this context, no one really knows how the pattern of human employment in law will unfold. There is no guarantee that legal professionals, even highly skilled lawyers, will still have jobs for life, or even jobs of any kind in the law. That said, law will not be the only sector in which skilled professionals will be impacted by disruptive technologies.

Modifying the standard sketch of law

Returning to the standard introduction to law, it already recognises that legal systems are no longer centred on courts and cases; it recognises that most laws are made by political institutions. Once upon a time, there might have been clear water between law and politics but, even in the standard introduction, it is recognised that this line is blurred and that not everything stands still. What both the courts and legislatures are engaged in, however, is 'governance'—that is to say, setting standards or codes of conduct, dealing with disputes, allocating authority to undertake particular governance functions, and so on. Governance is what legislative assemblies are doing; and governance is what the courts and judges are doing. However, it is not only the legislatures and courts that are engaged in governance. Governance is undertaken informally within families, small groups, clubs and associations, universities, and so on, as well as by commercial people and others who operate across national boundaries. In other words, governance is ubiquitous.

If we modify the standard introductory sketch to take account of both politics and governance in the way just indicated, then our introduction to law will be quite radical. However, to this, we must add technology as both a key contextual feature for law's governance as well as a critical agent of change. Whether it is the technologies that powered the industrial revolution or the technologies that transformed life in the last century or the leading-edge technologies of our time, the standard introduction does not treat any of this as being anything special or salient for either law or governance. However, the more that we automate processes and develop smart technologies, the more that we see that new technologies are not only economically and socially disruptive, but also disruptive of legal systems and law. On the one hand, new technologies present major challenges to lawmakers who, operating in the slow lane, have problems connecting with technologies that are being developed and applied in the fast lane; on the other hand, some of these technologies promise to outperform law's governance being more effective and efficient than human lawmakers and judges.

Threads of a radical introduction

So, whatever we think should be included in an introduction to law, and whichever topics we highlight for attention, we have the standard view in which technology is at best marginal and a radical counterpoint in which technology is central. If yesterday's introduction to law centres on courts, judges, and disputes, on codes of conduct, rules, and principles, then tomorrow's introduction centres on technological management of conduct and the automation of governance. This book is not so much a radical introduction to the same old world of law as a heads-up for a radically different world of law and governance.

In the chapters that comprise the opening part of the book, I will elaborate on three radical threads that have already figured in these introductory remarks—namely, viewing law as a mode of governance, appreciating what it is to think inside the box (thinking like a lawyer) and what it is to think outside that box, and highlighting the significance of technologies as a challenge for law's governance as well as an opportunity for improved governance. However, we will start with a fourth radical thread, one that has not yet been mentioned in this chapter.

This fourth thread is a response to the idea that law is not about civilising humans and, concomitantly, that young people who seek to become civilised persons should not be looking to law degree programmes for that purpose. As Lord Dyson, who was a member of the Supreme Court before becoming the Master of the Rolls (from 2012–2016) recalls:

> I was awarded a scholarship to read Law at Wadham College, Oxford. The Warden … who was a famous classicist, advised me to read classics rather than law. If you are going to spend your life as a lawyer, why read law? Broaden your mind!
>
> *(Dyson, 2018: 2)*

Faced with this advice from the Warden, young Dyson understandably switched to classics. Nevertheless, the fourth thread of this book rejects this implicitly negative characterisation of law. Radically, it will be argued that law's governance is all about civilising processes and that law school programmes should leave their students in no doubt about this. We might have to apologise for the under-performance of law's governance but we should never have to apologise for its intentions. The Warden surely was right in thinking it desirable that those who work in legal practice should at least be civilised persons, and he might well have been right in thinking that Oxford law degrees of that time were not ideal for that civilising purpose; but no one should doubt that law's governance and lawyers—yes, lawyers—can and should make a significant contribution to civilised community life. Indeed, let's not understate this point: as one City lawyer has put it, the law 'is the foundation of our civilization, our societies and our survival' (Wood, 2017: 4).

3

LAW AS 'CIVILISING'

Introduction

As a teenager, in the mid-1960s, I was not particularly 'academic'. My school examination results were sufficient for me to progress to university; but, I was not so engaged by any of the school's very traditional curriculum subjects that I wanted to take their study beyond 'A' level. In those days, it was easy enough to find work; leaving school to start work was the norm; and, with only a few of my school friends going on to university, I thought at one stage that I was going to be no exception to the usual rule.

However, the thought occurred that I might make a career in the law. I do not know where this thought came from. My maternal grandfather had been a London policeman and one of my paternal grandfather's brothers had been a solicitor in Manchester, but the former had died before I was born and I met the latter just once when I was very young. So, I am pretty sure that they played no part in bringing the law onto my radar.

At my school, there was no one who could give advice about the study of law at university or making a career in legal practice. I am not sure whether anyone there was aware that, many years before, at a time when there were still some boys who boarded at the school, one of its pupils was James Atkin. This was none other than *the* James Atkin who would go on to become a particularly distinguished Law Lord and who, as we noted in the introductory chapter, was the author of a legendary judgment in the great case of *Donoghue v Stevenson* (see https://en.wikipedia.org/wiki/James_Atkin,_Baron_Atkin). In fact, Atkin spent only a short time boarding at the school and when, some years later, he went to Oxford it was to study classics, not to study law. In Atkin's schoolboy days, as in my own, it was only a small

DOI: 10.4324/9781003507802-4

minority of teenagers who went on to university; and, of those who did go, students who enrolled for law degrees were few and far between.

A solicitor's advice

Fortunately, I was able to take advice from a local solicitor. I had two questions. First, I asked this solicitor whether he would advise taking up the opportunity to study at university. Secondly, I asked whether, if so, he would advise reading law. His responses to both questions were unequivocal. To the first question, his response was that the opportunity should be seized; with the benefit of a university education, a young person would undergo a process of 'becoming civilised'. However, in response to the second question, the solicitor advised that in no circumstances should I read law. That, he said, would defeat the object. Echoing the Warden's advice to young John Dyson (see Chapter Two), my local solicitor told me that to study law was no way to become civilised.

In the event, I half-followed the solicitor's advice—following his advice by going to university, but acting against his advice by enrolling for a law degree. While I have no reason to regret either of these decisions, the solicitor was undoubtedly correct. The principal objective of university law programmes in the UK was to train young people how to think like lawyers—nothing more and nothing less; and, in those days, this meant that students were being trained to think in a particular kind of way, to think in a particular box. This box, as I indicated in the introductory chapter, is designed to train students to stick to the legal sources, the statutes and the cases, in advising on the legal position. Often, the legal position will be clear but law school training tends to hunt out factual scenarios where the legal position is not clear. Recognising these more difficult cases, students will then be taught how to apply the law. Here, the smartest students, emulating the smartest legal practitioners and judges, will be able to write equally convincing opinions for both parties to any dispute. In academic legal circles, where this is the name of the game, being smart is knowing how to pirouette around the rules and principles, not about learning how to be a civilised human.

Law as a civilising influence

One of the rallying calls of this book is that no one should be deterred from studying law at university because they fear that it will not be a civilising experience. Quite to the contrary: one of the first lessons is to understand that all human communities need governance; that legal codes were a feature of some of the earliest civilisations; and that there has never been a greater need for governance than in the present century. At the same time, though, and in line with the radical approach taken in this book, it needs to be understood that law—with its various rules, principles, and standards, and its distinctive institutions and practices—is just one mode of *governance*. Having spelt this out, we then have the opening to draw in alternative (and, potentially, complementary) modes of governance in which today's technologies are implicated. Whether or not those technologies will have a positive or a negative impact on our chances of good governance and civilised community life is one of the big questions of our age.

It is extremely important, too, to understand that there is more to good governance than effective and efficient administration. Good governance should be in the interests of those who are governed; it presupposes integrity on the part of those who have governance responsibilities; and, it aspires to operate with fair and just procedures, and to adopt legitimate positions and policies. In modern societies, there is much to debate about these matters, such that law can become a hub for discussing good governance relative to the values, needs, and preferences of each human community. No doubt, there will be many different views about such matters and some differences will go deep and will be held intensely. Law cannot satisfy all views but good democratic governance deserves to be respected. As, now retired, Supreme Court Justice, Jonathan Sumption, rightly says:

> The only thing that ever has or ever will unite us is a common loyalty to a way of conducting our affairs that we can respect even if we disagree about the outcome. This means a process of decision-making that accommodates dissent, debate and a diversity of values.
>
> *(2021: 204)*

Similarly, and more generally, Sumption remarks that: '[W]hat holds us together as a society is precisely the means by which we do things. It is a common respect for a way of making collective decisions, even if we disagree with the decisions themselves' (237). The radical lesson here is very clear: law's governance might be imperfect but law and lawyers are not peripheral to civilisation, they are absolutely central.

Interviews, reputations, and generalisations

There was a time when law schools interviewed their prospective students. Typically, the interview would start with a gentle motivational question. Why, interviewees would be asked, did they want to study law? Nowadays, even if there is no interview, applicants will probably have to compose a personal statement which will address the question of what it is about the law that has attracted them. Is it the drama of the courtroom; or do they perhaps see themselves as campaigners for justice; or is it the pressure and buzz of the large law firm, or the prospect of a view from the corner office that appeals?

Imagine though that the motivational question is put in a more challenging form. Imagine that the interviewer asks the interviewee to read and then comment on a few lines from a famous law review article by Fred Rodell (1936). Here, recalling that the political theorist Harold Laski liked to quip that in every revolution the lawyers are liquidated first, Rodell elaborated in the following way:

> The reason the lawyers lead the line to the guillotine or the firing squad is that, while law is supposed to be a device to serve society, a civilized way of helping the wheels go round without too much friction, it is pretty hard to find a group less concerned with serving society and more concerned with serving themselves than the lawyers.
>
> *(42)*

How should an interviewee respond? Presumably, the seat in the white shoe law firm should be struck off the list of eligible reasons for wanting to study law. But, if Rodell was right, how would law students be able to fulfil their more noble aspirations?

Fortunately, at my own admission interview at the LSE, my interviewer—the distinguished public international lawyer and human rights activist, Cedric Thornberry (see, https://en.wikipedia.org/wiki/Cedric_Thornberry)—did not pitch me such a difficult question. Rather, he asked me how I would respond if someone were to suggest that 'all generalisations are false'. Not having been coached to spot, let alone to deal with, teasers of this kind, I replied that I would regard the statement as unremarkable, even trite. There was quite a pause while my interviewer figured out how to take this unexpected reply. Recognising his puzzlement, I explained that this must be so because, quite simply, it is in the nature of a generalisation to express a truth that, given its generality, is subject to falsifying exceptions. Indeed, had I known about Rodell's characterisation of lawyers as being less concerned with serving society and more concerned with serving themselves, I might have offered this up as a case in point. For, even if Rodell's assessment were generally true, there surely are some lawyers who are exceptions to his general characterisation—or, at any rate, so one would hope (compare, for example, Michael Legg and Felicity Bell's (2020: 1) much more positive assessment of lawyers as 'essential to social ordering … [as playing] critical roles in the administration of justice and in the maintenance of a free and democratic society … [and as enabling] the protection of human rights and facilitation of commerce').

Six decades on, the interview is a distant memory. However, Rodell's assessment of lawyers is not so easily forgotten. If law degrees are not about civilising young people, and if legal practice is largely self-serving, then if we suggest that we see law's governance as a civilising force and want to be a part of it, we are likely to be whistling in the wind. Clearly, if law is to be a force for civilisation, if we are not to feel the need to apologise for wanting to study and be a part of law, some radical changes are required.

Postscript

In the early 1980s, when I was Sub-Dean for undergraduate admissions in law at the University of Sheffield, I interviewed a couple of applicants who were already several years into their degree programmes in medicine and who wanted to transfer from the Medical School to the Law School. They told me that, during their medical studies, they had become aware of, and interested in, the legal liability issues that can arise in medical practice; and, having thought some more about it, they had decided to make a career change, from medicine to law. Now, it did not cross my mind to say to these applicants that, if they intended to make a career in legal practice, they should not transfer to the law programme. As Nicholas McBride (2022) observes in one of his 'letters' to a prospective law student, if we recognise that reading medicine at university is the best preparation for becoming a doctor then it would be astonishing if we did not also recognise that reading law at university is the best preparation for becoming a lawyer. Yet, at first blush, the advice that my local solicitor gave me might be understood as subscribing to just this astonishing view.

However, what my solicitor was saying was that, of course, we want our lawyers to know the law but we also want them to be civilised persons; and, undergraduate law degrees do not cut it when it comes to civilising people. As I have already indicated, I think that, provided we get our undergraduate law act together, this is seriously mistaken. McBride also offers a robust rejection of this mistaken view arguing as follows:

> Deciding to become a lawyer is just as morally worthwhile as choosing to become a doctor, or a teacher. This is because you can't have a functioning legal system without lawyers, and a society's legal system is as vitally important to the flourishing of the people living in that society as are that society's health or education systems. We tend to forget this in Western societies because we take our legal systems—and the benefits we obtain from living under our legal systems—for granted.
>
> *(27)*

I will not repeat what I have already said about this radical thread: suffice it to say that, on this extremely important point, McBride is absolutely right.

4

LAW AS GOVERNANCE

Introduction

In his book *The Future of the Internet* (2008), Jonathan Zittrain draws attention to the way in which the Dutch town of Drachten responded to dissatisfaction with the local level of traffic congestion and accidents. Quite simply, road signs and traffic signals were removed; the spaces shared by motorists, cyclists, and pedestrians were cleared; and parties were encouraged to assume personal responsibility for their safety and the safety of others in the town. On the face of it, this was a bold experiment but Drachten is not the only place that has turned with some success to such an approach (Senthillingam, 2014).

While the people of Drachten dispensed with the signs and signals associated with top-down imposed rules of law, they did not dispense with governance. Drachten is an example of governance by means other than by formal laws and other than by imposed rules. The people of Drachten did not decide that passage through the town's spaces should be a free-for-all; rather, a culture of care and responsibility, together with the development of informal protocols, replaced the previous regime of law's governance.

Elsewhere, the safety of pedestrians in town centres is assured not by informal governance but by hard architectural measures. Pedestrianised zones are created and protected not by rules that are directed at motorists, not by signs and signals, and not by informal governance and a culture of responsibility. Rather, physical barriers render it impossible for vehicles to be driven into these zones.

So, what we should take from these cases is that law's governance might be one way of achieving safety on the roads and in town centres but that it

DOI: 10.4324/9781003507802-5

is not the only way and, importantly, that law's governance might not be the most effective way. In line with one of the radical threads in this introduction, we should recognise that humans need governance but that law is just one possible mode of governance.

In this chapter, we will begin to elaborate this thread by speaking to the need for governance, to its different modalities, and to its conceptual limits.

The need for governance and its functions

Why do humans need governance? Or, putting this in a way that does not yet anticipate forms of governance other than by law, why do humans need law's governance? Why do humans need to be subjected to the governance of rules?

According to the great American common lawyer, Karl Llewellyn (1940), all groups need governance if they are to be viable. If members of groups are to interact and transact, if they are to act in the collective interest, if they are to manage conflicts and disputes, they need governance. The group needs a basic code of conduct to channel, control, and coordinate behaviour; it needs mechanisms to settle disputes; it needs to have a sense of direction or common purpose; and, it needs to allocate authority to group members for drafting the code, settling disputes, and maintaining the direction of the group.

In small groups operating in a stable context, once the basic code of conduct has been agreed, governance should largely run itself. However, in larger groups and particularly in groups where the context is more dynamic—where the group has to adjust to new technologies, new applications, and new circumstances, to new challenges and new opportunities, or where the group regularly contemplates a change of direction—then governance will be more challenging. Indeed, in many contexts, finding the right regulatory balance between stability and change will always be a work in progress—and, in our technological times, where there is a commitment to both law and order and democratic decision-making, then governance conversations are likely to be heavily contested.

So understood, the prospectus for law's governance will minimally promise to instate and maintain a well-ordered society. There will be rules; and the rules will be published, applied, and enforced. However, over and above the promise of order, the distinctive pitch might be to commit to a democratically ordered society, or to an order that aspires to (or that actually achieves) justice.

In relation to the minimal promise, our experience might be that law's 'order' does not work, or that it does not work in ways that we want or expect, or that it has inputs with which we are at odds. In relation to the commitment to a democratic order, we might complain that there simply is no 'democratic conversation', or that we are not parties to the conversation, or that the conversation is rigged, or that the conversation results in the wrong outputs (which then get fed into the order, aggravating our disenchantment with law). And, in relation to the promise of a just order (or a democratic and just order), it might be that the focal points for our disenchantment with law's governance relate to its (in)accessibility, its procedures and processes, or its substance, and there will be as many versions of discontent as there are contested theories of justice. Moreover, even before law's governance is put to the test, we might have our doubts about the scale and scope of its promise, whether because we view it as under-ambitious or as over-ambitious.

While we can recognise that there is doubt and discontent with law's governance, it does not follow that humans do not need governance. What humans need is at least adequate governance whether this is delivered by a better version of law's governance or some other (better performing) mode of governance.

Governance, rules, and law

Famously, another well-known American jurist, Lon Fuller (1969) characterised law as the enterprise of subjecting human conduct to the governance of rules. This chimed in with the widely held view that law is an affair of *rules* (Hart, 1961) and that legal concepts are to be understood in the context of systems of *rules*; and it enabled Fuller to develop his ideal of legality around the commitment to governance by *rules*. With all this attention to *rules*, the idea that law is about *governance* slipped into the background. So, when governance came back into the spotlight (alongside law and regulation), it could be viewed not so much as a human enterprise of which rule-based law is a particular kind but as a particular kind of direction or guidance to be differentiated from law—for example, by reference to its lesser formality, or lesser institutionalisation, or its less top-down nature, or its non-governmental or transnational or technological characteristics, and so on.

It follows that we might conceive of governance in a broad sense that includes a rule-based legal instantiation of governance or in a narrow sense that contrasts in some way with rule-based law. In the broad sense, we have a number of governance options of which law is one; in the narrow sense, law is to be contrasted with governance. For the purposes of this book, it is not necessary to comment on whatever competing conceptions of governance in the narrow sense might be up for debate; quite simply, for present purposes, it is the idea of governance in the broad sense that needs to be retrieved. Law might be an affair of *rules* but the key point—the radical thread in this narrative—is that law is a species of *governance*.

Turning to the concept of law—and this is something that we will discuss in some detail in Chapter 11—although this is a much-debated matter, the disputants follow Fuller in assuming as their common starting point that law is an enterprise of governance by rules. However, for the purposes of our radical introduction to law, the emphasis has to be on *governance* rather than rules. From this radical perspective, we will view law as one mode of governance; but, so too, are strategies that systematically employ technologies for governance purposes. As Lawrence Lessig (1999) pointed out, if the purpose of governance is, say, to channel motorists towards wearing seat belts, then there might be legal rules that require or encourage the wearing of seat belts; but, alongside these rules, there might also be support for the development of social norms favouring the wearing of seat belts as well as the offering of financial incentives for seat belt use—in other words, governance can involve a mix of both sticks and carrots. However, Lessig's principal point was that cars might be designed (or 'coded') in such a way that they would not operate unless the seat belts were engaged.

In the wake of Lessig's introduction of technology into governance thinking, there has been much agonising about whether 'code' or 'algorithmic governance' or 'technological management'—such as we have with the designed-in features of products, processes, and places—is 'law'. While this is a legitimate question, from a radical perspective it is not the highest priority. From this perspective, the essential point is that both 'law' and 'code' are modes of governance: to be sure, their interfaces at the point of governance are different—one presenting as rules to be complied with, the other not—but their intended purpose is the same; and that purpose is governance.

Recalling again the debate about the student use of AI tools, everyone agrees that we need governance. This governance might take the form of rules and regulations issued by universities and other educational institutions, or even rules of criminal law; and, if they are to be effective, these rules will need the support of peer pressure. This, however, might be only a part of the governance regime. Almost certainly, there will be tools that can be used to check the use of AI (just as there are tools to check for plagiarism); and, in a reversion to old-school examinations, students might be assessed in places and in ways that preclude the practical option of using AI tools.

The conceptual limits of law's governance

Although we can treat the idea of law's governance as having a broad bandwidth, it does have limits. We can comment briefly on three potential boundary-markers, namely: the limits set by the human and/or rule-based characteristics of law's governance; the limits set by bad governance; and the limits of authoritarian governance.

First, if we reduce the human and/or the rule-based features of governance, we move away from law and, at a certain point, we will move into another mode of governance. Although we do not need to take a position on precisely where the line lies between law's governance and a technological mode of governance that takes humans out of the loop and dispenses with normative signals (rules), we do need to understand that law, as a particular practice of governance, does not stretch out into infinity.

Secondly, an ostensible regime of governance might be so bad, so chaotic, so corrupt, so tyrannical that it barely qualifies as governance, let alone law's governance. There is a minimum threshold for law's governance. Again, though, for the purposes of this introduction, we do not need to take a position on how bad governance has to be before it should no longer be characterised as law.

Thirdly, while law's governance will claim to have 'authority', we will proceed on the basis that both authoritarian and democratic practices can qualify as examples of law. Hence, law's governance might be offered by a Leviathan—and, in some circumstances, this might be an offer that is not unattractive (compare Micklethwait & Wooldridge, 2014)—but it might also be offered by sponsors who are committed to democratic processes.

5

LAW AS RULES

Thinking inside the box, thinking outside the box

Introduction

During one of the vacations in my first undergraduate year, a sales representative who called at our house from time to time, asked me how my law studies were going. I said that I was, so to speak, all at sea: I simply did not have my bearings; and, even when we were having relatively focused discussions about the cases, I was puzzled. In response, the salesman told me that he had felt much the same when he had taken a correspondence course that dealt with sales (contract) law: just as you seemed to be getting a sense of what the law was on some point, he said, you found that the cases were contradictory. Finding it all frustrating, the salesman told me that he had given up. For me, that was not an option.

To overcome such frustration, it has to be understood that law schools are dedicated to training their students 'to think like lawyers'; to appreciate that this is being trained 'to think in a particular box'; and, ideally, to develop some distance from 'in the box' exercises so that one is also capable of 'thinking outside the box'. And, yes, it has to be recognised that, sometimes, the cases really are contradictory.

Puzzling cases

A typical 'in the box' exercise will present law students with a couple of cases, the facts of the cases looking similar, the question looking the same, but the outcomes being diametrically opposed. The puzzle is: how are these cases to be squared (or, as lawyers express it, 'reconciled')?

DOI: 10.4324/9781003507802-6

My introduction to this kind of exercise came very early on in our contract law classes when we were instructed to read two cases in which the question was whether the law would treat a sales contract as void and of no effect where the sellers claimed that they were mistaken as to the identity of the buyer. In these cases, the sellers were indeed mistaken because, as it turned out, the buyers had fraudulently misrepresented their identities.

In the first case, *Phillips v Brooks* (1919), the seller was a jeweller who sold some items to a buyer who fraudulently misrepresented himself as being Sir George Bullough with an address in St James's Square, London. Having written a cheque for his purchases, the fraudster persuaded the jeweller to allow him to take away one of the smaller items—this was a ring which, ostensibly, was a gift that the fraudster had bought for his wife. Of course, this was a complete fabrication and the fraudster promptly sold the ring to a pawnbroker. The cheque that the fraudster left with the jeweller was not honoured and the latter, having traced the ring to the pawnbroker, claimed that he was entitled to have the ring returned.

As a matter of contract law, the jeweller's claim against the pawnbroker would have succeeded if he had taken steps to 'avoid' the initial transaction *before* the fraudster sold the jewellery to the pawnbroker; but, not having taken such steps, the jeweller's claim would succeed only if the initial transaction with the fraudster was void for a mistake of identity.

Addressing the mistake of identity point, the judge took the view that the jeweller intended to deal with the person who stood in front of him in the shop. If cash had been tendered for the jewellery, there would have been no hesitation, no question about the identity of the buyer. Accordingly, although the identity of the buyer was a consideration, the mistake that was made was not as to the *identity* of the buyer as such but as to the *creditworthiness* of the buyer.

The principle of *Phillips v Brooks* seems to be pretty straightforward: a seller who, dealing face-to-face with a buyer, accepts a payment by cheque and then permits the buyer to walk away with some or all of the goods in their possession, will be assumed to have intended to deal with that person. Without more, the transaction will not be void for a mistake of identity.

So far, so clear. However, we now have a later case, *Ingram v Little* (1961), in which the sellers (two Bournemouth ladies who had advertised their car for sale) dealt face-to-face with a prospective buyer, who fraudulently misrepresented himself as one PGM Hutchinson from Caterham in Surrey. The Bournemouth ladies accepted a cheque in payment, and then permitted the buyer to drive away with the car. Just as in the earlier case of *Phillips v Brooks*, the fraudster disposed of the car to a downstream purchaser who bought the vehicle in good faith, leaving the original sellers to claim that the initial transaction with the fraudster was void. However, without saying that the principle in *Phillips v Brooks* was incorrect, the majority of the court in

Ingram v Little ruled that there had been a fundamental mistake of identity and that the transaction was void. The puzzle is to reconcile this later decision with the earlier case.

Thinking inside the box, thinking like a lawyer, there are two principal ways of trying to square the cases. The first is to 'distinguish the cases on their facts', finding in the facts some material difference that explains the contrasting outcomes; and, the second is to find some room for discretion or leeway within the governing rule or principle itself.

In my contracts class, it was the first of these strategies that was explored; and, what is more, it was explored at great length. I recall being truly amazed at the attention that was paid to the details of the cases, particularly to the matter of when precisely the fraudster gave a false identity and how much trouble the sellers had gone to in checking the identity that was given. Yet, it was not clear why, as a matter of legal principle, these factual details were important (or, as lawyers say, 'material'). If the fraudster introduced himself at once, or at some point before he proposed paying by cheque, this would seem to be no more than a courtesy and no kind of indication that the sellers were concerned about the identity of the buyer—that is, no indication that the identity of the buyer might be a deal-breaker. In other words, there is nothing here to suggest that the sellers would have declined to deal with the buyer if a cash sale had been proposed. Equally, if the fraudster only (mis) identified himself when payment by cheque was proposed, that suggests that the concern was about creditworthiness (and the risk of non-payment) rather than identity. As for the care taken by the sellers, if this is relevant, it suggests that sellers might be precluded from having the transaction declared void if they have failed to exercise due diligence in dealing with the buyer. However, this would only bite if the legal principle in *Phillips v Brooks* indicated that, normally, the transaction should be treated as void in cases of this kind—and, of course, that is exactly what the legal principle did *not* say.

Thinking like a lawyer, how are we to avoid chasing our tail when we are presented with puzzles of this kind? The answer is that we have to think outside the box that specifies that, in our various attempts to reconcile the cases, we can only refer to their facts and to the legal rules and principles. Once we think outside this box, we might not be able to square the circle but we can find a number of possible explanations for the different outcomes. For example, we might simply say that different judges decided these cases and that adjudication, albeit orientated towards legal rules and principles, is undertaken by humans. To the extent that this implies that the outcome of cases can vary from one judge to another, from one human to another, this is likely to provoke the objection that law is supposed to be the rule of rules and not the rule of humans (men or women). However, this objection fails to recognise the tension that humans can experience where the consistent application of legal rules and principles is perceived to lead to an unfair outcome in the instant case. For all lawyers, these 'hard cases', where the law points one way but justice points in the opposite direction, are a challenge. All lawyers, including judges, have to take a position, either favouring the consistent and predictable application of the law or making an exception for the sake of justice.

Following up on this, and now speaking from just outside the box, we can suggest that, in both *Phillips v Brooks* and *Ingram v Little*, the law had to make a tough choice between the interests of two innocent parties, the seller and the downstream buyer. The difference was that while, in *Phillips*, there was no obvious (additional) injustice in favouring the downstream purchaser (the pawnbroker), this was not the case in *Ingram*. Why so? Quite simply, this was because the sellers in *Ingram* were not dealing on the same footing as the downstream buyer: whereas the latter, a Blackpool car-dealer, was in the trade, the former were not. In other words, while we might reasonably assume that the car dealer who ended up in possession of the car would have the opportunity to recoup his losses in the course of his trading, it would not be reasonable to make the same assumption about the sellers, who were acting purely in a private capacity. On this basis, the key to explaining the different decisions in these cases does not lie in the minutiae of the way that the fraud was perpetrated or in the sellers' due diligence; rather, the key to the cases is whether the parties were acting in a business capacity (as the downstream buyers were in both cases and as the sellers were in *Phillips*) or in a private capacity (as the sellers were in *Ingram*). Prefiguring the explicit recognition some years later of a policy of protecting consumers, these cases suggest that protecting the interests of good faith private transactors will be prioritised over the interests of good faith business contractors.

We will return to this explanation in a moment but, if we are thinking outside the box, we might come up with further explanations. For example, where there is some failure to apply the law, it will in many cases be because an official has been 'bought off' (by corruption or so-called 'capture') or influenced by threats. Worldwide, these are familiar problems. However, where, as in the UK, there are processes that are designed to secure the 'independence' of the judiciary, no one would take seriously the proposition that classic case-law puzzles are to be explained this way. Any student who tried to reconcile the cases by proffering such an 'out of the box' explanation would be rapidly told to get back to thinking in the box.

The idea, however, that some judges are more responsive to individual justice than others cannot be so readily dismissed. In the 1960s, the law reports were full of contract cases where judges in the Court of Appeal were bending over backwards to find ways of protecting consumer purchasers who were not at all streetwise. At the time, it was the small print of the sales agreements used by dealers in the second-hand car trade that was the problem. The cornerstone principles of contract law—namely, freedom of contract and sanctity of contract—might have been against these consumer purchasers but justice was on their side.

By the mid-1960s, when I started studying contract law, this tension between the application of the general principles and achieving justice in the individual case was creating something of a crisis. This tension was brought to a head by an appeal to the House of Lords in *The Suisse Atlantique* (1967), a case that actually had nothing to do with consumers or second-hand cars but which was a dispute between a shipowner and a commercial charterer of a vessel. The judgments handed down by the House of Lords were analysed with great care and, when the case was presented in our lectures, the lecture hall was full with standing room only for many. Despite the sense of anticipation, the House of Lords fudged the issue: on the one hand, the cornerstone principles were reaffirmed but, on the other hand, it was emphasised that, where small print non-negotiable terms and conditions were presented to consumers, they needed to be drafted very clearly so that there should be no misunderstanding about their import. Of course, in practice, this made little difference: consumers back in the 1960s did not understand the small print of contracts any more than they do nowadays—especially when, if you want the particular goods or services, you have no choice other than to sign off on the sales agreement or click the 'I agree' button. With the judges having tried unsuccessfully to manage the tension but succeeding only in leaving consumers exposed to non-negotiable terms and conditions that were clearly drafted, it was left to Parliament in the late 1970s to introduce bespoke legislation that explicitly protected consumer contractors against the abuse of the classic principles.

Before we move on from the mistake of identity cases, we should note two other out-of-the-box reflections, both of which pick up on recent developments in technology.

First, reflecting on the way in which AI enabled by machine learning detects patterns in large sets of data, we might entertain the mischievous thought that the AI would have picked up the apparent significance of the contracting parties being professional, in the trade, dealers or private buyers or sellers long before we humans caught up with this distinction. In other words, what the AI picks out as being material facts in the precedents might not align with what, at the time, we humans treat as material; and, even when we humans do reassess the precedents, we view ourselves as making a fresh start rather than applying, as the AI would view it, the existing pattern of the precedents.

Secondly, we might reflect that, without the option of paying by cheque, the fraudster would have had to find another way to deceive the sellers. At the time of the cases, there would have been no support for the idea that we should put a stop to this kind of fraud by taking cheques out of circulation. Yet, one line of radical thinking is that governance should focus on eliminating practical options that facilitate crime. Today, we have moved on. On the one hand, there has been a dramatic decrease in the use of cheques and, on the other, there has been a significant increase in the options for payment. So, while we no longer need to take steps to eliminate the use of cheques (that will probably occur naturally), it might be that governance of the payment rails is key to controlling various kinds of fraud and deception.

Right answers

Moving on into my second year as an undergraduate, I still had not grasped that, in being educated to think like lawyers, we were being trained to play an 'in the box' game; and even less had I grasped what the ground rules of the game were. My lightbulb moments came early in that year in a torts class.

Our classes in tort law usually involved discussion of some hypothetical fact situations. These were not discussions at large but exercises in 'thinking like a lawyer'. Our task was to advise on the legal position. On the hypothetical facts, would a tort claim stack up or not? As I recall, the lightbulb tutorial presented us with a scenario in which there was an accident at a ski resort, someone was injured, there was an allegation that the accident was caused by a failure to maintain the equipment properly, and we were instructed to advise on whether the accident victim would have a claim in negligence. Our tutor invited me to have a first shot at advising on the legal position in this case.

I started by rehearsing the general principles of negligence law, namely, that accident victims will have a claim for compensation against a defendant where it is judged that the latter has failed to take reasonable care, where it is reasonably foreseeable that this failure would lead to a person such as the claimant being injured, and where the accident happens in a reasonably foreseeable way. On the facts, I said that it seemed to me that the claim would be sustained. However, while my tutor did not say that this was the wrong answer to the problem, neither did he say that this was the right answer and move on to the next hypothetical; rather, each of my fellow students was invited to present their view on the claim. This elicited a range of views, at the end of which I was unclear whether my answer was correct or, if not, what the correct answer was. At the end of the tutorial, I took this up with our tutor. I cannot recall the exact terms in which he responded to me, but the gist of it was that I clearly did not 'get it'—these hypothetical problems did not have right answers in the simple way that I assumed.

If there were no right answers as such, did this mean that anything went? No, it did not; some answers were definitely wrong. The general principles of negligence law could be stated correctly or incorrectly, and they were pretty much as I had rehearsed them. To this extent, I was not wrong. However, their application to the particular facts of a case was not always clear and straightforward; indeed, as the discussion in the tutorial had highlighted, there might be several readings of the legal position, each of which was plausible. The essence of being a good lawyer was to understand where the law was contestable and to develop the capacity to interpret the legal rules and principles in more than one way.

At last, I got it. As law students, we should approach our studies as if we were being trained to play a game. The object of the game was not to come up with the right answer to a legal problem, but to be able to advise on the legal position in a way that was sensitive to the interpretive options that were plausibly available in the relevant legal rules and principles. Playing this game, if we were asked to advise the claimant, our brief would be to read the law in a way that would be most favourable to the claimant's position; and, equally, if we were asked to advise the defendant, our brief would be to read the law in whatever way was most favourable to the defendant's position. Accordingly, if asked to advise on the legal position in a particular scenario, we might preface our response by saying that our advice would depend on whether we were instructed by the prospective claimant or the potential defendant. Or, as lawyers in practice often say, on the one hand, the law says such and such but, on the other, it also says such and such—with the latter indications being in tension with the former.

While there is no harm in law students viewing their training as game playing, once they have qualified as legal practitioners they will be working in a practice that is much more than a game. Thus, for example, legal practitioners might be instructed to advise on whether doctors at a hospital would be acting lawfully if they were to remove the feeding and hydration support from a patient who was diagnosed as being in a permanent vegetative state; or the question put might be whether there would be a breach of international law if there were to be 'pre-emptive strikes' against a rogue state that was feared to be intent on using weapons of mass destruction or causing a humanitarian crisis. If these or other questions were litigated, an arbitrator or a judge would have to reach a decision; sitting on the fence would not be an option. But, if plausible readings of the law are presented on both sides of the case, on what basis are decisions to be made? Judges do not normally say that one view is 'right' or 'correct'; they tend to say that they prefer a particular view or that one reading of the law is the 'better' view. What this coded language means is not clear and, if we are to decode it, we probably need to think outside the box.

Questions of fact and questions of law

The hypothetical situation that we discussed in our torts class presented us with a sketch of the facts. It probably was open to us to advise that we could not be confident about the legal situation without some further and better particulars concerning the facts; but, the main point of the tutorial was to direct us to the law, to its plasticity, and to its several potential applications. The judges who sit in our appeal courts, where disputes have been narrowed to particular questions of law, can articulate the legal position in more than one way. Thinking outside this box, however, and back in the real world it is evident that the facts can be the key to the case and to the legal position. For example, in Spring 2023, the press highlighted a trial being held in a Utah court in which an elderly skier, Terry Sanderson, claimed that the actress Gwyneth Paltrow had struck into his back, knocking him down, and causing him injury (Pavia, 2023). Broadly speaking, the legal position and liability in this dispute would be governed by the principles of negligence law that guided our classroom thinking. However, the key question in the case was whether Paltrow did or did not slam into Sanderson on the ski slopes in the way that he maintained. It took the jury only a couple of hours to decide that, on the balance of probabilities, they preferred Paltrow's account; hence, Paltrow was not liable. The crux of the case was the finding of facts, not making a choice between this or that reading of the legal principles.

The contrast between appeal court and trial court argument can be pronounced. Whereas the former starts with the findings made by the trial court, the latter is all about making those findings. In trial courts, in those cases where a judge sits with a jury, although the judge has control of the proceedings and, for example, can make rulings on whether the jury should or should not hear certain evidence, it is for the jury to decide which parties and which witnesses are honest, credible, reliable, and decent. Why a jury prefers the account of one party to that of another—why, for example, the jury preferred Gwyneth Paltrow's account of the accident on the ski slopes—we do not know. By contrast, in those cases where judges sit without a jury, then they will typically give a very detailed account of their impression of the parties and their witnesses. For example, in *Blue v Ashley* (2017), the question for the judge was whether an alleged promise made by Mike Ashley to pay Blue (a consultant for Sports Direct) £15 million if he could get the company's share price up to £8 per share, was made seriously or just in the course of pub banter. Here, the context (an informal business meeting in a pub where a considerable amount of alcohol was consumed) was critical as were the perceptions of the various parties at the meeting. After a lengthy assessment of the evidence given at the trial, the judge concluded that the promise was not intended to be taken seriously and the fact that Blue had convinced himself otherwise showed only that 'the human capacity for wishful thinking knows few bounds' (para 142).

Whether it is judges or juries who decide the facts, there is no denying the human factor that is involved. For those who think outside the box and who believe that the key to appeal court cases lies in their human decision-makers and not the rules (or the law), the parallel thought is that the key to trial court cases lies in their human decision-makers and not the facts. In other words, the sceptical out of the box view is that cases are not determined by either the facts or the rules but by humans who form an impression about the parties or the merits and then, if they are required to give reasoned decisions, bring the facts and rules into line accordingly.

6

LAW IN OUR TECHNOLOGICAL TIMES

Introduction

In the 1960s, the world was a very different place. To be sure, the industrial revolution had happened, leaving its mark on many of our landscapes; and, for my generation, the Cuban missile crisis of 1962 was an extremely salient reminder about the destructive power of modern technologies that are applied for military purposes. Although the world was a dangerous place, and although the need for governance was manifest, the challenge was not yet 'to govern so as to effectively ensure security in an environment of simultaneous *individual* empowerment and *individual* vulnerability' (Wittes and Blum, 2015: 10, emphasis added). Importantly, the world was still pre-digital. Josh Fairfield (2022) captures this well, when he says:

> [A]sk someone in two different decades what they would save from their house if it were burning down. In the 1950s someone might say a photo album. In the 2020s, someone is much more likely to say their phone or laptop. All the sentimental and personal value that people used to store in the objects around them is now stored inside of digital devices or in the cloud. Photo albums become photo apps. Letter exchanges become text messages.
>
> *(1264)*

But, in the UK, it was not only that neither the information society nor the digital society were in prospect. The fact of the matter was that we did not yet perceive ourselves as being in the age of any particular technology. In the 'swinging 60s', there might have been electric guitars and rock 'n' roll, but

DOI: 10.4324/9781003507802-7

the so-called 'consumer society' was still in its offline infancy, televisions were a black and white analogue novelty, and relatively few people owned cars or telephones let alone autonomous vehicles or multi-functional mobile phones. Suffice it to say that, although there was some political talk about the 'white heat' of technology, it had not burnt through to the university law schools. My induction to law took place in a zone that was largely technology-free and, having embarked on an academic career in 1968, it continued in that way for many years.

In the early 1980s, I was working on an article with a colleague who was away visiting Simon Fraser University in Canada. I had produced a first draft of the article using an old manual typewriter and, literally, cutting and pasting text that needed to be re-positioned. The process was slow and messy; but, unless you were the kind of person whose first draft was also their final draft, this was how articles were knocked into shape. Having airmailed the draft to my colleague, I waited to hear back from him. When he got back to me, I expected him to be making suggestions for revision but the main thing that he wanted to tell me was that, at Simon Fraser, they had some kind of computer (with word processing software as we would now say) that could 'magically' re-order and revise the text. It truly was magic and it was not until the mid-1980s that the Law Department at the University of Sheffield, where I was working at the time, acquired a similar piece of equipment. Even with this prompt, it was still to dawn on me that lawyers should be taking far more interest in the leading-edge technological developments of our time.

However, in the 1990s, this was to change. First, the UK enacted the Human Fertilisation and Embryology Act (HFE Act) to regulate the provision of assisted conception. This was fully a dozen years after Robert Edwards and Patrick Steptoe had developed a workable technique of in vitro fertilisation (IVF) as celebrated by the birth of Louise Brown; and, although by the time of the legislation, IVF itself was not headline news, its governance was clearly a matter of legal interest. Secondly, it was during the 1990s that developments in 'genetic engineering' and 'cloning', notably the birth of 'Dolly' the sheep, drew the attention of a broad sweep of commentators, including lawyers. What, I wondered, would criminal lawyers, IP lawyers, family lawyers, employment lawyers, medical lawyers, and so on, make of the new genetics? How would the new genetic technologies impact various fields of law (Brownsword, Cornish, and Llewelyn, 1998)? Thirdly, during the same decade, work on the development of the Internet, which had started quietly as a military project back in the 1960s, was close to creating an entirely new (online) space for social, economic, and consumer purposes (Brownsword and Howells, 1999). With these advances in both biotechnology and information and communication technology, it seemed that we were on the cusp of an exciting multi-pronged technological revolution—and the question of how law should engage with such a revolution was at last taking shape in my thinking.

At that time, the priority seemed to be to put in place legal provisions for the governance of these technologies and their applications—exactly as the HFE Act laid out a regulatory scheme for licensing clinics that would offer IVF services. However, this was only half the story: some of the technologies that were being developed also had potential applications as tools to be used for legal and regulatory purposes. Recognising the dual significance of technology, a radical introduction to law should highlight not just the general salience of technology as a feature of the context in which law's governance now operates but the importance of technology for law as both something that needs to be governed and as a tool for governance (Brownsword and Yeung, 2008).

In the stories that follow, two of which relate to a visit that I made to the European Patent Office (EPO) in Munich in the early 1990s, we will see some seeds of the realisation that technology has this double significance for law.

Law's governance of technology

In the 1980s, the US corporation Du Pont funded research that was designed to find ways of modifying the genetic characteristics of white laboratory mice. In due course, the researchers applied to the US Patent Office for a cluster of patents to protect their inventive work. These patents covered the techniques employed to introduce the modification as well as a modified mouse. The mouse, the so-called Harvard Onco-mouse, was modified in such a way that it would develop tumours that would then assist researchers in their attempts to understand the development of cancers in humans. The US Patent Office, having granted the patents, the researchers brought their claims to Europe, making their application to the EPO.

After some initial doubt about the application of European patent law to the claims being put forward for protection, the examiners at the EPO decided that the patentability of the inventions hinged on whether it would be immoral or contrary to ordre public for the techniques and the mice to be commercially exploited. If so, applying Article 53(a) of the European Patent Convention, even though the research processes and products were inventive, no European patent would be granted. This question provoked a huge controversy: while some thought that it was imperative that patent law kept pace with state of the art genetics, others thought that it would be plain wrong to grant patents, especially to grant a patent on a living thing, the genetically-engineered mouse. The EPO decided that these issues needed to be debated and a symposium was duly held to take soundings from a range of participants.

Arriving at the EPO's building, I encountered quite a gathering of students from the nearby Max Planck Institute. The purpose of this demonstration was to express solid opposition to the granting of patents on living things. Inside the EPO, at the symposium, there were voices that supported the grant, voices that opposed it, and voices that counselled caution. For example, the British ethicist, Mary Warnock, having remarked that biotechnology was now making things possible that previously had not been possible, said that the focal question was whether we *ought* to do the various things that we can now do (Warnock, 1993). The fact that we can now do something is one thing; but, whether we ought to do it is something else. Echoing the students, there were plenty of voices arguing that we categorically ought not to do this thing. Patents on life, it was argued, compromised human dignity; if we could not see that, there was surely something wrong with us. However, elsewhere, there was no shortage of voices arguing that we should go forward with genetics. Cancer is a killer and, if research into effective treatments could be facilitated by the modified mice, then the law should support the underlying research and development. If patents on the work were not granted, this might discourage investment in this kind of research; and human lives that might have been saved would be lost.

The symposium at the EPO was just the beginning of a saga that ran on for more than a dozen years. Eventually, after some amendments to the original claims, patent protection for the Harvard Onco-mouse was granted. However, this was just one instance of a mass of questions presented by both biotechnologies and information technologies for law's governance. The challenge facing law's governance was that a position needed to be taken and then defended even though the questions were divisive and even though not everyone would agree with the position taken.

Meanwhile the Internet was arriving

While developments in biotechnology were provoking deep debates, the infrastructure for the Internet and e-commerce was taking shape. So far as governance was concerned, it was the former rather than the latter that was seen as most challenging. Indeed, in *Our Posthuman Future* (2002), the American political scientist, Francis Fukuyama, argued that it was the developments in human genetics, not online information and communication technologies, that were really troubling. To be sure, there were some concerns about a 'digital divide' and about online privacy, and so on, but none of this was seen as particularly challenging. Accordingly, when Fukuyama embarked on an international 'roadshow' with Gregory Stock, another US academic who was also speaking to his latest book, *Redesigning Humans* (2003), it was the governance of the new genetics that was front and centre. When the debate came to London, it attracted an audience of almost 1,000 people who heard a lively exchange between Fukuyama's conservatism and the more liberal approach taken by Stock. However, Stock also suggested that if genetics gave humans more control over their own characteristics as well as the characteristics of their children, then we should not expect governance to be able to prevent this happening. In other words, there were two issues here: one was the Warnock question (with genetics we can do these things, but ought we to do so?); and, the other was whether law's governance could prevent these things being done even if we wanted it to do so. Although this latter question was not seen as the primary one, it was precisely the effectiveness of law's governance that was being challenged by the development of the Internet.

Thus, in a seminal paper on the regulation of online communications, David Johnson and David Post (1996) warned that, because '[g]lobal computer-based communications cut across territorial borders, creating a new realm of human activity and undermining the feasibility—and legitimacy—of laws based on geographic boundaries' then territorial law-makers and law-enforcers will 'find this new environment deeply threatening' (1367). This warning rapidly proved to be well-founded.

Speaking for the so-called cyberlibertarians of that time, John Perry Barlow famously issued a declaration of independence (www.eff.org/cyberspace-independence)_which opened in the following memorable terms:

> Governments of the Industrial World, you weary giants of flesh and steel, I come from Cyberspace, the new home of Mind. On behalf of the future, I ask you of the past to leave us alone. You are not welcome among us. You have no sovereignty where we gather.
>
> We have no elected government, nor are we likely to have one, so I address you with no greater authority than that with which liberty itself always speaks. I declare the global social space we are building to be naturally independent of the tyrannies you seek to impose on us. You have no moral right to rule us nor do you possess any methods of enforcement we have true reason to fear.
>
> Governments derive their just powers from the consent of the governed. You have neither solicited nor received ours. We did not invite you. You do not know us, nor do you know our world. Cyberspace does not lie within your borders. Do not think that you can build it, as though it were a public construction project. You cannot. It is an act of nature and it grows itself through our collective actions.

Acting on this cyberlibertarian rejection of the authority of national legal systems, a generation of Internet separatists took the law into their own hands. Cocking a snook at whatever restrictions copyright law imposed, millions of young people took advantage of the latest file-sharing technologies.

Copyright was being violated around the world and on an industrial scale. In online environments, as Joel Reidenberg (2005: 1953–54) put it, different rules applied:

> The defenses for hate, lies, drugs, sex, gambling, and stolen music are in essence that technology justifies the denial of personal jurisdiction, the rejection of an assertion of applicable law by a sovereign state, and the denial of the enforcement of decisions….In the face of these claims, legal systems engage in a rather conventional struggle to adapt existing regulatory standards to new technologies and the Internet. Yet, the underlying fight is a profound struggle against the very right of sovereign states to establish rules for online activity.

Despite lawmakers having tried a range of approaches to reinstating the Rule of Law in cyberspace, and even though it is widely recognised that the Internet needs governance, the sense remains that they have enjoyed only limited success.

Meanwhile, lawmakers have also had to contend with the operations of big tech, with the harvesting of huge amounts of personal data, and with the pursuit of information capitalism. This is another major challenge. It might well be, as Julie Cohen (2019: 267) has argued, that 'institutions for recognising and enforcing fundamental rights should work to counterbalance private economic power rather than reinforcing it. Obligations to protect fundamental rights must extend—enforceably—to private, for-profit entities if they are to be effective at all'. It might well be that it should be a condition of the Rule of Law (the Rule of Law 2.0, as Cohen terms it) that the *private* use of technical measures, machines, and technological management should be compatible with the general principles for their (public) use. This applies whether the private regulators are operating at a distance from public regulators or, as is increasingly the case in some contexts (such as the development of 'smart' cities) in partnership with them. The $1000 dollar question, however, is how private enterprise is to be controlled. How are effective regulatory interventions to be made? Will the governance of technologies itself have to rely on technologies to do the governance work? Will the governance of technologies have to resort to governance by technologies?

Governance by technologies

Returning from the symposium at the EPO, and in an absent-minded professorial way, I managed to walk from the arrivals lounge at Munich airport right through to my gate without first having checked-in to obtain my boarding pass. At the gate, the BA staff for my flight were astounded that I had been able to do this. 'How is that possible?' they asked. To which the answer was that it was possible because, quite simply, I had been able to do it. My intentions were entirely innocent; I was travelling light without luggage to check-in and so I walked straight past the area where my boarding pass would have been issued; and, between there and the gate, whoever was supposed to check that I had a boarding pass evidently failed to do so.

At an international airport in the 2020s, this would not happen because it could not happen. Nowadays, the architecture and design of many airports ensures that progression from the arrivals lounge onwards is not possible without passing through gates which will open only once the barcode on a boarding pass has been successfully scanned (or once facial recognition technology has confirmed passage). The architecture and design of international airports, in conjunction with the automation of processes, controls the flow of passengers. This is governance by technology, governance by technological management of the airport spaces together with the use of smart machines (including the use of AI to profile passengers and assess the risk that they might present).

Reworking Mary Warnock's remarks at the EPO conference, the fact that we can now use new tools to channel the conduct of passengers at airports is one thing; but whether we ought to use these tools, at airports or more generally as mechanisms of social control, is altogether a different question. For example, in August 2023, on the day that the trial judge pronounced a whole life sentence on Lucy Letby who was convicted of seven charges of murder and attempted murder of babies at the Countess of Chester hospital, there was much criticism of the fact that she could not be required to be in court to hear the judge's sentencing remarks and, concomitantly, suggestions that the relevant rules should be changed. However, one of the more pressing questions for the committee of inquiry set up after this case surely will be to consider whether technological safeguards, such as CCTV in neonatal units, might be installed in order to prevent such a tragedy occurring again.

My experience at Munich airport flags up two potential weak spots in law's governance: first, that governance relies on humans; and, secondly, that governance relies on rules (or protocols). We might try to mitigate these weaknesses in various ways but, at modern international airports, they are addressed head-on: humans are taken out of the governance loop (their functions are taken over by machines and automated processes); and, reliance on rules is replaced by technological management which focuses on controlling the options that are actually available in a regulated space. To be sure, those who are subjected to governance are humans, and they are likely to be a heterogeneous group of travellers with a plurality of different preferences, principles, and priorities. On occasion, the airport's technological mode of governance will provoke some discontent, the plurality will be agitated; but, so long as security and safety is recognised as the highest priority, and the more that humans are accustomed to being herded through terminal buildings, the more efficient and effective the airport's order will be.

Summing up

In our times, law students and lawyers need to be increasingly alert to the governance of, and by, a raft of new technologies. In relation to the former, one of the principal challenges concerns the positions that law's governance takes in relation to whether the development and application of these technologies is to be permitted. Here, we find intense debates about the acceptability or legitimacy of particular applications and then as to the legal position. Another major challenge concerns the effectiveness of governance. As we have seen already, there can be a push-back against the authority of law and, even when there is no push-back, there are problems of the kind anticipated by Johnson and Post.

In relation to governance by technology, the design of international airports gives an indication of how humans might be more effectively channelled by technological management rather than by rules. But, even if we can now channel humans more effectively, there remains the question of whether we ought to do so. What we see crystallising, then, is a tension between, and potential trade-off between, our interest in effective governance and our interest, as humans, in being in control of our governance.

PART 2

Legal landmarks

7

THE LANDSCAPE OF LAW

Legal London

Introduction

If we search for a map of walks around the 'legal district' of London—such as the map at www.google.com/maps/d/viewer?mid=1yn5ouRinFtmUtxK2B2oLD----28&hl=en&ll=51.51405854203101%2C-0.11050682012938573&z=16—we will probably find that it centres on an area on the North bank of the Thames, running between Waterloo bridge and Blackfriars bridge, and extending about half a mile to the North. While there is a huge amount of legal history in this small area, it does not extend Eastwards to the City and downriver to Canary Wharf where many of the major law firms are headquartered, and nor does it extend West to Westminster and Whitehall where most of our laws are formulated and enacted.

So, if the law students at, say, King's College London, duly supplied with a copy of the aforementioned map, were to be offered a traditional guided tour of the local legal landscape then, setting off from the Law School in Somerset House, they would head East, their first port of call being the law library in Chancery Lane. In law libraries, as we noted in Chapter 1, the shelves are filled with the principal sources of law, with the rules, principles and standards that are set out in the legislation and in the case-law, as well as with the many journals and reviews that publish articles and case comments of legal interest. If we want the *ipsissima verba* of a statute or of a passage in a leading case, this is where traditionally (in pre-digital times) we would expect to find it. From this point, however, there would be a choice as to the direction and emphasis of the walking tour.

One option would be to stick with the map, staying close to the library, highlighting the Courts and the historic Inns of Court—Inner and Middle

DOI: 10.4324/9781003507802-9

Temple, Lincoln's Inn, and Gray's Inn—that are clustered in the vicinity. As to the Courts themselves, the tour would certainly include the nearby Royal Courts of Justice on the Strand and the Old Bailey just beyond the end of Fleet Street, and possibly (reminding students about the everyday routine processing of criminal justice) the former Bow Street Magistrates Court. All the talk would be about courts, judges and barristers—although solicitors might get a mention as the party walked past the Law Society Hall (which is right across the street from the law library) or one of the law firms that has its offices in the area.

Another option would be to put the map to one side and head in the opposite direction, going West, to Westminster and Whitehall where it would be Parliament, 10 Downing Street, the Ministry of Justice, the Cabinet Office, and the apex court, the Supreme Court, that would be the landmarks. The talk here would be about politicians and the Cabinet, about long nights in the House, and possibly about the anomalous location of the Supreme Court in the shadow of the political branch—I say 'possibly' because there are other capital cities where the apex court is located right by the legislative building.

Whichever option we took, the tour would highlight the rules, principles and standards that are the stuff of legal argument and analysis. However, while one tour would treat the centre of gravity of law as being in the courts and the cases, the other would treat it as being in legislation and politics. While the former would draw a sharp line between law and politics, the latter would not. Crucially, on neither tour would technology get a mention. For radically minded law students, this invites two questions. First, what exactly is the relationship between law and politics; and secondly, where would we take our guided tour if we wanted to locate governance by technology?

Law and politics

Although the UK Supreme Court is located in, so to speak, the political quarter of London, the Justices emphasise that the Court operates at arm's length from the political branch, that they are independent, and that they leave their personal and partisan politics behind them when they enter the courtroom. In saying this, the Justices speak not only for themselves but also for the judicial branch generally in the UK.

Inevitably, though, the judges are called upon from time to time to make decisions about legal questions that are politically contentious. For example, in March 2023, the government introduced the unfortunately named Illegal Migration Bill, this being designed to stem the rising tide of asylum seekers and migrants who were coming across the Channel in small boats in an attempt to enter the UK. Unusually, the government conceded that it could not be certain that the measures in the Bill were consistent with international human rights law and, seizing on this concession, the opponents of the Bill claimed in no uncertain terms that the measures were unlawful. In due course, this led to the Rwandan case (2023), where the lawfulness of the government's plans to remove asylum seekers to Rwanda was challenged. Speaking for a unanimous Supreme Court, Lord Reed and Lord Lloyd-Jones set out the remit in the following terms:

> In this appeal, the court is required to decide whether the Rwanda policy is lawful. That is a legal question which the court has to decide on the basis of the evidence and established legal principles. The court is not concerned with the political debate surrounding the policy, and nothing in this judgment should be regarded as supporting or opposing any political view of the issues.
>
> *(para 2)*

Ruling that the policy was not lawful, the Court could find plenty of legal support for its judgment; and, it is surely one of the functions of the Court to ensure that governments stay honest in relation to the limits on their law-making powers that they themselves have accepted. Nevertheless, the political ramifications of the decision are all too obvious and, if the government responds (as it has done) by, in effect, trying to redraw those limits or assert its sovereignty, then we could be in for a series of cases in which the courts will find it very difficult to put clear water between the law, which they say that they are simply declaring and applying, and the politics into which they are being drawn. Indeed, no matter how judges rule in such cases, some will accuse them of being 'political' (Gibb, 2023).

Nowhere was this problematic interface of law and politics more apparent than in the questions referred to the courts following the Brexit referendum in 2016. Of course, it is not suggested that the judges did not have their own views about the wisdom of calling the referendum as well as about its outcome and nor is it suggested that it is inappropriate for judges, as members of a political community, to have a political view; the question is whether judges are able to insulate their legal judgments from their political convictions.

In the first of the big Brexit cases, *Miller 1* (2016), the question was whether the government was acting constitutionally in proposing simply to notify the EU of the UK's intention to withdraw without also taking the proposal through the usual legislative process. Article 50 of the EU Treaty provides that withdrawal should be in accordance with the (withdrawing) member state's 'own constitutional requirements'; but, in the absence of clear constitutional provision on the matter, the nature of the UK's requirements were legally moot. The government argued that notification of the UK's intention to withdraw was within the so-called 'prerogative power' to conduct foreign relations and, as such, was not a matter for the courts. However, the Miller team argued that there was more to it than this: the Article 50 notification was the first step in a process that would lead to changes in domestic law and that would impact on domestic rights—indeed, more than that, by de-recognising the EU legislative and judicial institutions as sources of law within the UK, the process that was being set in motion would lead to major changes in the UK's constitutional arrangements. This, the applicants argued, required the authorisation of primary legislation. By a substantial majority, the Supreme Court confirmed that primary legislation was indeed required, this prompting the wrath of Brexiteers and, especially, the Brexit supporting press.

By the time of the second case, *Miller 2* (2019), the story had moved on. Theresa May had been replaced as Prime Minister by Boris Johnson; Brexit was going to happen; and the only question was whether the UK would leave with or without 'a deal' having been agreed with the EU. Insofar as there was any common ground, it was that the UK should leave with the best deal available (which, for some, meant that the UK should leave with 'no deal' if that were better than the best deal on offer from the EU). With exit due to take place on October 31, 2019, the Prime Minister advised the Queen that Parliament should be prorogued on a date between September 9 and September 12 (this having the effect of closing the current parliamentary session on that day) and that it should stay prorogued until October 14 (when the new parliamentary session would start with the announcement of the government's legislative programme and its priorities for the session). To prorogue Parliament for more than about ten days (in this case for 34 days) was unusual and the government's reasons for taking such action were unclear. However, given the government's negotiating strategy, its thinking probably was that its chances of securing the best deal for the UK would be to have a clear run without 'interference' from parliamentarians—hence the proposed extended prorogation.

Whatever the best reading of the government's thinking, the Supreme Court was now asked to rule on its lawfulness. Giving the unanimous judgment of the Court, Lady Hale and Lord Reed were at pains to emphasise right from the outset that the Court was not being asked to decide 'when and on what terms the UK is to leave the European Union' (para 1). Also, there was no doubt that a decision to prorogue Parliament is based not on legislative authority but on an historic prerogative power, that such a decision is essentially of a political nature, and that it is not for the courts to supervise the exercise of such powers where they are clearly within scope. Nevertheless, the Court emphasised that any exercise of a prerogative power has to be compatible with fundamental constitutional principles—in particular, an exercise of the power to prorogue Parliament should not have the effect of incapacitating the legislative body and nor should it disable the government's having to account to Parliament. In the circumstances, the Court was not persuaded that the government needed to prorogue Parliament for five weeks in order to sketch its legislative intentions for the Queen's Speech at the opening of the new session. Hence, the Court ruled that, on the evidence put to it, there was no reasonable justification—or, to be precise, there was not 'any reason—let alone a good reason' (para 61)—to support this exceptional exercise of the prerogative power. Despite the Court's protestations that this was not a political decision, purely a matter of constitutional law, Brexiteers might beg to differ. When some see the adjudication of constitutional disputes as political and others see it as legal, we have a problem—and, we have a problem whether, like Stephen Sedley (2018: 134), we see it as being 'the politicisation of legal issues' or, to the contrary, 'the legalisation of political issues'.

Away from the drama of high constitutional law, how plausible is it to suppose that judges maintain a clear distinction between their personal politics and the application of the law? In *The Politics of the Judiciary* (1977), a book that caused considerable controversy at the time, John Griffith argued that judges are not able to shake off their somewhat similar educational and professional backgrounds as a result of which their decision-making tends to be 'conservative', supportive of the status quo, and pro-'Establishment'. Griffith's thesis was not that judges are guided by the latest manifesto of the Conservative party but, more subtly, that legal culture tends to be 'conservative' in a way that aligns with Conservative politics. The lesson here is that judges who, in good faith, simply apply the law will necessarily apply whatever politics is inscribed in legal principles and doctrines. When those principles and doctrines derive from the historic case-law, they might well reflect the interests of, say, the landed or industrial classes but the line between law and politics would still be relatively clear. However, once Parliament becomes the principal maker of laws, and once judges are being asked to interpret and apply legislation, the legal principles and policies that are inscribed in those laws means that applying the law is necessarily an application of positions taken by political bodies.

Across the Atlantic, the political nature of judicial appointments makes it difficult to draw a bright line between law and politics in adjudication. When the members of the US Supreme Court are interviewed, they might profess to apply the law of the constitution and nothing but the law, but the polls indicate that the majority of Americans believe that, when constitutional cases—such as the Obamacare cases where the flagship policy of the administration was challenged—are highly charged, then the decisions of the Supreme Court will 'be more "influenced" by "politics" than "based solely on legal merits"' (Zirin, 2016: 19). Similarly, it was no surprise when, in *Dobbs v Jackson Women's Health Organization* (2022), the Court with a clear Republican majority finally overturned the decision in *Roe v Wade* (which Democrats had defended as a bastion of women's reproductive autonomy and liberal rights generally).

Locating governance by technology

If, instead of a traditional tour, our guide was looking for a more radical view of the landscape, the choice between what Lawrence Lessig called an East coast-style of governance and a West coast style would be much more pronounced. On the East coast, governance is rule-based and traditional. By contrast, on the West coast, governance is far more reliant on the latest technologies. There are courts but most disputes are resolved online by automated processes—in the way, for example, that millions of disputes on eBay are resolved every year. On the West coast the landscape of governance is not dominated by fine buildings but by smart machines humming away in maintaining order and resolving disputes.

If the question is 'Where do we find governance by technology in central London?' then one answer is 'Everywhere. CCTV cameras are ubiquitous; and it is estimated that, on average, Londoners are captured on CCTV 300 times each day'. However, although surveillance technologies contribute to governance, they do not limit the practical options that are available to those who are governed. CCTV does not go as far as physically limiting the options available to the students and their guide. That said, any one of London's mainline train and Underground stations exemplifies a level of technological management. In my student days, it was possible to walk into and out of these stations as well as ride the trains without having a ticket. There were random ticket inspections but the architecture of the stations did not make it difficult to enter or exit without a ticket as is now the case. If, once upon a time, governance relied on trust (on passengers doing the right thing by paying for their rides), technological management now does the regulatory work. So, perhaps, a more effective induction would be to forget about walking and take the train to Heathrow airport where West coast governance is the order of the day. Anyone who doubts this should try, having got through to the departures lounge at Terminal 5, to retrace their steps back to their point of arrival.

However, technological governance is to be found not just in the architecture of the Metro or at airports. In his book, *The Digital Republic* (2022), Jamie Susskind offers readers a glimpse of what everyday technological governance might look like, being embedded in places and spaces, products and processes, and so on. One example is electronic scooters. These scooters are designed for governance in the sense that '[e]very journey is tracked from start to finish. No matter how hard the throttle is pressed, the scooters will not go above a particular speed. They refuse to leave designated urban areas. And there is no haggling over the fare: an app deducts a precise sum depending on the length of the journey' (35). Another example is the late return of library books. If the library operates an e-collection, there is no longer a problem: quite simply, once the time is up on the loan, the digital copy will cease to be available on the reader's device (35–36).

With technologies being put, directly or indirectly, to governance use in both the public and the private sector, we might wonder where we can see the relevant governance decisions being made. At Westminster, we can see where our laws are made; and, at the Bundestag in Berlin, the architecture of the building is conspicuously designed for transparency. At the Royal Courts of Justice, we can also observe the processes of law at work; and, we can even watch some proceedings in the Supreme Court as online viewers. We know roughly where the key nodes of law are and we can see how they work. However, West coast governance is widely distributed, opaque to the extent that it takes place behind closed doors and with trade secret or IP protection, and some of the technologies (notoriously AI) function as black boxes. How we capture the landscape of, let alone control the application of, this radical form of governance by technology is a very good question.

8

THINKING LIKE A LAWYER

Introduction

No one questions that one of the roles, arguably the principal role, of law schools is to train students 'to think like a lawyer'; but, we rarely pause to interrogate the idea of 'thinking like a lawyer'. One of the radical threads in this introduction is to insist that we should pause to ask precisely this question. Accordingly, if we are asked what, as a lawyer, we make of such and such a matter, we should always point out that this depends on our mode of thinking like a lawyer; and that, in the current landscape of law, there are several modes of such thinking.

In this chapter, we will distinguish between three ways of 'thinking like a lawyer', namely: thinking like a doctrinal coherentist, thinking in a rules-based regulatory way, and thinking in a techno-regulatory way. When I say that law students are traditionally trained to 'think in a box', it is the doctrinal coherentist mode of thinking to which I am referring. In other words, as traditionally and persistently understood, training students 'to think like lawyers' equates to training law students to think and reason in a doctrinal coherentist way.

The purpose of this chapter is to sketch the three modes of thinking that represent distinct takes on what it is to think like a lawyer (Brownsword, 2020). Each mode of thinking belongs to a distinctive paradigm of law's governance, namely: Law 1.0 (doctrinal coherentism), Law 2.0 (rule-based regulatory), and Law 3.0 (techno-regulatory).

DOI: 10.4324/9781003507802-10

Law 1.0

In the legal landscape where Law 1.0 is dominant, new technologies are not viewed as having any particular significance or salience. The same applies to ethics that are not already doctrinally inscribed in private law concepts or doctrines (such as 'good faith' or tests of fairness and reasonableness) or public law values (such as equality, human rights, or human dignity). The application of legal rules and principles to new technologies is simply doctrinal business as usual; there is no need to ask whether the rules are fit for purpose; and the thought that these technologies might be applied in ways that support or replace legal rules and principles has simply not occurred.

Where Law 1.0 is the mode of engagement, the focal question is the one that lawyers ask when confronted by a particular fact situation irrespective of whether new technologies or novel applications are involved. In common law jurisdictions, that question is how the precedents and the historic principles of the law apply to, or fit with, the technology or situation. For example, we might ask how the general principles of tort law apply to defamatory content that is hosted online; or how the principles of contract law might be applied to so-called 'smart contracts' or to those platforms in which the relationship between, the roles, and the responsibilities of the parties are not clear; or we might ask how copyright law maps onto creative works generated by AI or by those who engage in remixing; or we might ask how traditional concepts of property, assignment, and novation map onto cryptoassets. The list of potential questions is not endless, but it is long and it gets longer with each new technology and its applications.

Often, this kind of question will be asked (and answered) by lawyers who are advising clients on their best reading of the legal position. However, where such questions are referred to courts, the flexibility of the law notwithstanding, there is a tendency towards conservative rulings coupled with no more than incremental development of the law. So, for example, although patent offices were able to adjust their understanding of patentability and disclosure to accommodate new products and processes in biotechnology, the common law courts were not so quick to recognise body parts, embryos, and gametes as property in order to ground tort claims. On the other hand, as Joshua Fairfield (2021: 54–59) points out, at any rate in some US jurisdictions, there was judicial development of the old idea of 'trespass' to apply in cyberspaces (for example, to respond to the problems of spam mail), this suggesting that traditional legal concepts and principles are flexible enough if only the members of the judiciary are imaginative enough.

This is not to say that practitioners of Law 1.0 are uncritical of the state of the law. To the contrary, the 'coherence' of the body of legal doctrine is a matter of intense and enduring concern. Contradictions and inconsistencies in the body of doctrine are not to be tolerated; precedents and principles should not simply be ignored; legal doctrine should not be distorted; law should be applied in a way that respects its integrity—all of this being regarded as desirable in itself. Indeed, for many lawyers, Law 1.0 reasoning speaks to the essence of the Rule of Law (the rule of rules) and it exemplifies the virtues of 'legality'. Given this culture, there is a good deal of nervousness about stretching legal principles, or about creating ad hoc exceptions in order to accommodate a hard case, or about correcting the law where it is plainly not fair, just, or reasonable. Similarly, at times of rapid economic, social, and technological disruption, the concern for doctrinal coherence can inhibit major development of the law. While critics will say that the law should move with the times, judges will tend to exercise restraint and be mindful of being accused of assuming an unauthorised legislative role. Accordingly, while the courts will give an answer to the Law 1.0 question that is put to them, they do not have either the resources or the mandate for expansive lawmaking or for setting new policies (compare Goddard, 2022). This means that the burden of responding to questions that invite a serious overhaul of the regulatory environment moves elsewhere.

Law 2.0

The first disruption to the legal landscape occurs when it is recognised that the challenges presented by emerging technologies to traditional legal rules and principles are significant and salient. Accordingly, the paradigmatic question in a Law 2.0 mode of engagement, the kind of question that regulatory scholars and various kinds of regulatory agencies typically ask, is whether existing rules are fit for purpose, whether the rules are effective and appropriate in serving regulatory policies, and whether perhaps new rules are required. In short, the question is whether the regulatory environment is fit for purpose. This is an exercise in setting and serving policy, and the reasoning (with its focus on effectiveness and efficiency) is predominantly one of instrumental rationality. In practice, the engagement with this question will be in the political arena.

The answers given to the headline questions in Law 2.0 are not constrained in the way that we find in the courts. It is not a matter of finding an answer from within a limited set of materials; there is no pressure for consistency with the jurisdictional history and nor for doctrinal coherence. Regulation can make a fresh start and regulators can develop bespoke responses to particular questions in a way that would offend doctrinal coherentism. So, for example, regulators can adopt any number of absolute or strict liability offences (relating to health and safety, the environment, and so on) that would offend the classical code of criminal law in which it is axiomatic that proof of mens rea is required (Sayre, 1933). Or, if the protection of the investment in databases does not fit well with standard IPRs, a bespoke regulatory regime can be put in place (as was the case with Directive 96/9/EC); and, if innovation policy is not well served by limiting patents to *human* inventors (thereby excluding AI invention), the limitation should, and *could*, be removed (Abbott, 2020: Chs 4 and 5). In Law 2.0 circles, there is no need to justify a departure from an historic legal principle or classificatory scheme; in Law 2.0, regulators operate with a new brush which, if they so wish, they can use to sweep the law clean.

Although much regulatory discourse is focused on finding what works, modern scholarship in law, regulation, and technology sometimes undertakes a broader critique. In this articulation of Law 2.0, it is not simply a matter of regulation being effective in serving its purposes; those purposes and the means employed must be legitimate, and there needs to be a sustainable connection between regulatory interventions and rapidly changing technologies and their applications (Brownsword, 2008). It follows that this invites a more complex critical appraisal of the fitness of the regulatory environment. So, the law needs to make its regulatory moves at the right time (neither too early nor too late); and, even if regulation seems 'to work', there might be questions about the acceptability of the position that has been taken up in relation to a new technology.

With regard to the acceptability of the legal position, a key question is whether the regulatory environment strikes the optimal balance between providing support for beneficial innovation and providing adequate protection against the risks of harm that might be caused by an emerging technology. Accordingly, much of the regulatory theory and practice in Law 2.0 circles is focused on avoiding both over-regulation (and stifling innovation) and under-regulation (and exposing consumers and others to unacceptable risks). As we will see in later chapters, if we are to avoid discontent with law's governance, we will need to rise to the challenge of getting regulation right in an age of rapid technological innovation; and, moreover, we will find that keeping it right is a case of constant regulatory work in progress.

Finally, ethics has a place in this landscape; it is now salient and significant for law's governance. As we have said, the regulatory environment that is set for new technologies needs to be broadly acceptable, and to some extent the acceptability of the governance regime (what is prohibited, what is permitted, and so on) will reflect not only the general ethics of the community but also, and increasingly, the ethics found in professional codes of conduct (especially the codes of the medical profession). In practice, *judges* do occasionally emphasise the importance of their decisions being adequate both legally and ethically; but, for legislators, ethics can intrude very explicitly on lawmaking where a vote is seen as a matter of conscience but also implicitly where regulatory policy is being debated.

Law 3.0

The second disruption to the legal landscape occurs when we begin to wonder, in a characteristically Law 3.0 manner, whether new tools and technical measures might be deployed for governance purposes. The greater the potential utility of these tools as regulatory instruments, the more salient and significant they look. Where the constitutionality of using these tools is contested, then whatever the ethics that are already implicated in public law provisions, they will be relevant; this is as in Law 1.0. However, as in Law 2.0 debates, the legislative and regulatory debates of Law 3.0 that focus on the acceptability of using these tools will draw in ethical views irrespective of whether they are inscribed in legal doctrine. Moreover, with the technology industry joining the professions in promulgating their own ethical codes, we find some foreshadowing of a tension between the interest of technologists in self-governance and the protection of the public interest through public governance. In this landscape, whether we view ethics from the legal or the technological perspective, it is a salient and significant feature of governance.

Where Law 3.0 is the mode of engagement, the headline questions might be whether new technologies might be used in support of the rules relied on to serve particular regulatory policies, whether technologies might be used to assist those who are undertaking legal and regulatory functions, and whether the technologies and technical measures might actually supplant the rules and the humans who make, administer, and enforce them (Deakin and Markou, 2020). In all cases, though, we are looking at technologies as potential instruments of governance rather than (as in Law 2.0) tools and applications that need to be subjected to law's governance.

When governance is on the cusp of Law 3.0, it will still be *humans* who lead in the use of new regulatory tools; and, it will still be compliance with *rules* that is assisted by these tools. However, from that point on, broadly speaking, Law 3.0 thinking develops two spearheads. The first spearhead aims to automate rule-based governance. Those who are subjected to law's governance are directed by legal rules and it might be found that governance is assisted by technologies (such as facial recognition technologies, CCTV surveillance, DNA profiling and so on) that nudge humans towards compliance. However, the ambition is to take humans out of the governance loop by employing the full range of technologies in order to automate the detection of rule-breaking, the identification of the rule-breaker, and the administration of the penalty. The second spearhead no longer relies on rules to direct the conduct of those who are subject to governance. Instead, governance is achieved by employing 'technological management' of the places and spaces in which the governed act (Brownsword, 2019). The focus here is on designing environments, as well as products and processes, in such a way that there is no practical possibility of acting in ways which those who govern view in a negative light. That said, while technological management in this sketch is about limiting the options that are practically available, in principle, it might also be employed in a less restrictive way to remove the cause of conflict (for example, overcoming scarcity of resources by digitising texts or by using other technologies).

It is not altogether clear who should respond to the questions that are on the agenda in Law 3.0, nor who should be parties to the regulatory conversation. Because the technological solutions will often be developed in the private sector, there seems to be a need for a public/private partnership or some form of co-regulation where public bodies set the desired regulatory objectives but leave it to industry to develop the best technological means. However, of one thing we can be quite sure: this is that, where governance is guided by Law 3.0 thinking, technical specifications and standard-setting will move from back-stage to centre-stage. Given that Law 2.0's governance promises to bring the public into the conversation, and even if we are discontent with the performance of this promise, any transition to Law 3.0 governance will need to reckon with an expectation that, at minimum, the public should be consulted (Micklitz, 2023).

What is more, there are likely to be challenging issues relating to public engagement when the technologists are working on taking humans out of the loops of law and regulation (as with governance by machines) or rules being replaced by technological management. For humans at least, where they interface with such technologies, the displacement of humans needs to be 'socially acceptable' and this raises deeper questions about the compatibility of such forms of governance with the community's fundamental values and with the global responsibilities of those who govern.

In short, Law 3.0 presents a very different legal landscape in which we can contemplate a wide spectrum of regulatory deployment—with technologies being deployed both in support of rules and in place of rules, to assist human decision-makers and to replace human decision-makers, to interface with both regulatees and with regulators, to support legal officials and to supplant them, and to supervise both regulatees and legal officials, and so on—as a result of which, in various ways, the needle shifts from governance by rules to governance by machines and technological management.

Summing up

Summing up, we can detect three distinct but co-existing modes of legal engagement with emerging technologies. Each mode has its own particular framing, its own range of focal concerns, and each relates to a particular input into the regulatory environment as we should now conceive of it. We can also say that each mode of thinking has its own strengths and weaknesses: Law 1.0 reflects the virtues of legality (predictability, consistency, and so on) but it is not geared for agile and responsive governance where technologies are disrupting the social and economic order; Law 2.0 asks the right questions but, because regulatory decisions will be made in the political arena, it is subject to the usual political pathologies; and Law 3.0, by potentially taking both humans and rules out of the equation, promises greater efficiency, consistency, and effectiveness but, at the same time, might be feared as dystopian control of humans by machines. To the extent that ethics has the potential to constrain the application of emerging technologies, it is in the conversations of Law 2.0 and Law 3.0 that we see how it can enter the regulatory mix and guide law's governance. If Law 1.0 is the box in which young lawyers are trained, then it is the three co-existing modes of legal engagement that are represented by Law 1.0, Law 2.0, and Law 3.0, that should become the new frame.

9

HANDLING STATUTES

Introduction

Increasingly, our laws are found in a legislative form. In the early years of my academic life, when I walked students around the materials in the law library, I would say that they could expect there to be as many as 100 Acts of Parliament (statutes) each year. Nowadays, although the headline number is very much lower, the statutes themselves tend to be longer. At first glance, these laws are pretty daunting—and they do not get much more accessible on a second or third look. For whom, we might wonder, are such complex and convoluted documents drafted?

In addition to the statutes (which have gone through the usual processes of parliamentary scrutiny, debate, and voting) there are several thousand statutory instruments each year. Although the making of these statutory instruments will have been authorised by provisions in a statute (the so-called 'parent Act'), the text of statutory instruments is not subjected to the same level of scrutiny as the text of statutes. Whether or not this is a satisfactory situation, whether or not so-called 'delegated legislation' of this kind is compliant with the Rule of Law, is a matter for recurrent debate. At all events, legislative texts, in both statutes and statutory instruments, require interpretation and application in ways that invite law students and lawyers alike to take a view on the legal position.

Knife crime

Consider the question of statutory interpretation that arose in the case of *Fisher v Bell* (1961). Concerns about knife crime are not new, and back

DOI: 10.4324/9781003507802-11

in the 1950s, legislation was introduced to try to control the sale of flick knives and other dangerous weapons. The relevant statute, the Restriction of Offensive Weapons Act 1959, made it a criminal offence to 'offer for sale' various kinds of offensive weapons, including flick knives. A shopkeeper in Bristol, having displayed a flick knife for sale in his shop window, was charged with the offence. The shopkeeper did not deny any of the facts, including the fact that the flick knife that was displayed had a price tag attached to it. Nevertheless, the shopkeeper's lawyer argued that no offence had been committed within the meaning of the Act because the display of the knife in the shop window did not signal that the shopkeeper was actually 'offering' it for sale. It was conceded that the knife was 'exposed' in the shop window with a view to its sale but this, it was argued, fell short of 'offering' the knife for sale. Given the clear purpose of the 1959 Act, this argument might seem to be one having little merit and yet the magistrates accepted this defence and their decision was upheld on appeal by Lord Parker. So, the Bristol shopkeeper was found not to have committed the offence and, in order to close this loophole in the law, Parliament had to pass a statute, the Restriction of Offensive Weapons Act 1961, making it clear that the offence is committed where the defendant exposes a flick knife for the purposes of sale.

Strangely, law students usually read, and view, *Fisher v Bell* as a leading case in contract law rather than as an example of statutory interpretation. The reason for this is that the case exemplifies a three-step process that contract lawyers treat as the template for the formation of a contract, namely: (i) the prospective seller *invites* offers for the goods to be sold; (ii) a prospective buyer *offers* to buy the goods; and (iii) the seller *accepts* (or, of course, sometimes declines to accept) the offer. If the offer is accepted, there is (other things being equal) a contract. Given this model, when the Bristol shopkeeper displayed the flick knife in his shop window, he was simply inviting offers from prospective buyers; and, he was not himself offering the flick knife for sale. Similarly, when the sellers in *Ingram v Little* (see above Chapter 5) advertised their car for sale, they were not offering it for sale but, rather, inviting prospective buyers to make an offer. Accordingly, on this analysis, sellers are not committed by their shop window display or their adverts to selling to a prospective buyer; it is the buyer who makes the offer and, preserving freedom of contract, the law recognises that the seller may accept or decline whatever offers are made. In other words, even if a prospective buyer had walked into the shop in Bristol and tendered cash for the flick knife (as per the indicated price in the window), the shopkeeper would still have been within his rights to decline to accept the offer (to decline to sell). On the facts of *Fisher v Bell*, this might seem implausible. Are we seriously suggesting that the shopkeeper would have declined to sell the flick knife to an adult customer who tendered the indicated price? Surely not. Moreover, even if it is conceded that contract law needs to make room for responsible shopkeepers who want to ensure that any knives that they sell (lawfully) do not get into the wrong hands, this seems like a weak consideration to set against endorsing a loophole in the criminal law that would allow for flick knifes to be displayed by irresponsible shopkeepers.

What we have in *Fisher v Bell* is a tension between the policy of the particular criminal law statute (to prevent flick knives being so easily available) and the usual model of formation of contracts in contract law. In contract law, there are circumstances in which the default model will be displaced because it is clear that the prospective seller is not reserving the right to decline a buyer who tenders the indicated price. This being so, we might wonder not only why the model was not displaced within the logic of contract law itself but also why contract law was allowed to obstruct the clear purpose of the criminal law as expressed in the Act. Surely the provisions of the criminal law should prevail over the private law of contract?

The rules of statutory interpretation

In standard introductions to law, students are taught that statutory interpretation is guided by certain well-recognised rules. If there are rules of statutory interpretation, perhaps they hold the key to cases like *Fisher v Bell*.

Typically, law students are introduced to three 'rules' of statutory interpretation. First, there is the literal rule according to which the language of legislation is to be given its plain meaning even though this might lead to absurd or mischievous results. The second is the so-called golden rule which follows the literal rule by requiring that the legislative language should be given its ordinary meaning but then adds the important qualification that this meaning should not be applied where it leads to results that are so absurd or inconvenient that it could not have been the intention to use the language in this way. The third rule, the 'mischief rule', directs judges to identify the mischief (problem) at which the legislation was directed and then interpret the statute in a way that will 'suppress the mischief and advance the remedy'.

Equipped with these rules, how would we apply them to the question in *Fisher v Bell*? Our first question is whether we judge that the language of the statute is plain. If we were to ask members of a jury whether they understand the term 'offering for sale' as covering the display of goods in a shop window, we can be pretty sure that they would so understand it; but, if we were asking contract lawyers the same question, they would say something like, 'This depends on whether we are speaking as non-lawyers or as contract lawyers because, in the latter case, the display was merely an invitation to treat, the shopkeeper's invitation to others to make an offer'. Immediately, we have a fork: if we act on the jury members' use of the English language, the words are plain; but, if we act on the lawyers' use of the language, the meaning is not plain. If we take the former approach, the case will be entirely straightforward: the literal meaning is clear; there is no absurdity or inconvenience in applying this meaning; and, given the mischief of flick knives, this meaning is the way to advance the remedy. However, if we take the latter approach, we have a problem: neither the literal nor the golden rule, both of which are predicated on there being a plain meaning, is relevant. This leaves the mischief rule as a possible back-up in the event that there is no plain meaning and this is a plausible approach where, as here, we have a plain mischief and remedial policy. On this reasoning, we would end up with holding that the offence has been committed; but, of course, Lord Parker, albeit reluctantly, held that no offence was committed.

Thinking inside the box of the rules of statutory interpretation, the court's decision in *Fisher v Bell* seems puzzling. However, if we expand the frame of our thinking, the rule applied in the case seems to be that where the meaning is not plain, defendants (at any rate in criminal cases) should be given the benefit of the doubt. But, if we are committed to the control of crime, this makes little sense: indeed, if anyone is to be given the benefit of the doubt should it not be prosecutors, the state, and the potential victims of crime rather than the criminal classes? However, civil libertarians and liberals, who are committed to due process will take a different view: citizens are entitled to be given a fair warning that their acts amount to a criminal offence and, in the event that they are not given a fair warning, then they should not be convicted of a crime. To be sure, it seems unlikely that the Bristol shopkeeper was misled by the language of the statute into thinking that no crime was being committed by the display of the flick knife; but there might well be cases where defendants have been misled.

Consider, for example, the case of *Smith v Hughes* (1960), where the defendants were charged with soliciting 'in a street or public place' for the purposes of prostitution, this being contrary to section 1(1) of the Street Offences Act 1959. At the time of soliciting, the prostitutes were inside buildings adjacent to Curzon Street in London and they were directing their solicitations at passers-by who were in the street. Had the defendants been standing in the street, the offence would have clearly been committed; but, they argued that, by positioning themselves inside buildings, they were no longer in a street and that, effectively, they had not had a fair warning that soliciting from buildings would also be an offence. Despite this, Lord Parker—the same Lord Parker who sat in *Fisher v Bell*—had no time for such a defence. Even though the text of section 1(1) was unclear, Lord Parker reverted to the purpose of the legislation. Thus:

> Everybody knows that this was an Act intended to clean up the streets, to enable people to walk along the streets without being molested or solicited by common prostitutes. Viewed in that way, it can matter little whether

> the prostitute is soliciting while in the street or is standing in a doorway or on a balcony, or at a window, or whether the window is shut or open.
> *(at 861)*

So, in *Smith v Hughes*, the mischief rule is in effect the default where the legislative language is not plain; and if, in *Fisher v Bell*, Lord Parker had said that everybody knew that the Act was intended to make the streets safer places, to enable people to walk in public places without fear of being a victim of knife crime, and so on, and if he had then ruled that the offence was committed, then there would be no puzzle. But, he did not say that; he took a quite different approach; and what we have is one puzzle piled on another.

Drawing together these threads, it is clear that the rules of statutory interpretation will be of no avail once the cases are anything other than easy. In easy cases, the statutory language will be plain, its application will be straightforward, and the decision made will not be in any way inconvenient, unfair, or troubling. However, where the language is not plain, neither the literal nor the golden rule assists with the interpretation of the law; and, although the mischief rule might give guidance where the background policy or intention is clear and well-known, its application is subject to counter-considerations (such as the fair warning principle) that might prevail. Thinking outside the box, it is tempting to conclude that there is no clear pattern here because each judge exercises his or her discretion in their own way and because even the same judge is not always consistent in their decision-making.

Questions of fact and degree

Thus far, we have encountered problems with the phrasing of legislation—with the meaning of 'offering for sale' and soliciting 'in the street'—and this is very much in line with the stock example of an hypothetical rule that prohibits vehicles from entering a park (Hart, 1961). In relation to this stock example, there might be a preliminary question about whether a particular place or space qualifies as a 'park'. However, discussions of this rule typically treat the principal interpretive question as turning on the scope of the word 'vehicle' (for example, whether the rule covers both motorised and non-motorised modes of transport), the purposes that the rule is intended to serve (for example, whether the rule is designed to ensure safety for park-users or is about the level of noise and disturbance in the park), and how the rule might be applied in unanticipated circumstances (for example, whether the rule applies if an ambulance needs to go into the park in order to deal with a medical emergency). There is, however, nothing special about this example. Many other apparently simple rules give rise to similar interpretive affordances or leeways.

In many cases, the affordance is not so much within the text of the rule (it is not a case of ambiguity) or in relation to unanticipated circumstances but in its application to scenarios that involve questions of fact and degree (Wilson, 1969). Typically, these are cases where the facts fall somewhere between two particular characterisations or categories which, according to the rule, have different legal consequences. So, if the facts of problem case, P, are classified as A, they will have consequence Z but, if they are classified as B, they will have consequence Y; and, the question is whether the material facts of P are more like A than B, or vice versa. For example, according to section 20 of the Local Government (Miscellaneous Provisions) Act 1976, a local authority may require the owner or occupier of a 'relevant place' to provide toilets and washbasins, free of charge; and, section 9 of the Act indicates that one such 'relevant place' is that which is normally used for the purpose of selling food or drink to members of the public 'for consumption at the place'. But, where premises, such as sandwich bars, are used for both take-away sales and for sit-in customers, how do we decide whether a particular place falls within the statutory definition? Does it depend on how many seats there are for sit-in customers, or what proportion of customers sit-in or take-away, or which is the dominant income stream for the business? And, if all these factors are relevant, are they all of equal weight? On such questions, lawyers can, and do, disagree.

In these cases, lawyers will sometimes admit that their best understanding of how the rules apply to the facts is largely a matter of impression; or, they might say that questions of this kind are ones about which lawyers can *reasonably* disagree. However lawyers may choose to express it, and no matter how we wrap it up, it is the normative affordances of rules (here in their application) that are the source of our differences.

Then and now

Where lawyers are called on to interpret rules that allow for more than one plausible reading, they will often present their reading as the 'better view'. Of course, they would not say anything else. Nevertheless, it is not clear that this amounts to saying anything more than that the view presented, while not the only plausible reading, is more plausible than others. So, for example, if the rule has been made by a legislative body but the form of the statutory words dates back a couple of centuries, then the interpretation that is claimed to represent the better view might be one's best historical reading of the text, or of the purpose and intent of the rule (as conceived by the originators), or of its meaning and purpose by present-day standards, and so on. On the face of it, each approach has some plausibility.

According to the late Justice Antonin Scalia, who was a key figure in shaping the modern jurisprudence of the US Supreme Court, the better approach is to stick with the 'original' meaning of constitutional documents. However, as Scalia declared quite candidly in a seminal address (Scalia, 1989), his preference for originalism (rather than for 'non-originalist' approaches) was somewhat a preference for the lesser of two evils. Formally, this signalled that the focus of interpretation should be on text rather than purpose and on original meaning rather than original intent. However, if the original meaning was wholly unacceptable, Scalia admitted that 'in a crunch I may prove a faint-hearted originalist. I cannot imagine myself, any more than any other federal judge, upholding a statute that imposes the punishment of flogging' (at 864). Other judges, of course, might take a different view about originalism and, indeed, the modern British approach is more likely to treat legislative intent as dynamic, such that Victorian statutes should be treated as 'always speaking' (*Reg. v. Ireland* (1998)).

Much the same could be said about contextual readings of the case-law that can develop around statutes and their interpretation. Should judges be guided by older established cases or by more modern revisions to the jurisprudence? More than one approach, more than one reading, is plausible. The criteria that determine whether one plausible reading of the law is better than another are rarely made explicit and, even if they were made explicit, the view will be accepted as better only by those who accept that the criteria used are appropriate. So, the idea of the better view papers over the cracks of the interpretive affordances; and the surface interpretive affordances associated with rules cover a potentially deeper problem, namely the lack of authoritative criteria for operating the affordances.

Four radical (technological) thoughts

This introduction to statutory interpretation prompts four radical thoughts about how new technologies might be deployed to respond to the puzzles and problems that we have indicated. With each thought, we find ourselves more deeply immersed in Law 3.0's technological approach to governance.

The first thought is that lawyers might be assisted by AI tools that have been trained on a database of thousands of cases of statutory interpretation. Where lawyers do not feel confident about how a particular question of statutory interpretation might be decided, they might be guided by an AI tool that is designed to predict the outcome. Of course, there might be some cases where the personal knowledge and experience of lawyers makes them better, and more confident, predictors of how the law will be interpreted but, even in those cases, they might routinely check their prediction with that presented by an AI tool.

Secondly, a similar AI tool might be used by judges who, when sitting alone, are unsure about how to interpret a statute. The tool would give the judge an indication of how other judges would be expected to respond. We should not think that the indication given by the AI tool would be the 'correct' reading of the law. As we have explained in Chapter 4, legal questions do not have correct answers in this sense. The most that the AI tool can do is advise a judge about the interpretation that other judges, rightly or wrongly, plausibly or implausibly, would be likely to adopt.

A third thought is that the problem with judges is that they are humans and, as such, they are prone to all kinds of subconscious bias, influence, tendency, and inconsistency. Educating judges to guard against these factors can go so far, but what we really need is to hand over the interpretation of statutes to smart machines. To get the best out of these machines, the law will need to be reduced to machine-readable terms, and this will have ramifications for the legislative process. For this to be viable, laws would need to be cast in forms that are capable of being coded and rendered machine-readable. How far there is a realistic prospect of doing this is moot: coding the law, it might be conceded, will be possible in easy cases (but not particularly beneficial because humans also find these cases easy); but, the question is whether we can code the law and automate its interpretation in those cases that human interpreters find more difficult.

Finally, we might consider resorting to technological management to eliminate the possibility of acts that might raise questions as to their lawfulness. For example, if the relevant rule is that 'vehicles' are not to be taken into the park, then there might be a question about whether electric scooters would fall under this rule. As we noted in Chapter 7, the design of these scooters already governs many aspects of their use. If we take this a step further, designing electric scooters so that they cannot enter parks, then the affordances of rules, both interpretive and practical affordances, are no longer relevant. But, then, if this is to be the high-tech solution to a pervasive governance problem, even if we no longer need to decide whether an electric scooter is a vehicle, it will fall to someone to make a design decision about whether electric scooters should be disabled from entering parks. And, by whom, and how, would such a decision be taken?

10

HANDLING CASES

Introduction

Consistency in judicial decision-making is seen as one of the virtues of law's governance. Judges apply the rules and the principles of law; and, where those rules or principles are enshrined in earlier case-law, then judges follow the precedents. This practice of consistent and calculable decision-making enables parties to know both where they stand and what to expect—it aids both reliance on the case-law and predictability of judicial decisions. Moreover, not only does this practice observe the principle of procedural justice that like cases should be treated alike, it also is efficient—if the legal point at issue has already been decided by a previous decision, there is no need to re-argue the point. On the face of it, if there is a precedent on the point at issue, it makes sense simply to follow it—or, at any rate, it makes sense unless there are some unusual circumstances that give us pause.

Precedent: The standard introduction

Traditional introductions to English common law highlight the fact that judges display considerable respect for previous decisions and determinations of the law; and, the higher the level of the deciding court, the greater its authority within the court hierarchy, and the greater the respect for its precedents. Hence, in the English legal system, where the precedent is from the highest court, the Supreme Court, then all other courts should follow it and even a later, differently constituted panel of Supreme Court Justices should overrule a prior decision of the Court and treat it as mistaken only in exceptional circumstances. At the next level down, decisions made by the

DOI: 10.4324/9781003507802-12

Court of Appeal will bind lower courts and will usually bind later courts at the same level (although there are some limited exceptions to this usual rule and the matter has been contested). For judges sitting in trial courts, such as the High Court, precedents at the same level should be given serious consideration but they are not treated as binding in quite the same way that appeal court precedents are.

If this account suggests that decision-making in courts, where there is a large library of precedents, is relatively 'mechanical', then the radical induction already undertaken will surely have raised a doubt as to whether this is the reality. In traditional accounts, two important indications are given that invite the thought that there might be more 'wiggle-room' than a mechanical picture of precedent suggests. The first is the distinction between the 'ratio decidendi' of the precedent case and mere 'obiter dicta'; and the second is that previous cases might be 'distinguished on their facts'.

As traditionally put, the point of the first qualifier is that later courts will not be bound by remarks made by the precedent court which were not strictly necessary for its decision; and the point of the second qualifier is that the rule or principle of the precedent court and the way in which it was applied in the precedent case will not bind later courts where the facts of later cases are 'materially different'.

For readers who are already thinking in a radical way, these qualifiers will be viewed not so much as minor footnotes to a model of the mechanical operation of precedent but as crucial openings to marginalise an earlier decision. In other words, the radical take will home in on openings for interpretation around whether some remark in the previous case was 'strictly necessary' for the decision and, similarly, around whether the facts of the precedent case were 'materially different' to those of the instant case. Indeed, the sceptical view will be that, with these openings, judges will characterise remarks in a precedent case as 'ratio' if they want to follow them but, otherwise, as obiter; and, similarly, judges who want to follow the precedent rule or principle will decline to distinguish the cases on their facts whereas those who do not wish to be bound will characterise the facts as materially different.

This, however, is far from the full story. Even if we accept that the earlier case-law establishes a rule or principle that is binding in the instant case, it does not follow that application of the rule or principle is mechanical. Far from it: there might well be scope for interpretation in our reading and application of the rule that binds. For example, a number of cases in the nineteenth century laid down the rule that, in the event of a breach of contract, the innocent party should be compensated for the breach by being placed, so far as money awards (damages) can do so *in the same position* as if the contract had been performed. Although courts in the present century will respect this as the rule to be applied, there are scenarios that persistently raise the question of what we mean by placing the innocent party in 'the same position' as if the contract had been performed. Typically, these are cases where a contractor has failed to carry out work in accordance with the contractual specification (for instance, failing to construct a swimming pool with the specified length, breadth, or depth, or failing to include some decorative feature) but where the cost of correcting the breach far exceeds any difference in the market value of the work. The question is whether the 'same position' principle means that the full cost of correcting the work must be paid as damages or whether the (lower) difference in market value satisfies that principle. The question is not whether the same position principle is ratio or obiter; it is accepted as ratio. The question is how this ratio is to be interpreted—and, in the leading case in the modern English law of contract, *Ruxley Electronics v Forsyth* (1996), the House of Lords applied the principle in a way that reflected neither the difference in value nor the cost of cure, but a figure somewhere between the two. In the result, *Ruxley* might be the leading case but it is a precedent with no clear ratio and which invites being distinguished on its facts.

If we are to make some sense of our radical instincts, we need to start by differentiating between cases that are easy (where the law and its application are straightforward) and those that are harder; then we need to look at really hard cases (where the law is clear but its application strikes us as manifestly unfair); after which we can recall puzzling conjunctions of cases such as those we have discussed already in Chapter 5; and, finally, we can think radical thoughts about robot advisers and decision-makers.

Easy cases and harder cases

Most contracts are for the supply of goods or services for an agreed price. If the goods or services are supplied in accordance with the contract, but if the customer does not then pay the agreed price, the supplier has a straightforward action for breach of contract; the action is simply to be paid the agreed sum; and, payment of the agreed sum will put the supplier in the same position as if the contract had been performed by the customer in the first place. So far, so easy. However, as we have already seen, if the breach is on the side of the supplier (if, for example, the goods or services supplied do not match up to the contract specification), it might not be so easy to put the customer in the same position as if the contract had been performed. This is not to say that there cannot also be easy cases here: there can be, for instance, where the supplier fails to deliver goods and the customer is compensated for whatever additional costs have been incurred in buying substitute goods. But, if the case is not an easy one of this kind, then as we have said the damages rule in contract law can present judges with harder cases.

Taking the contract rule back a level, we can say that the idea of putting the innocent party in 'the same position' as if the contract had been performed reflects the general principle that, in the event of breach, the innocent party should be fully compensated. This seems fine but what do we make of cases where the contract-breaker makes a gain but without causing the innocent party to suffer any financial loss? How might this happen? Suppose, for example, that A contracts to sell goods to B for, let us say, £1,000. However, before A has delivered the goods to B, C offers to pay A £1,500 for the goods. A accepts and, in breach of contract relative to B, A delivers the goods to C. C pays A £1,500 as agreed. If B has to pay more than £1,000 to obtain substitute goods, then the law will require A to cover the excess; so, if B has to pay, let us say, £1,200, then A will be ordered to pay B £200 damages and this will reduce the gain of £500 that A would otherwise make by breaking the contract. But, what if B can obtain the substitute goods at exactly the same price as the original contract price with A? In those circumstances, B seems to be in the same position as if the contract had been performed by A (except that it was not now A who supplied these goods to B, and B might now regard A as unreliable). So, in these circumstances, does it follow that we should treat B as needing no compensation?

We might think that it is one thing for A to take advantage of a better offer in the course of routine commercial dealing (as in the above scenario); but what if this is not routine commercial dealing; what if A has explicitly promised B that he will not sell the goods to C? What if, as in the case of *Attorney-General v Blake* (2000), A was a notorious spy who, in breach of contract with the Crown, published his memoirs and stood to make a very substantial financial gain thereby? To be sure, the Crown (B) might not have suffered any financial loss as a result of Blake's conduct; in which case, there was no need to order Blake to compensate the Crown for financial losses caused by the breach. That said, Blake's financial gain was made on the back of a blatant breach of contract. So, would it be right for contract law to stand by and do nothing about this? Even without knowing that, in recent decades, English contract law has been deeply troubled by this point, we can appreciate that the precedents that engage with this question will be harder cases.

Really hard cases

Even where the rules seem, on their face, to be just, it does not follow that we will always be comfortable with their application in the particular circumstances of the case at hand. For example, in *Ingram v Little* (above, Chapter 5), the court had to choose between the interests of two entirely innocent parties, both parties being the unsuspecting victims of a third-party fraudster. In a split decision, the Court of Appeal ruled that the sellers were still the owners of the vehicle because the transaction with the fraudster was void. But, whichever side lost this case, it would seem less than just that an innocent party should have to bear the full financial cost of the fraud. Might it not be fairer, as one judge suggested in the case, to apportion the loss? In fact, why not simply operate with a default that apportions the loss 50/50 between the innocent parties? Granted, this is not perfect; but law's governance, we have to accept, is often imperfect.

If *Ingram v Little* is one kind of hard case, another is that in which we acknowledge that the precedents and principles clearly favour one party but where the merits seem to lie with the other party. In such cases, the dilemma is a familiar one, namely: should the courts be consistent, stick with the precedents, and fulfil the reasonable expectations of those who have relied on them, or should they bow to the sense of what would be fair and reasonable in the particular context of the dispute and the circumstances of the case? If the law is to be credible but also coherent, some hesitation is in order (compare Latour, 2010: Ch 4).

One source of such hard cases is found in the rules of contract law that restrict claims by third parties. For example, where a contract is made between A and B with a view to conferring a financial benefit on C, what view should the law take if one of the parties (let us suppose that this is A) fails to perform the contract as a result of which C does not receive the intended benefit? The obvious answer is that B should step in to protect C's interest by suing A for breach of contract. However, what if this is not practicable? Then, where the third-party rules are restrictive, should judges accept that C has no claim or should they find a way around the restrictions to enable C to recover? In some legal systems, where the rules of contract law are restrictive, the rules of tort law are broad enough to assist C, even though C's claim is for purely financial loss (rather than for physical or psychological injury, or damage to property, or the like, which we commonly find in tort claims); in this way, when the case is viewed through the lens of contract law it looks hard, but through the lens of tort law it is more straightforward.

In English jurisprudence, some cases look hard whether they are viewed through the lens of contract law or tort law. For example, in the case of *White v Jones* (1995), B instructed a solicitor, A, to change his will so that B's daughter, C, would benefit. A failed to act on B's instructions in a timely manner; B died; and, under the unrevised will, C was not a beneficiary. The merits clearly favoured C who was the intended beneficiary; but, the law—whether the rules of contract law or tort law—would require some considerable manipulation to assist C. These doctrinal obstacles notwithstanding, the majority Law Lords felt that practical justice compelled not a contract-based but a *tort*-based remedy against A in favour of C. According to Lord Goff, 'it is open to your Lordships' House … to fashion a remedy to fill a lacuna in the law and so prevent an injustice which would otherwise occur on the facts of cases such as the present' (at 268). For the minority Law Lords, however, the price of justice in this particular instance was too high: if there was no claim in contract law for what was essentially a breach of contract by A, tort law should leave well alone; and, the deployment of tort law in this case failed to respect the integrity of the (typically restrictive) principles of negligence law that govern the recovery of compensation for purely economic losses. We might also ask: if there was 'a lacuna in the law', should it not be left to Parliament to reset the law?

Really puzzling cases

From hard cases, we can move on to cases which, while not hard in themselves, are puzzling when they are set side by side. These are cases, like *Phillips v Brooks* (1919) and *Ingram v Little* (1961) which, thinking inside the box, defy reconciliation.

Imagine that, at the last minute, the coronation of King Charles III had been postponed because he had tested positive for Covid-19. Contracts that had been made in anticipation of the coronation, the celebrations, and the national holiday would be thrown into disarray. In many cases, the contracts might be subject to express terms and conditions that would provide for the rights and obligations of the parties in these changed circumstances. In other cases, parties would agree to treat the original contract as cancelled and make new arrangements. However, in the absence of express provision or mutual agreement, some parties might look to contract law to be released from their obligations by the doctrine of 'frustration'. How might the law respond?

In the early years of the last century, a scenario of just this kind arose when the coronation of King Edward VII had to be postponed. In the wake of this postponement, there were many cases taken to court where the question was whether the contracts in question were frustrated. Generally, the problem was not that the contracts were literally impossible to perform but that their purpose was, in a colloquial sense, frustrated. The question was whether these contracts were also frustrated in a legal sense. Two of the coronation cases, *Krell v Henry* (1903) and *Herne Bay Steamboat Company v Hutton* (1903), give rise to a classic puzzle because the material facts seem to be identical, the same panel of judges heard the two cases, and they heard the cases on the same day. Yet, while the court ruled that the contract was frustrated in *Krell v Henry*, they held that it was not frustrated in *Herne Bay*. How do we square that circle?

Approaching the puzzle from inside the doctrinal box, the best reconciliation is that the contractual purpose can be frustrated to a greater or lesser degree. In *Krell v Henry*, where the contract was for the hire of a room on Pall Mall overlooking the route of the coronation procession, the hirers it is true could access the room on the day but, realistically, they got little or nothing of what they had bargained for. So, the contract was frustrated. By contrast, in the Herne Bay case, where a boat had been chartered for a couple of days when a royal naval review was planned to take place at Spithead (near Portsmouth harbour), the fact that the review was cancelled did not entirely frustrate the purpose of the contract. The boat was available for a period when it could be used. In other words, the hirer had got something of what he had bargained for. We can protest that this does not seem altogether convincing; but, a not implausible in the box response would be to the effect that the principle of frustration calls for judgments of fact and degree, that cases of this kind are a matter of impression and that, while *Henry* fell on one side of the line, *Herne Bay* fell on the other.

If we approach the puzzle instead from an, at that time, outside the box perspective, we might suggest that the facts of the cases actually are materially different. How so? Whereas, in *Henry*, the hire of the room was for private (non-business) use, purely for the enjoyment of the hirer, in *Herne Bay*, the hirer was a local businessman from Southampton who saw the opportunity to take paying customers around the bay in the chartered boat. In the event, while the hirer in *Herne Bay* was not able to make the profit he expected, the hirer in *Henry* was not in any kind of business, profitable or otherwise. Today, the law explicitly recognises that B2B contracts (such as that in *Herne Bay*) are to be governed by different legal principles to those that apply to B2C contracts; and it would not be too much of a stretch now to suggest that purely private (P2P) transactions also should be governed on their own terms. Today, one of the first questions that we will ask when we are thinking inside the box is 'In what kind of capacity did this party contract? Were they dealing in the course of their business or not?' This does not mean that we will no longer meet really puzzling cases; occasionally, we might still need to think outside the box to explain the apparent tensions in the jurisprudence.

A radical thought: Robot advisers and adjudicators

In a well-known article, Ben Alarie (2016) envisages AI tools being employed, first by citizens and then by lawyers and legal officials, to clarify how particular rules of law apply to specified facts. The particular example on which Alarie focuses is that of the rules which determine whether a 'worker' is an employee or a self-employed contractor, this having many practical implications for the tax and benefit responsibilities and entitlements of the parties as well as for employers' liability. Over the years, the tests supported by the common law jurisprudence have changed somewhat but, even when the tests are relatively stable, they are not always easy to apply because each case has its own distinctive features. Moreover, where the question is posed in relation to legislative provisions the application of which hinges on the interpretation of the term 'worker'—for example, as in the *Uber* (2021) case in the UK, where the private car hire drivers argued (successfully) that they were 'workers' within the meaning of the relevant statutory employment law—we not only hear echoes of the common law jurisprudence but also of the background employment purposes and policies. On the face of it, if AI tools can enable parties to know where they stand in particular cases, this seems to be entirely beneficial.

Imagine that, long before the Uber test-case, Smith, one of Uber's drivers, uses an AI tool to clarify the legal position on a particular matter, to predict how the legal rules will be applied to a specified set of facts—for example, to clarify (as in Alarie's example) whether a particular working arrangement will be treated as an employment relationship or as a relationship between a client and an independent contractor (perhaps with a view to clarifying whether Uber would be vicariously liable for Smith's negligent driving); or, perhaps, Smith uses the AI tool for some entirely unconnected matter such as whether the noise coming from building work on an adjoining property (and which is disturbing Smith's daytime sleeping) is so unreasonable as to constitute a common law nuisance. Assuming that the AI tool is reasonably reliable, such uses of the tool seem to be unproblematic. It is up to Smith to choose whether to use the tool and what to do with the advice given by it.

Let us suppose that Smith is advised by the tool that the claim (or defence) he has in mind is arguable but that the legal position is not entirely clear and predictable. On the basis of this feedback, Smith decides that he needs to take professional advice by consulting a lawyer. Possibly the lawyer to whom Smith turns for advice will also consult an AI tool; but, the lawyer's advice to Smith is more than a rehearsal of what the AI tool has advised. Again, assuming that the tool is reliable and provided that Smith knows exactly what he is getting for his money, this all seems to be unobjectionable.

Taking this a step further, imagine that Smith, now as a taxpayer, seeks guidance from the Revenue on whether a particular scheme will be treated as a lawful and permitted scheme of avoidance or as an unlawful evasion of liability. The status of 'guidance' given by the Revenue is somewhat problematic but, even treated as merely informal guidance, the fact that a tax official is using an AI tool might raise some reservations. In particular, unless it is common knowledge that the Revenue uses tools in this way, there is likely to be a requirement that the Revenue should notify Smith that they have relied on a particular tool, or taken the tool's view into account in giving guidance back to Smith. If the guidance given by the Revenue becomes a formal decision, then we would certainly expect the use of AI tools to be regulated and, of course, there would be procedures for appeal.

Assuming reliability, voluntariness, and transparency, we have not yet detected a point at which we want to draw red lines against the use of AI tools, but how much further would we be prepared to go? Tools that trawl through the precedents and that offer advice on the legal position are one thing—although, as we noted earlier, the way in which AI tools read the precedents, identify the material facts, distinguish and reconcile cases, treat particular cases as 'mistaken', and so on, will be quite different to humans who are trained to think like lawyers; but what would we make of disputes being resolved by machines (governance by machines) as well as conduct being channelled and confined not by prescriptive rules but by technological management? This is the West coast vision of governance to which we have previously referred; in this technological vision, the regulatory enterprise is no longer rule-based and human-directed in the way that we traditionally conceive of law. Crucially, while regulatees might know precisely where they stand, this is no longer relative to a regime of rules but relative to an array of technologies that design out the practical option of 'non-compliance'. Once the practice of automated governance takes humans out of the legal and regulatory loop and once technological management replaces rules to channel conduct, we have a very different version of law—indeed, we might think that this is such a departure that it is no longer a case of *law's* governance (recall the discussion in Chapter 4).

It should be emphasised that the equivalence between AI tools being used to apply legal rules and principles and the traditional 'coherentist' legal reasoning of Law 1.0 is only approximate. The AI tools might have been trained by reference to many examples of humans applying legal rules and principles but the tools lack the authenticity of a human who is trying to construct a compelling narrative that justifies reading the law in a particular way. In other words, the AI tools might simulate an exercise in coherentist legal reasoning but the logic that drives the tools is not coherentist in the same way. Accordingly, while AI tools might outperform humans in a straightforward predictive context, and while applying the general principles of the cases to particular facts is functionally equivalent to coherentist reasoning, it does not follow that AI tools outperform humans in reasoning like a coherentist lawyer. The process, and the processing of the case, is not the same. We might or might not be troubled by this. However, if legal and regulatory decisions are to be delegated to smart machines, this is a sea change in the mode of governance and we need to be alert to this shift from the East coast to the West coast.

PART 3
Key concepts

11

THE CONCEPT OF LAW

Introduction

Arriving for freshers' week at the London School of Economics in September 1965, I found that students in the metropolis had a language of their own—for example, the word 'esoteric' seemed to be a favourite and sentences regularly ended with 'and so on and so forth'. Of course, in the law school, we were soon to be introduced to a whole new language as well as to legal conventions—such as spelling the reasoned decisions handed down by judges as their 'judgments' rather than their 'judgements', making the correct use of square and round brackets when citing the year of a law report or a journal, and underlining case names (which, so I was told, was a signal to copy-editors and type-setters that the names should be italicised). As to the language of lawyers, some residual Latin was still employed and, in the history of English land law, there seemed to be lots of 'men of straw' and fictitious Roes and Does; but there were other words that lawyers liked to use—'discretion' is the one that sticks in my mind—where I was unsure about the spelling and even more so about the significance of the term (which, with hindsight, was actually not a bad instinct because there is a lot to ponder about judicial discretion).

While we could change much of the language and convention of the law without impacting on the traditional (Law 1.0) mode of thinking like a lawyer, there are certain conceptual features that set the frame for this kind of legal reasoning. These are the features that constitute the 'box' in which students are being taught to think like lawyers. Accordingly, the target for this radical introduction is not so much the way that lawyers might talk but the conceptual framework that shapes the way that they pose their

DOI: 10.4324/9781003507802-14

questions and their assumptions about which considerations are relevant to answering those questions. It is not so much that, in our times, lawyers need to talk about 'governance' in the broad sense and nor that they need to talk about technology but that they must think beyond the traditional Law 1.0 box.

In this part of the book, we introduce a range of concepts that are characteristic of legal thinking. We start with the traditional thinking (and contestation) around the concept of law itself and, after a short detour to introduce the idea that our thinking as lawyers should meet a standard of 'coherence', the Rule of Law. Then, having given this thinking some radical twists, we introduce the concept of the 'regulatory environment' which, like the concept of governance in a broad sense, opens the field of legal interest to technologies that can perform law-like functions. While there are many nice distinctions to be drawn when we view law as governance by rules, this traditional conceptual field might be by-passed in a regulatory environment that relies on technological management (rather than rules) to control the practical options available to regulatees.

In the chapters that follow, we consider both the organising concepts of legal systems and those concepts (like reasonableness) that allow for some flexibility in the operation of law. This leads to a pair of chapters in which we consider the principal signals given by rules (where, stated simply, rules signal red-light prohibition or green-light permission) as well as the rights, duties and enabling powers that are conferred or imposed by law's rules. We, then, discuss some concepts that are central to the criminal code and, likewise, to the regime of property law.

Finally, focusing on the concepts of precautionary and preventive governance, both of which are somewhat unfamiliar to traditional reactive law, we reflect on how they might be viewed from a more radical perspective.

The concept of law

We have already said quite a bit about law's governance, emphasising that for the purposes of this radical introduction what matters is that law is a particular species of governance. Nevertheless, even if this is conceded, there is still a question to be asked about the characteristic features of the species that we call 'law'. How should we conceive of law as a particular form of governance?

Generally speaking, those who debate this question are agreed that one of law's characteristic features is that it relies on rules. Law, as Lon Fuller (1969) famously characterised it, is the enterprise of subjecting human conduct to the governance of rules. Legal systems are systems of rules; and laws are instances of particular rules—the rules of criminal law, the rules of contract law, the rules of intellectual property law, and so on.

This minimal characterisation does not yet differentiate between the rules of law and other rule-based forms of human governance. For example, what is the relationship between the rules of law and the rules of morals; and what is the relationship between the rules of law and the informal rules that groups might observe? These questions invite the development of particular conceptions of law along two axes. The first axis plots the extent to which law is necessarily moral in its governance; and the second axis plots the extent to which law is formal and to be identified with the high-level governance institutions of nation states.

We can start by considering these two axes before beginning to map the conceptual space occupied by law and thinking about how governance by technology might fit with that map.

The first axis: law and morality

With regard to the first axis, we might conceive of law as being quite distinct from morals or as having some connection with morals. In some places, notably in the Islamic world, the law is a body of religious rules and principles such that there is no distance between law and morals. However, in other parts of the world, such as the UK, where law made a historic break with religion some centuries ago, the connection between law and morals is a matter for debate. On one side, we have so-called 'legal positivists' who deny any necessary connection between law and morals; and, on the other, we have 'legal idealists' who maintain that there is a necessary thread of connection between morals and law.

In the nineteenth century, the British jurist John Austin famously argued that, while the existence of law is one thing, its moral merit or demerit is something else. It does not follow from this that the rules of law which exist (the so-called positive law) will not reflect the moral beliefs of their makers (or, indeed, the wider community to which the rules apply) but morality figures in the law only contingently, to the extent that lawmakers choose to be guided by it. So, in recent times, when lawmakers, recognising the importance of human rights, have incorporated human rights standards into the law, the law connects to a particular stream of liberal moral thinking; but Austin's point is that, while we might believe that legal rules that reflect moral thinking (in this case, by incorporating human rights) have some merit, they are no more law than legal rules that do not reflect such moral beliefs. Or, turning this around to put it more pointedly, even where legal rules do not reflect human rights or any other moral standard, they are no less law for that reason. According to the legal positivists, law is what it is and its rules are what they are (laws) regardless of any moral criteria (other than those that might happen to be incorporated in a particular legal system).

Opposed to these legal positivist positions, we have legal idealists who argue that we should conceive of law as an articulation of some independently secured moral standards. Notwithstanding the formal separation of Church and Law (see Wood, 2017), some versions of legal idealism still are rooted in an overarching religious view; but, other versions are purely secular. In relation to the latter, some legal idealist conceptions argue that law must be compatible with guiding moral standards or values, for example with human rights or human dignity; however, in other versions, the necessary connection with morals impinges on the fairness of legal procedures and processes.

The debates between legal positivists and legal idealists are complex and nuanced. However, the standard way of highlighting the difference between these conceptions of law is to ask how they would characterise a rule that licenses acts that, by common consent, are not just immoral but violate the interests of humanity. For example, what would the protagonists say about a rule that licenses acts of torture or genocide or slavery, and the like? Let us suppose that our protagonists agree that such acts are egregiously immoral and have no merit. The question then is what follows for the status of the rule as an ostensible law? For legal positivists, nothing follows. Whether or not the rule in question is legally valid does not depend on whether it is compatible with moral standards; law has its own internal tests of validity and, in principle, if the rule satisfies the system's own criteria of legal validity, it is a law notwithstanding that it is egregiously immoral. By contrast, for legal idealists who, as we are supposing, accept that the rule is egregiously immoral, it fails to meet a necessary criterion for its legal validity. For legal idealists, immorality does entail legal invalidity.

On the face of it, there is an obvious risk that the practical project of law's governance—the project of establishing and maintaining 'order' in society—would be compromised if we adopted the legal idealist view. If each person, following their own moral lights, were able to declare which rules were legally valid and which were not, each person would have their own individual legal code to observe. However, the degree of practical difficulty presented by a legal idealist conception of law will vary from one context to another. In communities where most people share their moral views, most people will share the same legal code. Granted, there might be some differences around the edges of a shared moral code but there is no reason to jump to the conclusion that this would be unmanageable—any more than that the situation is unmanageable where legal systems incorporate contested moral standards such as human rights. In short, in morally homogeneous groups, legal idealism is not problematic but the more pluralistic the group the more challenging the context for legal idealism.

Even in pluralistic groups, though, we should not assume that legal idealist thinking will lead to widespread non-compliance and problems of order.

For one thing, an individual might judge that the moral evil of complying with the rule is outweighed by the moral evil of provoking disorder; and, in practice, even legal idealists will often be guided by prudential and pragmatic considerations. In other words, in the debating chamber, legal idealists might argue for their moral conception of law but, outside the chamber, where they are faced with what they judge to be immoral rules and sanctions for non-compliance, they might continue to think that the rules are not legal but comply with them nevertheless—not because the rules are laws but because of the exigencies of the circumstances.

Whatever we make of the practical arguments, we might wonder whether either legal positivist or legal idealist conceptions of law give us any compelling reason for recognising the authority of law. While legal idealists, as we have seen, will recur to moral criteria to judge whether a rule is legally valid, legal positivists will check whether the rule is authorised by the system's own criteria (which will indicate who is authorised to make and enforce the rules). The challenge for legal idealists is to give compelling reasons for taking moral reason seriously and for treating a particular set of moral criteria as determinative when there are so many different views about this amongst moralists. At the same time, the legal positivists base themselves on the 'actualities', on the constitution, on official practice, and on what is generally recognised. They can try to sweeten reliance on these social facts by constructing narratives about social contracts and acceptance but, for those who do not accept the particular arrangements, they can offer no further reason for treating the de facto criteria of authority as decisive. This is a matter which we will return to in a later chapter but, at first blush, both legal positivist and legal idealist conceptions of law seem to stand on questionable foundations.

The second axis: formal law and informal rules

Working along a second axis, we can conceive of law in a way that assumes a greater or lesser degree of formality and institutionalisation. Fuller's specification of the legal enterprise as being that of the subjection of human conduct to the governance of rules is neutral as between these features. Nevertheless, if we are asked to indicate the kinds of things we have in mind when we refer to legal systems or the law, we are likely to point to the making of rules by national legislative assemblies and the handling of disputes by courts. Such is the focus of our benchmark on this axis, the so-called Westphalian view of law, which treats the high-level governance institutions (the legislature and the courts) and the rules of nation states as the paradigm of law. Against this view, there are various kinds of 'legal pluralism' and 'transnational law' which purport to find law in much less formal governance as well as both below the nation state level and across state boundaries.

First, legal anthropologists have found a wide variety of governance practices, particularly practices of dispute settlement, in 'simpler' societies (see, e.g., Roberts, 1979). Where these societies lack any centralised state apparatus, they necessarily deviate from the Westphalian model.

Secondly, as Fuller himself recognised, governance by rules can be undertaken at many levels below the commanding heights of the nation state. This possibility is very clearly expressed by Karl Llewellyn whose views about governance we have already drawn on in Chapter 4. According to Llewellyn's well-known 'law-jobs' theory (Llewellyn, 1940), all groups must set out their basic code of conduct, agree upon processes for resolving disputes between members of the group, and also agree who shall have authority to make the rules, decide the disputes, and give the group its direction. In this way, we can recognise that the rules of clubs and associations, or simply the 'house rules' are de facto the law within their limited sphere of application. While such rules and group practices might simply supplement national law, in other cases they might be oppositional (for example, where the group is a drug cartel or the Mafia).

Exemplifying the proposition that 'law is always local', Eugen Ehrlich (1913), writing in the early years of the last century, famously highlighted the role of the 'living law' in what was then the Austro-Hungarian empire, where the rules that were actually followed in the provinces were not the same as those decreed centrally. Similarly, in Robert Ellickson's (1994) study of the informal norms of 'neighbourliness' and 'live and let live' recognised by the close-knit group of ranchers and farmers of Shasta County, California, we find that there is some distance between the rules that actually guide a group and the rules recognised at state or national level.

Thirdly, some groups will (lawfully) operate with their own rules rather than with the default rules provided by national law. For example, many of the rules of contract law are put in place as defaults to apply unless the contracting parties make their own provision or adopt the rules of particular markets. Where contracting parties self-govern in this way, they are guided, not by the formal general rules of contract law but by their own bespoke trading codes.

Fourthly, some groups, finding that the rules of national law do not adequately protect their interests, will supplement the formal rules of law. For example, where the rules of intellectual property law do not adequately support the interests of comedians or chefs, they will self-govern informally to protect their jokes and recipes. For them, it is the informal code that governs and that is, as it were, 'the law'.

So much for governance that is orientated to rules other than those of the nation state. Beyond this, however, we also need to recognise the many rules that arise from 'transnational' custom and practice or more formal articulation of the relevant rules. Historically, merchants who crossed national borders carried with them codes that applied in marketplaces; and, transnationally, there are many examples of clubs and associations that are in effect like local clubs or associations except that their scaling up involves going beyond the boundaries of nation states. In the age of the Internet, we also have striking examples of private rule-making and dispute-settlement (notably at ICANN on domain names) that is not part of national law and which also crosses borders. So, for example, the rules that apply to persons who use social media networks such as Facebook are subject to Silicon Valley 'law' whether they are in California or elsewhere in the US or beyond the US borders; and, the fact of the matter is that online intermediaries can, and do, operate as rule enforcers by denying essential online services to those who are identified as rule-breakers, irrespective of their physical location.

Mapping law

If we reduce the conceptions on each axis to the two polar cases—on one axis legal positivist and legal idealist conceptions of law and, on the other, Westphalian and pluralist conceptions of law—we will have the makings of a 2 x 2 four square matrix in which to map and place conceptions of law. Thus, our conceptual options and answers to the question, 'Where do you stand in relation to debates about the concept of law?' are as follows:

A: Legal positivist and Westphalian
B: Legal idealist and Westphalian
C: Legal positivist and pluralist
D: Legal idealist and pluralist

Insofar as there is a general view in the UK, it is A: Law is to be differentiated from morals and it is to be identified with the rules made by Parliament and by the courts. Such is the legacy of Hart and post-Hartian jurisprudence. In the UK, B (because of its espousal of legal idealism) is very much a minority view; but, the revisionist pluralism of view C has plenty of support within the socio-legal research community where the tension between the background rules of (positive) law and the foreground informal norms of the group (whether the group is a profession, or the police, or business people, or car drivers, or street artists, or whoever) has given rise to a large literature that contrasts the law-in-the-books with the law-in-action. Finally, we have view D which rejects both legal positivism and Westphalianism. Although this is probably the most radical of the four views, and although I would count myself as subscribing to this view, this is not the radicalism that is reflected by this introduction to law. Rather, in the bigger picture of governance, the really radical thought is that law, whichever conceptual view we take of it, is not the only game in town.

The radical sketch

In the present context, the radical response to the question 'What is law?' has two striking features. First, as I have just repeated, it places law (on any of the above conceptions) within the broader field of governance; and, secondly, it emphasises the role that technologies now play in undertaking governance functions.

Recalling Fuller's characterisation of law as the governance of rules, we see that the seeds of a sketch that starts with governance have already been sown. However, if what we accentuate in this characterisation is the *rule-like* nature of law, then we might relegate its *governance* function to the background. So, the first task for the radical sketch is to retrieve the idea that our interest is in the human enterprise of governance. Of course, Llewellyn's law-jobs does this but neither Fuller nor Llewellyn were writing at a time when, as now, technologies were being applied to undertake governance functions. In the last century, when Fuller and Llewellyn were developing their understanding of law, the alternative to rule-based governance was the arbitrary exercise of power or the disorder of the Wild West. At that time, technology had not really presented itself as a tool of governance.

With its broader lens, the radical sketch now recognises not only that there is more than one way of doing governance but also that technology has promising applications for the purposes of governance—or, as we put it in Chapter 14, we should think about the 'regulatory environment' as (potentially) a mix of both rules that guide and technologies that govern. In a seminal contribution to this line of thinking, Lawrence Lessig (1999) identified four regulatory modalities that bear on the governance of human conduct. Each of these modalities—the rules and standards of the law; social norms; pricing and other market signals; and the coding of hardware and software—and combinations of these modalities can govern human conduct. Although we might want to differentiate between, on the one hand, the coding of hardware and software and, on the other, rules (like rules of law or social norms) that govern human conduct by signaling what ought or ought not to be done, the point here is simply that we might rethink our field of interest and inquiry. Indeed, taking a broad view of what counts as a technological approach, we might rethink our field of interest in such a way that it includes not only rules and standards that prescribe what we ought or ought not to do but also architecture and design (of places, products, and processes) that shape the environments in which humans act and which determine which actions are practically available and which are not.

Accepting the radical view, we will have a broad concept of governance, which allows for governance by rules but also governance by other means (such as technology), within which we will conceive of law as a particular rule-based species of governance; and, if we are interested in refining our conception of law, we will have a choice between the four particular views outlined above. From the perspective of the radical view, there is still a debate to be had about the concept of law. However, this is not a debate about whether law should be or should not be conceived of within a broad notion of governance; and it is not a debate about whether law should be conceived of as a rule-based form of governance. What is up for debate is limited to whether we are with the legal positivists or the legal idealists, and the Westphalians or the pluralists, in specifying the particular features of law as an articulation of rule-based governance within the broad field of governance. While this is a debate for those who are specialists in traditional jurisprudence, for those lawyers who have a broader interest in good governance there are, so to speak, other fish to fry.

12
COHERENCE

Introduction

The general pattern of undergraduate law programmes has been to start with and build on a number of compulsory modules which map onto the professional exemption subjects. In this way, students gain some familiarity with the 'core' areas of law, with their concepts, classifications, rules, and principles, all the time being trained to think in a Law 1.0 way. Having studied these core subjects, students are then presented with a range of optional law subjects, some of which might be quite theoretical but others of which are densely doctrinal.

In line with this pattern, at the LSE, the first two years of the law degree programme were made up of compulsory subjects but, in the third year, students had some choice as to their subjects. However, this optionality was with the exception of Jurisprudence, which was the one compulsory third-year subject.

The Jurisprudence module sketched the various concepts of law that we find in classical thought (notably in the thinking of Plato and Aristotle), before reviewing the scholastic idea of law associated with Aquinas, and then moving on through the thinking of Hobbes, Locke, Bentham, and Austin to the (then) contemporary theories of Kelsen and Hart. As we embarked on this journey through the history of the idea of law, one of my fellow students remarked during a particular lecture—and, remarked somewhat loudly—that 'It simply does not cohere'. At the time, I did not know what he meant but, in retrospect, I take it that he was puzzled about the relationship between the central questions of the Jurisprudence course and the exercise of thinking like a lawyer that seemed to be the principal preoccupation of the

DOI: 10.4324/9781003507802-15

law degree. For my own part, I was still struggling to get to grips with thinking like a lawyer but, for those students who understood how to think that way, it might well have made little sense to engage in jurisprudential reflection on what law is and, concomitantly, on what it is to think like a lawyer. If we already know how to think like a lawyer, why spend time reflecting on what it is to think like a lawyer? As my fellow student exclaimed, it does not cohere.

Again, with the benefit of hindsight, the sense that this way of doing things did not cohere might have gone deeper. Here, the thought would be that it makes no sense to train students to think like a lawyer without first alerting them to the possibility that, given more than one conception of law, there might be more than one way of thinking like a lawyer. In other words, the cart was being put before the horse; the questions that were posed by the Jurisprudence module needed to be on the table before students were trained to think like a lawyer. After all, if we take Jurisprudence seriously, we might not accept the legal positivist view (view A in the previous chapter) that underpinned our legal education; instead, we might be attracted by a different conception of law, one that would entail a very different understanding of what it is to think like a lawyer. We will come back to this matter shortly but, before that we need to note the difference between doctrinal coherence and regulatory coherence.

Doctrinal coherence and regulatory coherence

In Chapter 8, we noted that, where lawyers are reasoning in a Law 1.0 way, they will be particularly concerned with the internal consistency and coherence of the body of doctrine. Thinking in this way, lawyers will endeavour to apply the traditional rules and principles of the relevant legal system to particular factual situations. In easy cases, this is a straightforward exercise. However, where there is apparently more than one way of reading the law, lawyers will argue for a view that fits best with the cases and the jurisprudence and that presents the body of doctrine in the most coherent light; and, where there is a tension between the application of clear and settled rules or principles and the merits or individual justice of the case, lawyers will accept that the ideal of doctrinal coherence places limits on how far they can stretch or ignore doctrine.

So, recalling the mistake of identity cases that we introduced in Chapter 5, our desire for doctrinal coherence demands that we go to extraordinary lengths to find a convincing way of distinguishing *Ingram v Little* from *Phillips v Brooks*. Unless we can find a narrative that displays the coherence of these cases, we have to concede either that the earlier decision was mistaken or that the later decision was ad hoc. Similarly, recalling the case of *White v Jones*, a textbook hard case, the minority Law Lords resiled from crafting a remedy for the claimant because they feared that this would leave the body of doctrine in a state of incoherence.

By contrast, when we approach questions in a Law 2.0 policy-focused way, it is recognised that regulatory interventions might not cohere with the principles that give shape to the historic codes and cases. Regulators are focused on achieving particular policy objectives and, to the extent that policy requires it, regulatory interventions can simply 'correct' or ignore traditional legal principles. Hence, when regulators pursue a policy of, say, consumer protection it might be necessary to limit the application of the founding principles of the general law of contract; and, when policies of market harmonisation are pursued in the EU, the Regulations and Directives that implement these policies might cut into the distinctive legal principles and cultures of the member states.

Although, when we are thinking in a Law 2.0 way, we are not constrained by coherence as understood in the Law 1.0 paradigm, there is an important sense in which regulatory interventions should be coherent. However, this is coherence relative to the policy objectives that guide regulators. Accordingly, it is important to regulators that the various interventions that they make cohere in a sense that they each contribute in their way to the policy objectives and that we do not have one regulatory intervention pulling against another. So, coherence continues to matter in regulatory thinking, but it is not the coherence that animates the thinking of Law 1.0.

Conceptual coherence

To return to our thinking about the concept of law, if more than one concept of law is on the table, how should we choose between them? According to Hart (1961), we might be guided by practical considerations or we might believe that one concept of law has better theoretical credentials than others.

Guided by practical considerations, a common view is that the legal positivist concept of law that underpins Law 1.0 thinking is to be preferred to a legal idealist concept of law. The argument is that those who conceive of law in a legal idealist way might tend to adopt undesirable practical attitudes (whether assuming in an uncritical and reactionary way that everything that is declared to be law is morally obligatory and should be obeyed, or adopting a revolutionary stance that denies any obligation to comply with rules that one judges to be immoral). In the same way, it might be argued that a legal idealist conceptual view would be unworkable because it would disrupt the process of training students to think like Law 1.0 lawyers—instead of learning how to argue from and around the cases and the statutes, students would be diverted into discussing whether the particular cases and statutes should be characterised as law in the first place.

Whatever we might make of these practical arguments—and, as we suggested in the previous chapter, what we make of them will depend a good deal on the context that we assume—they seem like second-best kinds of arguments. For if there are non-practical, theoretical, reasons to believe that one particular concept of law is rightly viewed as the concept of law, that view surely should be adopted. However, the question is: what might our theoretical reasons look like? And, this is where we get back to coherence.

Put simply, the idea is that we humans rely on a range of conceptual frameworks (for example, concerning space and time) to interpret what we see and experience in the world. Without concepts, we experience the world through our senses but the meaning of what we experience is given by our concepts. On one view, we can operate with whatever conceptual schemes we like provided that the concepts that make up those schemes are internally consistent and coherent. So, it is our choice whether we conceive of law in one way or another provided that our conceptual thinking is coherent. It follows from this pragmatic approach that one conceptual view of law is theoretically superior to another if it coheres with other parts of the protagonists' conceptual thinking in a way that rival conceptual views do not. However, to the extent that the only constraint on our conceptual choices is that they are coherent overall, this does not really settle the dispute. What we are looking for is some fixed non-optional reference point with which all our conceptual thinking must cohere; and this raises the question of whether there is any such reference point that is the ultimate test of the coherence of human conceptual thinking. While I do not think that my fellow student was making such a claim when he pronounced that what he was hearing in our Jurisprudence lectures did not cohere, I will suggest in Chapter 22 that there are some matters—the conditions for the possibility of viable human community—that it would be incoherent for any human to fail to recognise and that provide a necessary ground truth for our conceptual thinking.

13

THE RULE OF LAW

Introduction

I have already confessed that, in my first term as an undergraduate law student, I did not really get to grips with Contract Law. The same could be said for my engagement with Constitutional Law where, during the first term, we were focusing on 'high' constitutional conventions, customs, and parliamentary practices. Courts, cases, and judges did not figure much in these lectures or classes; and, so, my reasons for not 'getting' this branch of the law were not the same as those in Contract Law. Indeed, my reasons were more to do with wondering whether high constitutional law, with its debates about various 'conventions' (which, it was always emphasised, were not legally binding), was really a branch of the law at all. In an attempt to clear the mist, I read, cover to cover, Sir Ivor Jennings' book, *The Law and the Constitution* (1964). No doubt, it is a constitutional 'classic' but it went straight over my head. By the end of the first term, I was none the wiser.

Leaving London in December 1965, I hitch-hiked back along the A5 to my home city in North Wales. At some stage of that long journey, I was given a lift by a driver who could have been, and for all I know was, a constitutional lawyer. Having ascertained that I was a law student, he asked me what I thought about the War Damage Act 1965. Alas, I did not know anything about this Act or the furore that it was causing. My driver set about educating me. Briefly, during the Second World War, the British Army destroyed some installations that were the property of the Burmah Oil Company; they did this in order to prevent the installations falling into the hands of the advancing Japanese army. In the post-war years, legal proceedings were launched to establish whether the Company was entitled to

DOI: 10.4324/9781003507802-16

be compensated by the government for this 'war damage'. In the landmark *Burmah Oil Company case* (1965), the House of Lords ruled that the company was entitled at common law to be compensated. Responding to this decision and being concerned about the compensatory burden that would now fall on the public purse, the government enacted the War Damage Act 1965. To the extent that the Act provided that, *in future*, there would be no common law entitlement to such compensatory payments, it was not constitutionally contentious; Parliament is a sovereign body and the scope of its *prospective* law-making powers is unlimited. However, the immediate purpose of the Act was to overturn the award made to the Burmah Oil Company, which is to say, the Act was drafted explicitly to reverse, *with retroactive effect*, the decision of the House of Lords. Constitutionally, this was quite another matter. The idea that politicians should retrospectively change the law as declared by a court attracted widespread criticism both inside and outside Westminster. As my driver put it to me in no uncertain terms, this was a dark day for the Rule of Law.

Looking back, had I been thinking about law as being in the business of governance, had I appreciated that law is just a particular species of governance, and had I understood that we should all be aspiring to good governance, then the pieces of constitutional law would have fallen into place. Constitutional conventions might not be law in a strict sense but they are an essential feature of governance at Westminster; and, when legislatures do not observe the Rule of Law, we diminish our efforts at good governance. So, how do we traditionally understand the idea of the Rule of Law and how should we view it through a radical lens?

The Rule of Law

Traditionally, thinking about the Rule of Law starts with the idea that the legal enterprise is committed to governance by rules, the rules being published and then faithfully administered. The Rule of Law marks the end of arbitrary governance, the end of might being right; law's governance is the rule of rules; governance should be by law not by men.

Within this traditional paradigm, debates about the Rule of Law are largely between those who advocate sticking with a 'thin' and 'formal' (or 'procedural') version of the Rule of Law and those who argue for a 'thicker' more 'substantive' version. While the virtue of the former is that it conduces to order and predictability, its weakness is that it gives those who govern a blank cheque in relation to the rules that they make. Conversely, the virtue of the latter is that it invites a development of the Rule of Law that goes beyond the justice of treating like cases alike (by consistently applying the rules), but its weakness is that it invites contestation around the substantive justice of law's order (Raz, 1977).

Elaborating on the distinction between the rival conceptions, Paul Craig (1997: 467) explains that, whilst formal (or thin) conceptions of the Rule of Law

> address the manner in which the law was promulgated (was it by a properly authorised person, in a properly authorised manner, etc.); the clarity of the ensuing norm (was it sufficiently clear to guide an individual's conduct so as to enable a person to plan his or her life, etc.); and the temporal dimension of the enacted norm (was it prospective or retrospective, etc.),

they do not 'seek to pass judgment upon the actual content of the law itself.' By contrast, substantive (or thicker) conceptions 'wish to take the doctrine further. Certain substantive rights are said to be based on, or derived from, the rule of law. The concept is used as the foundation for these rights, which are then used to distinguish between "good" laws, which comply with such rights, and "bad" laws which do not'. Needless to say, even as traditional debates are revisited and played out in the present century, technology does not figure in them.

Recognising that in these debates there are many versions of the Rule of Law, the ideal should be understood as reflecting a bilateral compact: on the one side, rulers demand that citizens respect the rules; on the other side, citizens demand that rulers act in accordance with the rules. Thus, from a citizen's viewpoint, the Rule of Law goes to the heart of constitutionality; its focus is on the authorising rules, on the constitutive (or secondary) rules that set the terms and conditions to be observed by the rulers.

According to this traditional view, the War Damage Act 1965 flouted the Rule of Law by changing the rules retrospectively. Even on a formal or thin conception, the legislation was a serious deviation from our commitment to the rule of rules. Even on a thin conception, the Act was evidence of the UK falling short in any aspiration for good governance.

A radical take on the Rule of Law

From a radical perspective, we can make sense of debates and discussions that simply went over my head as a novice law student by placing constitutional law and practice in the larger frame of governance. In that frame, the Rule of Law, as traditionally conceived, does have some critical purchase on governance. However, in the present century, we need to revise our traditional understanding in the following ways (compare Brownsword, 2022a: Ch 5).

First, we have to understand that the Rule of Law is an ideal for all forms of governance. This means that, where law's governance by rules is assisted by new technologies or where governance by technology takes over law's functions, we have to apply the ideal of good governance. Precisely how the Rule of Law should be articulated for governance by machines is a matter for debate. Granted, it might not be possible mechanically to apply the Rule of Law as articulated for governance by rules to a regime of governance by machines. Nevertheless, the spirit of the Rule of Law as a compact between those who govern and those who are governed should persist.

Secondly, we have to reject the idea that, with new technologies, there are some technical zones and spaces where the Rule of Law does not apply. It follows that we cannot accede to the claims made by the cyberlibertarians and the Internet separatists (see Chapter 6) that the writ of the Rule of Law does not run to cyberspaces.

Thirdly, to the extent that the traditional understanding of the Rule of Law is that it constrains the arbitrariness of public governance, and only public governance, some correction is required. The Rule of Law applies to all those who take on governance functions whether public bodies and institutions or private enterprises. We cannot have it that the discipline of the Rule of Law applies only to public governance, allowing private enterprises to undertake governance without constraint. Given that it is private enterprises that have the resources and know-how to develop state of the art tools for governance, it is particularly important that the scope of the Rule of Law is not cramped and confined to public governance.

Finally, we need to think beyond the traditional paradigm, and the debate between those who advocate a formal version of the Rule of Law as opposed to those who argue for a more ambitious substantive version of the ideal. In Chapter 22, we will identify some conditions which speak to the possibility of governance. These conditions are so foundational to governance itself and to the possibility of engaging in debates about governance that no human can reasonably deny the importance of according special protection to those conditions. Just as the Internet relies on the integrity of a critical infrastructure, all human activity relies on the integrity of a set of infrastructural conditions. Following this line of thinking, good governance starts with, and builds on, these essential conditions and, if we view the Rule of Law as reflecting an ideal of good governance, then this is the core demand of the idea. Precisely how each viable community of humans then elaborates its own local understanding of the ideal, its own formal and substantive constraints on governance, will lead to its own particular articulation of the Rule of Law. So, from a radical perspective, the choice between a procedural and a substantive version of the Rule of Law is for each community to make but what all communities must respect are the infrastructural conditions on which the entire enterprise of governance depends.

14

THE REGULATORY ENVIRONMENT

Introduction

With governance (which includes law's particular form of governance) as our field of interest, we can explore the impact of changes that are made to the ways in which those who govern try to channel and guide the conduct of those who are governed. Or, if we put this in the language of regulation, we can explore changes that are made to the regulatory environment as those who govern rely on various combinations of rules, technological assistance, and technological fixes.

We can start by saying a few words about the nature of the regulatory environment; and, then, we can explore the significance of changes made to the regulatory environment, our extended example concerning the governance of golf carts at a fictitious golf club, Westways, where, having tried rules, and rules supported by surveillance technologies, the club eventually resorts to a technical fix.

The nature of the regulatory environment

In a well-known article, Clifford Shearing and Phillip Stenning (1985) highlighted the way in which, at Disney World, the vehicles that carry visitors between locations actually govern which areas of the theme park can and cannot be accessed by visitors. At Disney World, there are rules but also restrictions that are embodied in the design of the facility. However, theme parks are no longer a special case. We find similar regulatory environments in many everyday settings, where along with familiar laws, rules, and regulations, there are signs of technological management—for example, we find

DOI: 10.4324/9781003507802-17

mixed environments of this kind in homes and offices where air-conditioning and lighting operate automatically, in hotels where the accommodation levels can only be reached by using an elevator (and where the elevators cannot be used and the rooms cannot be accessed without the use of security key cards), and perhaps par excellence in what geographers refer to as the 'code/space' that we find at airports.

Entering a modern terminal building, while there are many airport rules to be observed—for example, regulations concerning smoking in the building, or leaving bags unattended, and so on—there is also a distinctive architecture that creates a physical track leading from arrival and check-in to departures and boarding. Along this track, there is nowadays an 'immigration and security zone', dense with identifying and surveillance technologies, through which passengers have little choice other than to pass. Moreover, if we ever have the misfortune to reach the departure lounge but then find that there is no plane to board, we will soon realise that there is no simple track that will allow us to retrace our steps back to the arrivals area and exit the building: the pathway at the airport is designed to be one-way only, taking passengers from arrivals to departure, not the other way round. In this conjunction of architecture and surveillance and identifying technologies, we have the design or 'coded' dimensions of the airport's regulatory environment—the fact of the matter is that, if we wish to board our plane, we have no practical option other than to follow the technologically managed track.

Similarly, if we want to shop at an Amazon Go store, we have no choice other than to subject ourselves to the technologically managed environment of such stores; and, of course, if we visit Amazon or any other platform online, we will probably do so subject to both the specified terms and conditions for access and whatever technological features are embedded in the site. Needless to say, this is a far cry from the Law 1.0 questions about contractual offer and acceptance that are presented to novice law students in relation to the layout of early self-service stores that departed from the traditional across-the-counter model. In our technologically managed retail environments (whether online or offline), the key questions are not about when the offer is made and when it is accepted but about who controls the practical options available to consumers.

If we treat the regulatory environment as essentially a signalling and steering environment, then each such environment operates with a distinctive set of regulatory signals that are designed to channel the conduct of regulatees within, so to speak, a regulated sphere of possibility. Of course, one of the benefits of technologies is that they can expand our possibilities; without aircraft, we could not fly. Characteristically, though, the kind of technological management that we are contemplating is one that restricts or reduces existing human possibilities (albeit, in some cases, by way of a trade-off for new possibilities). In other words, while rule-reliant regulation is directed at actions that are possible—and that remain possible—technological management engages with spheres of possibility but in ways that restructure those regulatory spaces and redefine what is and is not possible.

To recall our earlier discussion in Chapter 8, the technological measures contemplated in Law 3.0 are varied. Some measures serve the channelling function by supporting compliance with, and enforcement of, the rules; some assist human decision-makers who are authorised to settle disputes by reference to the rules; and, others take this a step further by automating the detection of rule-breaking, enforcement of the rules, and settling disputes in relation to the rules, in each case taking humans out of the governance loop. Other measures are designed to achieve channelling and prevent disputes arising by replacing reliance on rules (so that channelling is carried out by other means). Where technological management is employed in this way—as at Disney World, or the Metro, and at airports—the focus is on the places and spaces (particularly online spaces) in which humans act as well as the products they use and the processes that they undergo in such places. Accordingly, governance of this kind does not operate on the basis that the key to an effective regulatory environment lies in having the right mix of rules, incentives, and disincentives; rather, it proceeds on the basis that the key is to control the practical options that are actually available to those who are governed.

Typically, such measures are employed with a view to managing certain kinds of risks by excluding (i) the possibility of certain actions which, in the absence of this strategy, might be subject only to rule regulation or (ii) human agents who otherwise might be implicated (whether as rule-breakers or as the innocent victims of rule-breaking) in the regulated activities. Moreover, technological management might be employed by both public regulators and by private self-regulating agents (such as corporations protecting their IP rights or supermarkets protecting their merchandise and their trolleys).

It also should be emphasised that the ambition of hard technical measures is to replace the rules by controlling the practical options that are open to regulatees. In other words, technological management goes beyond technological assistance in support of the rules. Of course, regulators might first turn to technological instruments that operate in support of the rules. For example, in an attempt to discourage shoplifting, regulators might require or encourage retailers to install surveillance and identification technologies, or technologies that sound an alarm should a person carry goods that have not been paid for through the exit gates. However, this is not yet full-scale technological management. Once technological management is in operation shoppers will find that it is simply not possible to take away goods without having paid for them.

Westways and a changing regulatory environment

Imagine a fictitious golf club, 'Westways'. The story at Westways begins when some of the older members propose that a couple of carts should be acquired for use by members who otherwise have problems in getting from tee to green. There are sufficient funds to make the purchase but the green-keeper expresses a concern that the carts might cause damage to Westways' carefully manicured greens. The proposers share the green-keeper's concerns and everyone is anxious to avoid causing such damage. Happily, this is easily solved. The proposers, who include most of the potential users of the carts, act in a way that is respectful of the interests of all club members; they try to do the right thing; and this includes using the carts in a responsible fashion, keeping them well clear of the greens.

For a time, the carts are used without any problem. However, as the membership of Westways changes—particularly as the older members leave—there are some incidents of irresponsible cart use. The green-keeper of the day suggests that the club needs to take a firmer stance. In due course, the club adopts a rule that prohibits taking carts onto the greens and that penalises members who break the rule. Unfortunately, this intervention does not help; indeed, if anything, the new rule aggravates the situation. While the rule is not intended to license irresponsible use of the carts (on payment of a fine), this is how some members perceive it; and the effect is to weaken the original 'moral' pressure to respect the interests of fellow members of the club. Moreover, members know that, in some of the more remote parts of the course, there is little chance of rule-breakers being detected.

Taking a further step to discourage breaches of the rule, it is decided to install a few CCTV cameras around the course at Westways. However, this proves problematic in more than one respect. First, some members sense that the cameras signal a lack of trust. Secondly, the camera coverage is patchy so that it is still relatively easy to break the rule without being seen in some parts of the course. Thirdly, old Joe who is employed to watch the monitors at the surveillance control centre is easily distracted and members soon learn that he can be persuaded to turn a blind eye in return for the price of a couple of beers. Fourthly, the cameras pick up some embarrassing cases of cheating during play—the most prevalent example of this is members who, having marked the position of their ball on a green, pinch a few inches, when they replace the ball. Everyone knows that some members do cheat and a certain level of cheating is tolerated but members would rather manage this without being confronted by the camera evidence. Members, preferring to let sleeping dogs lie, push back against the existing cameras. Extending the camera coverage would not be acceptable. Once again, the club fails to find an effective way of channelling the conduct of members so that the carts are used in a responsible fashion.

It is at this juncture that the club turns to a technological fix. The carts are modified so that, if a member tries to take the cart too close to one of the greens (or to take the cart off the course), they are warned and, if the warnings are ignored, the cart is immobilised. At last, thanks to technological management, the club succeeds in realising the benefits of the carts while also protecting its greens.

As we trace the particular history at our fictitious club, Westways, we see that the story starts with an informal 'moral' understanding. In effect, just as in the early days of eBay, regulation rests on the so-called Golden Rule: that is to say, the rule is that members should use the carts (or the auction site) in the way that they would wish others to use them. It then tries to reinforce the moral signal with a rule (akin to a law) that sends a prudential signal (namely, that it is in the interests of members to comply with the rule lest they incur the penalty). However, the combination of a prudential signal with a moral signal is not altogether a happy one because the former interferes with the latter. When CCTV cameras are installed, the prudential signals are amplified to the point that they are probably the dominant (but still not fully effective) signals. Moreover, one of the unintended effects of the camera coverage is that it interferes with the members' own governance of cheating. Finally, with technological management, the signals change into a completely different mode: once the carts are redesigned, it is no longer for members to decide on either moral or prudential grounds to use the carts responsibly; at the end of the story, the carts cannot be driven onto the greens, members cannot claim to be responsible for compliant use of the carts (see, further, Chapter 17), and the signals are entirely to do with what is possible and impossible.

What the story at Westways illustrates is the significant changes that take place in the 'complexion' of the regulatory environment; with each regulatory initiative, the 'signalling register' changes from moral, to prudential, and then to what is possible. With each move, the moral register is pushed further into the background; and, with each move, the doubts that moralists might have about the direction of travel will be intensified.

15

ORGANISING CONCEPTS

Introduction

The basic structure and organisation of a legal system can usually be discerned from the provisions of its constitution. Even in the UK, where there is no written constitution, it is understood that law's governance has three principal branches: the legislative branch to enact the rules; the executive branch to determine policy and direction; and the judicial branch to adjudicate. Famously, we find this threefold conceptualisation of the branches of governance reflected in the theory of the 'Separation of Powers', according to which each branch should have its own institutional identity with its own discrete personnel. Although the UK recognised these three distinct branches of governance, its traditional practice tolerated some striking deviations from a strict separation of powers—notably, in the person of the Lord Chancellor who not only headed the judicial branch but also was a high-profile member of both the legislative and the executive branches. Despite resistance by some political pragmatists who saw some advantages in the Lord Chancellor's role, this historic office was abolished in 2005 in a package of reforms that brought practice closer to the ideal of the Separation of Powers (Reynolds, 2019).

In this chapter, we can note some of the features of the way in which we traditionally organise our thinking about the *internal* structure of a legal system (for example, by drawing a central distinction between public law and private law) and, at the same time, we can outline how we conceive of the relationship between nation-state law and other law or non-law phenomena. However, in our radical introduction to law, we need to understand

DOI: 10.4324/9781003507802-18

how such traditional conceptual thinking is shaken by the disruptive effects of emerging technologies.

The internal structure of law and its external relations

Rather like a large departmental store, law benefits from its internal structure and organisation. In the case of law, we start with the distinction between the public dimension of governance and the private: whereas the former concerns the (vertical) relationships between those who have executive and legislative responsibilities and those who are subjected to governance (citizens in modern states), the latter concerns the (horizontal) relationships between citizens.

There are two main pillars to the public dimension of law's governance: first, the criminal law and the criminal justice system; and, secondly, the rules and principles of judicial review (of public decision-making) and the administrative justice system. By contrast, while the civil justice system is the pillar of the private dimension of law's governance, the civil law includes many of the core legal subjects (such as contract law, tort law, property law, and equity and trusts) as well as a multitude of other sets of rules (concerning, for example, companies, children and families, consumers, employment, insurance, intellectual property, medicine and health, probate, and succession, and so on).

While there is a sense in which, relative to the legal rules, acts are either 'lawful' or 'unlawful', these headline concepts invite further analysis. Where an act complies with legal requirements, it will be lawful; but, it will also be lawful where it is simply permitted (and not subject to legal requirements). Similarly, an act that fails to comply with a legal prohibition will be unlawful; but, we will also treat an act as unlawful where it exceeds the scope of an authorising permissive rule. Moreover, the significance and practical effects of acting unlawfully are far from uniform and depend on whether the setting is the criminal, the civil, or the administrative justice system. So, where a criminal offence is committed, the crime is an unlawful act, and the offender will be punished; where a civil wrong is committed, such as a breach of contract or the commission of a tort, the act is also unlawful but the legal response is to compensate the innocent party, not to punish the wrongdoer; and, where a public body exceeds or abuses its authority, its act will be unlawful but the primary response is neither to punish or compensate but to declare the act invalid.

Turning away from its own internal structure and organising concepts, law's governance will have a narrative about how it stands in relation to its near neighbours in the world of governance. For example, while some national legal systems subscribe to a 'monist' theory which treats the provisions of international law as automatically part of domestic law, others (including the UK) take a 'dualist' view such that international law does not take effect within domestic law unless and until it is specifically incorporated in the latter. Similarly, each legal system will have a view about its relationship to regulation, politics, ethics, religion, and the like, which also seem to be in the business of governance as well as to science, technology, and architecture which, unless we take a radical approach to law, will seem to be in a quite different business.

Looking beyond all this, law's governance will also have a certain understanding about, so to speak, the human condition which hinges on conceptual distinctions between humans and non-human animals, humans and tools, born humans and the unborn, and so on.

Whether we are thinking about these organising concepts and classifications as a matter of the internal organisation of law's governance, or its external relations, or its take on the human condition, there can be some difficult questions at the interfaces of law, where the lines become blurred, or where traditional certainties are disrupted.

For example, as a matter of internal organisation, lawyers sometimes talk about 'the common law of obligations', this comprising the law of contract, the law of torts, and the law of restitution. Each member of this common law trio has a distinct remedial role to play: for contract law, the role is to compensate the innocent party for the losses occasioned by a breach of contract; for tort, it is to restore the innocent party to the position they were in before the tort took place; and, for restitution, the remedial role is to reverse an enrichment unfairly obtained at the expense of another. In Chapter 10, we met two cases that were problematic because they arose at the interfaces between these bodies of law. In *White v Jones* (1995) it was the interface between contract law and tort law that was the problem. For the House of Lords, the question was whether tort law should be employed to deliver a just outcome (for the daughter who was the intended beneficiary of her father's will) when contract law blocked that result. In *Attorney-General v Blake* (2000), it was the interface between contract law and restitution law that was the problem. Here, the question for the House of Lords was whether a restitutionary remedy (depriving the notorious spy, George Blake, of his ill-gotten gains) was appropriate in an action for breach of contract which, as usually understood, is geared to compensate for the losses incurred by the innocent party. Similarly, the internal organisation of the law is challenged when criminal courts, in addition to their powers to punish offenders (by ordering custodial sentences, probation, community service, fines, and so on), are authorised to make compensation orders for the benefit of the victims of crime and, conversely, when civil law courts make awards of damages that go beyond compensation by being explicitly exemplary or punitive in nature. Or, again, the neat internal organisation of the law is confounded where, in cases involving questions about the compatibility of decisions or actions with human rights law, the courts have to determine whether a body is essentially public or private. If there were clear water between public sector provision (subject to human rights requirements) and private sector provision (not subject to human rights requirements), this should not be a problem; but, in a world where private sector enterprises and bodies undertake public functions, the line between the public and the private becomes blurred.

Much of the messiness that we see in these examples can be explained without having to introduce technology. However, from our radical introductory perspective, once technology is in the mix, the disruptive effect is magnified and of a quite different order. As Guido Noto la Diega (2023: 5) says in relation to the Internet of Things (IOT):

> The impact of the IoT on the law is not limited to the rethinking of the concept of law to include techno-regulation. The IoT disrupts many of the dichotomies upon which the law was built, most notably good-service, hardware-software, tangible-intangible, consumer-trader, consumer-worker, human-machine, security-cybersecurity, online-offline.

Moreover, this disruption impacts our understanding of where law, its rules, and its essentially human enterprise stand in the world.

In what follows, we can begin to grasp the scale of the disruption by discussing law's changing relationship with technology; then we can review the question of whether, where AI is responsible for creative work and inventive products, it should be the human author of the AI or the AI itself which should be treated by the law as having the relevant intellectual property rights; and, finally, we can note the way in which future technological applications might challenge our thinking about the relationship between law's governance which has been articulated for the 'real' world and novel virtual online worlds.

Law and technology

As an undergraduate law student, I found that law shut itself off from all external distractions. In the outside world, law was very much involved with business and commerce but, inside the law school, students needed to be blinkered—they needed to think only in-the-box thoughts—if they were to learn to think like lawyers. To be sure, at LSE, law students were not exempt from the requirement that they should have some basic literacy in economics, but the connections between law and economics were not drawn explicitly and the latter seemed to be a distraction from our in-the-box training. Law was our world; learning to think in a Law 1.0 way was the object of our education; and, whatever else there was in the world beyond law, we should put it out of our minds. If technology was part of that world, it was not relevant. Law was 'autonomous' and it made no attempt to reach out to technology. At that time, if a dinner party had been arranged with a view to starting a conversation between lawyers and technologists, I cannot imagine that it would have got very far. However, as emergent technologies have captured the interest of the legal community—now being seen as both a regulatory challenge (in a Law 2.0 way) and as a governance opportunity (in a Law 3.0 way)—this picture has changed.

The transformative process might start with a number of threads of interest being spun out from particular areas of law to particular developments in technology. For example, medical lawyers become interested in articulating a new legal framework for the technologies of assisted conception and embryology; environmental lawyers become interested in regulating the research and development as well as the commercial exploitation of genetically modified crops; and intellectual property lawyers become interested in the application of patent law to innovative processes and products in human genetics. Similarly, we find tort lawyers asking questions about the liability rules for harms brought about in novel online environments, contract lawyers taking an interest in the facilitation of e-commerce, and criminal lawyers engaging with 'cybercrime'.

These discrete threads begin to form a tapestry of interests often in a particular stream of technology (such as biotechnologies or nanotechnology), but also there might be a convergence of threads as they come to focus on the application of a particular technological feature (as happened when lawyers coming from different areas of law came together to focus on the implications of developments in human genetics for their particular legal specialities) or they focus on a particular type of application (as is the case with the interest in human enhancement where a variety of technologies might be implicated). In the examples given in the previous paragraph, some of the threads come together to represent an interest in Law, Regulation and Biotechnology; and others come together to represent an interest in Law, Regulation and Information and Communication Technologies. In short order, these groups are joined by legal and regulatory interests in nanotechnologies, in neurotechnologies, in convergent technologies, and so on. However, we have still not reached the stage at which lawyers and regulatory scholars take a more generic interest in technology and its application.

At much the same time, a thread of interest in criminal justice and a range of new technologies takes shape. This is not an interest in the criminalisation of conduct around new technologies so much as an interest in deploying new technologies for the more effective achievement of crime control. Here, it is the use of DNA profiling, of surveillance and identification technologies (such as CCTV and facial recognition), of geo-locating technologies, and of automated vehicle recognition, and the like, that attracts attention.

Consolidating this evolving legal interest in emerging technologies, we reach a point where we can say that our thinking about the relationship between law and technology is that there are two dimensions of technology—one a dimension of challenge, the other a dimension of opportunity—that are of interest to legal and regulatory scholars. The dimension of challenge presents technology as a problem, as an object to be controlled by laws and regulations. One of the challenges here is to figure out how to apply older laws, legal principles, classifications and templates to these newly emergent technologies; and the other challenge is to articulate regulatory frameworks that are sustainable and appropriate in relation to such technologies. In both cases, the aim is to connect law, old or new, to these technologies. By contrast, the dimension of opportunity presents technology as a potential solution, as a tool to be used for the more effective performance of legal and regulatory functions.

This view of the relationship between law and technology is fortified by a stream of new technologies (including additive manufacturing, augmented and virtual reality, cloud computing, blockchain, quantum computing, robotics, artificial intelligence, and machine learning) which add further challenges and opportunities for lawyers and regulatory scholars to ponder.

This relationship now evolves jurisprudentially. One set of thoughts and questions here is analogous to the threads of connection that we described above. These are thoughts and questions that are formulated by jurists whose theoretical views about the Rule of Law, the authority of law, respect for the law, and so on, now need to be revisited and re-imagined in a context where technology has a role to play in the performance of legal and regulatory functions. The other set of thoughts and questions derives from the appreciation that technology is not only disruptive of society and economy but also of law. Crucially, one of the disruptions is to the field of interest: first, the field of traditional legal interest is disrupted so that it includes technology (our interest is in 'law and technology') but then it is overtaken by a larger interest in governance within which we locate both 'law' and 'technology' (as potential modes of governance). With this, we are at, so to speak, Law 2025 and the need for a new introduction to law.

AI, patents, and copyright

In October 2017, when Saudi Arabia announced that it was recognising the robot, 'Sophia', as having citizenship, this attracted worldwide comment and attention (see, https://en.wikipedia.org/wiki/Sophia_(robot)#:~:text=In%20October%202017%2C%20Sophia%20was,given%20a%20United%20Nations%20title); and, at the time of writing, there is a growing interest in virtual influencers, such as Noonouri, who routinely feature in (and are accepted as being a part of) the digital landscape (Marr, 2023). If virtual influencers can attract as many human 'followers' as human influencers, we might ask whether there is any material difference between virtual and human influencers.

Prior to such technological developments, we humans proceeded on the basis that we are the paradigmatic cases of intelligent agency. To be sure, we debate what we see as borderline cases of intelligent agency in the non-human animal world (whales, dolphins, apes, and so on) but, after Sophia and Noonouri, we also have to address the status of AI-enabled robots and virtual persons. Moreover, the question is more than academic, for the way in which a group responds to these new 'persona' will not only change the way in which law's governance views the relationship between humans and tools but also the legal groundrules. For example, if a group adopts a declaration of robot rights in much the way that declarations of human rights have been adopted, then law's governance will need to be compatible with respect for these (robot) rights (however specified).

While we might think, the cases of Sophia and Noonouri notwithstanding, that it will be some time before we reach such a point, questions about the IP status of 'artificial' inventors or creators are now being tested out in many jurisdictions—these are questions in relation to both patents and copyright, in both of which instances the question is whether AI can be treated as, respectively, the 'inventor' (or 'deviser') of an invention or the 'author' of creative work (Abbott, 2020: Ch 4). In both cases, if it were a person rather than a machine that was identified as the inventor or author, the legal position would be straightforward; but, where we have a person working with an AI tool, the legal position is more complex.

In the UK, the IP question was tested in *Thaler v Comptroller General of Patents Trade Marks and Designs* (2021, 2023). For the members of both the Court of Appeal and the Supreme Court, it was clear that, given both the history and the scheme of the Patents Act 1977, it was only a person who could be treated as the inventor. Humans could invent machines and be assisted by machines; but the machines (in this case, Thaler's AI machine, DABUS) could not qualify as inventors. Evidently, the case advanced by Thaler 'was frequently put on the basis of what the law ought to be rather than what it was' (2021, para 29); but, as Arnold LJ said, the task of the court was to apply the law of the UK; and 'at the risk of stating the obvious, we must apply the law as it presently stands: this is not an occasion for debating what the law ought to be' (para 114). In that vein, the Court of Appeal reached its conclusion

> without any need to examine the policy arguments raised by both parties. Machines are not persons. The fact that machines can now create inventions, which is what Dr Thaler says happened in this case, would not mean that machines are inventors within the meaning of the Act.

> Assuming the machine is the entity which actually created these inventions, it has no right to be mentioned as the inventor.
>
> *(para 55)*

In other words, even if DABUS had made an 'inventive' contribution to the two items (a food container and a flashing light) for which the patent applications were filed (and, each of which was on the face of it patentable), DABUS was not an 'inventor' within the meaning of the law.

Yet, to the extent that the policy of intellectual property law is to incentivise and support beneficial research and development as well as the creative arts, it is not so clear that a narrow focus on the statutory meaning makes sense. On the other hand, for a *court* to depart from that meaning might well provoke criticism. The matter surely invites further debate—but it needs to be a legislative and regulatory debate. As Lord Kitchin (giving the unanimous judgment of the Supreme Court) remarked (2023, 48–49):

> 48. This appeal is not concerned with the broader question whether technical advances generated by machines acting autonomously and powered by AI should be patentable. Nor is it concerned with the question whether the meaning of the term 'inventor' ought to be expanded, so far as necessary, to include machines powered by AI which generate new and non-obvious products and processes which may be thought to offer benefits over products and processes which are already known.
>
> 49. These questions raise policy issues about the purpose of a patent system, the need to incentivise technical innovation and the provision of an appropriate monopoly in return for the making available to the public of new and non-obvious technical advances, and an explanation of how to put them into practice across the range of the monopoly sought. It may be thought that the rapid advances in AI technology in recent times render these questions even more important than they were when these applications were made.

Similarly, if it is proposed that the input of the machines should be acknowledged (raising questions about their 'personality'), this invites further debate (Chesterman, 2021: 131–138). Again, though, this will be a regulatory, Law 2.0 and Law 3.0, engagement with the question of whether the law is fit for purpose and, if not, what governance measures need to be taken.

Technologically enabled worlds and the real world

In the early days of the Internet, we were able to differentiate with some confidence between the offline, real world and the online, technologically enabled world. However, the line between one world and the other has been blurred somewhat by always-on technologies that permeate our real-world environments as well as by wearables that physically connect us to online worlds. With the development of augmented and virtual reality, and technologically enabled environments such as the Metaverse, we might find that anchoring our laws and human experiences in the real world becomes even more problematic.

To focus on the Metaverse, how should we conceive of the gap between the real and the virtual world? Even where the interactions or transactions in the Metaverse are 'as if human to human' (as if H2H), there might still be a gap between the H2H situation in the real world and how it might be perceived in the virtual world; and, indeed, one of the attractions of the Metaverse might be precisely that it allows humans to change, or overcome, the limitations of what, still thinking in a traditional way, they treat as their real world situation.

Let us suppose that humans can participate as if themselves in some Metaverse places and spaces, interacting and transacting with other humans who are also participating as if themselves. Alternatively, humans might participate in some Metaverse places and spaces, interacting and transacting with others through the medium of their alter ego avatars (AEAs). So, in principle, interactions and transactions in the Metaverse might be (i) as if human to human (as if H2H) or (ii) alter ego avatar to alter ego avatar (AEA2AEA) or even possibly (iii) as if human to alter ego avatar (as if H2AEA).

One form of the gap puzzle will arise where, in the real world, the transaction or interaction between humans does not take place in the presence of one another but interactions or transactions in the Metaverse are of an 'as if H2H' nature. Here, although the parties do not experience a shared presence in the real world, their in-Metaverse experience is that of being in one another's presence. Now, there will be various kinds of real-world legal rules that hinge on humans acting in one another's presence. For example, the rules of contract law might differentiate between transactions that are made 'inter praesentes' and those that are not so made—recall the cases of mistake of identity that we met in an earlier chapter; the rules of succession or land law might specify that a document (such as a will or a conveyance) must be signed by one party 'in the presence of' one or more witnesses; and, the rules of evidence might demand that witnesses give their evidence in court in the presence of others. The puzzle is how as if H2H dealings in the Metaverse—where the immersive experience of the humans is that they are in one another's presence—will be treated for the purposes of these various real-world legal rules. Will the non-Metaverse actuality be decisive such that, if the parties are not dealing face-to-face in the real world, this will not qualify as 'inter praesentes' even if the phenomenological perception of the parties is that they are in one another's presence? Or, will judges perhaps build creatively on existing exceptions to the general principles?

Let us suppose that it has been decided that as if H2H 'inter praesentes' dealings in the Metaverse are not equivalent to H2H 'inter praesentes' dealings in the real world. In this case, it would follow that, where alter ego avatars are used, their AEA2AEA dealings would also fail to be treated as equivalent to 'inter praesentes' dealings in the real world. However, if it has been decided that, in principle, as if H2H 'inter praesentes' dealings in the Metaverse should be treated as equivalent to H2H 'inter praesentes' dealings in the real world, then the use of AEAs is a complication. It is one thing to treat the avatars used for as if H2H dealings as an extension of their human operators but, where humans have taken steps to distance themselves from their avatars, or to disguise their real-world identity, it is more difficult to identify the human operators with their AEAs. On the other hand, the fact that we can differentiate between the human operator and their AEA might make it easier to treat the latter as an 'agent' who is acting in the Metaverse for an undisclosed human principal in the real world.

While lawyers, reasoning in a Law 1.0 way, might spend some time wrestling with puzzles of this kind—and we can certainly imagine novice law students being confronted with questions about when an acceptance of an offer that is made in the Metaverse takes effect—no legal system will tolerate uncertainty about these issues where humans need to know where they stand with their transactions and documentary compliance. Hence, if reliance is jeopardised by uncertainty, it will not be long before clarity is demanded and a Law 2.0 response is made.

The gap between the virtual world of the Metaverse and the real world might also give rise to puzzles where acts or omissions that are judged to be wrongful by Metaverse standards lead to harm that is experienced by a human in the real world. For example, in Second Life (which we can regard as an early prototype for the Metaverse), the participants used the word 'griefing' to signify unacceptable, often abusive, behaviour by participants acting through their avatars. Suppose, then, that in the Metaverse one avatar (A2) is stalking another (A1). Within the Metaverse, there might well be governance arrangements that enable the platform management to block the acts of A2 or to shield A1 from A2's acts—for example, following the well-known case of Nina Jane Patel, Meta created a personal boundary functionality for users of Horizon Venues, that is designed to prevent one avatar from invading the personal space of others (Sharma, 2022). However, to hypothesise a clear test case, let us suppose that, before A2 can be blocked, H1 (who operates A1) has already been distressed by A2's stalking of A1, and that H2 (who operates A2) intends the stalking to cause distress to H1. How would such griefing be viewed?

On the one hand, it might be argued that 'what is said or done in the Metaverse stays in the Metaverse'. On the other hand, where H2 intends to cause distress to HI, and where the Metaverse is simply the medium through which that distress is occasioned, there will be pressure to protect victims. Where the real-world community demands protection, then judges might be prepared to be creative in applying existing criminal offences to cover such cases and this might suffice; but, even with this, it might be thought desirable to introduce bespoke offences to cover griefing that is intended to cause distress to a known human operator. If, however, H2 does not intend to cause distress to H1, then (following the pattern of real-world tort thinking) the question is likely to be whether H2 owes a duty of care to the operators of avatars in the Metaverse and has failed to take reasonable care not to cause reasonably foreseeable distress to HI. Here, there might also be a question about the application of the terms and conditions on which humans participate in the Metaverse. What if the terms and conditions do stipulate in effect that what happens in the Metaverse stays in the Metaverse? How far are these terms and conditions governing?

Potentially, the development of online environments such as the Metaverse problematises not only our organising distinction between the real world and the virtual world (should we, instead, be thinking about a continuum between the real and the virtual?) but also our assumption that real-world laws shall govern. However, once our organising thinking has been disrupted, the sovereignty of law's real-world governance might also be disrupted.

16

FLEXIBLE CONCEPTS

Introduction

Governance starts with the group agreeing on its basic rules. Even at this initial stage, some members of the group might feel the need for some flexibility (or tolerances) in the rules; and, as time goes by, it will be clear that governance needs to be able to make adjustments for cases that are hard or for circumstances that are quite different from those anticipated by the rules.

In this chapter, we can focus on the concept of 'reasonableness' which, once included in the formulation of a rule, immediately introduces some flexibility into its application—compare, for example, a rule that provides that the victim of a breach of contract should take all possible steps to minimise the loss occasioned by the breach (and should never increase such loss) with a rule that simply requires the victim to take reasonable steps to minimise their losses (and not unreasonably to increase them). Then, we can look at some examples of parties being given some wiggle room in relation to their legal commitments—not only as a result of those commitments being expressed in terms of, or qualified by, reasonableness but also by the idea of a margin of appreciation (and proportionality) for compliance with human rights.

Reasonableness in contracts

In Chapter 5, I mentioned that, as I was commencing my undergraduate studies in English contract law, the judges were having considerable difficulty in reconciling the foundational principles of freedom and sanctity of contract with the sense that dealers were engaging in sharp practice by

DOI: 10.4324/9781003507802-19

hiding behind their standard terms and conditions to take unfair advantage of consumers. Eventually, Parliament stepped in to provide that the most unreasonable of such terms and conditions were always invalid and could never be relied on by dealers; and, they backed up this non-negotiable rejection of the worst kind of exclusions and restrictions of liability by putting the burden on dealers to persuade judges that other exclusions and restrictions in standard form transactions were fair and reasonable terms to be included in the contract. While this gave the judges considerable discretion in allowing or disallowing terms that were subject to the 'fair and reasonable' test, it gave rise to two obvious questions: first, by reference to what or whom should the fairness and reasonableness of a term in a contract be judged; and, secondly, how much uncertainty can the law of contract tolerate for the sake of a 'fair and reasonable' test?

To start with the reference point for reasonableness, in principle, this might be assessed in more than one way—for example, by reference to the viewpoint of a reasonable business contractor, or to that of a reasonable consumer contractor, or to that of some impartial and reasonable member of the community. However, whichever viewpoint is adopted, the obvious objection is that there is no reason to privilege it over the alternative viewpoints; and, what is more, even if it is conceded that the privileged viewpoint is a reasonable place to start, within the class in question—whether it is the class of business contractors, or consumers, or impartial members of the community, or whoever—there are likely to be many shades of reasonable opinion. Bearing in mind these objections, consider the question that faced the UK Supreme Court in *ParkingEye Ltd v Beavis* (2015), namely: whether the terms for parking at a retail shopping area were reasonable in allowing two hours of free parking but then charging £85 for anything in excess of two hours. The business case for imposing £85 for overstaying was that the retailers needed to discourage commuters from leaving their cars in the parking area all day and making it difficult for shoppers to park there. Against this, the argument for consumers was that the charge was non-negotiable, excessive, and inflexible—indeed, so much so that no consumer who was in a position to bargain and who was properly advised would have agreed to such a charge. While the business case does not look unreasonable, the question for the majority judges who accepted this argument and held that the charge was fair and reasonable, was how they could justify taking the business rather than the consumer's or some other viewpoint; and, conversely, while the minority judge who accepted the consumer-focused arguments and held the term unreasonable, could muster some strong consumer protection arguments, the question was how he could justify favouring the consumer viewpoint over others—to which the answer perhaps would simply be that the policy of the relevant body of law was tilted towards the protection of consumers. Then, even if we accept the consumer viewpoint, we need to recognise that there are consumers and there are consumers. In EU law, the viewpoint of the average consumer (who is reasonably well-informed and circumspect) is the benchmark but, while this is not an unreasonable position to take, what about less well-informed and perhaps more vulnerable consumers?

In an attempt to reduce the uncertainty that inevitably comes with a reasonableness standard, one strategy is to set out statutory guidelines for the application of the test, or informal guidance. So, for example, in the original protective legislation, the Unfair Contract Terms Act 1997, Schedule 2 sets out a number of considerations—such as the relative bargaining strength of the parties, whether any inducement was given to accept the terms in question, whether alternative deals (without the questionable terms) were available, and so on—to which regard should be had. Given that consumer contractors would typically be in a much weaker bargaining position than the dealer, and given that the terms would usually be non-negotiable, the guidelines would tend to favour the consumer. However, the guidelines give less of a steer in commercial disputes where both parties are business contractors and, of course, if (as in *ParkingEye*) judges start taking the business perspective, or if they try to 'balance' the business and the consumer perspective, it becomes more difficult to know how they will call it in particular cases.

Reasonableness and the law of negligence

Typically, actions for negligence start with the claimant seeking to show that the defendant failed to take reasonable care. However, a defendant may argue that, even if a failure to take reasonable care were to be conceded, it would still be unreasonable to hold the defendant accountable (and liable) to the claimant. In fact, this was precisely the defence that was relied on in the famous case of *Donoghue v Stevenson* that I mentioned early in the book. At that time, nearly one hundred years ago, the general rule in English law was that, where A was careless in undertaking work *pursuant to a contract* with B, then A was accountable only to B. So, if A injured B, A was liable to B; but, if A's carelessness resulted in injury to C, A was not liable to C. Contractual relationships were, thus, personal to the parties in two ways: first, it was only B who could sue A for breach of contract; and, secondly, it was also only B who could sue A for negligence in the performance of the contract. In *Donoghue*, Lord Atkin, to whom I also referred early in the book, wrote a historic judgment saying that this rule was over-restrictive and that A should be answerable to C where it was reasonably foreseeable that A's acts or omissions would cause injury to C. With the contractual defence having been removed, and with it being recognised that a manufacturer of bottled ginger beer (A) could reasonably foresee that careless quality control might cause injury to the ultimate consumer of the drink (C), the focus shifted to the question of whether C could establish that A had failed to take reasonable care (in, as it was alleged, allowing the decomposed remains of a snail to enter one of its bottled drinks) and, then, whether it was these remains that caused the gastroenteritis subsequently suffered by the claimant (C).

In a case such as *Donoghue*, how would we assess whether a manufacturer has taken reasonable care? Three benchmarks of reasonableness suggest themselves: first, as manufacturers might argue, the benchmark should be set by the standards of their fellow manufacturers; secondly, as consumers of products might argue, the benchmark should be set by the reasonable expectations of consumers; and, thirdly, it might be argued that the test should be an impartial one of 'economic efficiency' (where the relevant considerations would include how much it would cost the manufacturer to prevent toxic agents entering their products, the likelihood of such an agent entering a product and causing harm, and the seriousness of the resulting harm). The problem with the first benchmark is that manufacturers might set the bar too low; the problem with the second is that consumer expectations might set the bar too high and, in turn, lead to an unwelcome increase in the price of products; and, the problem with the third is that it might be translated into an econometric calculation that is remote from the thinking of most people. Moreover, we might wonder whether a benchmark that makes sense in the manufacturing (or food and drinks) sector would make sense in another context such as, say, health care and medical negligence.

Following up this point, in English law, for many years the key case was *Bolam v Friern Hospital Management Committee* (1957). Stated simply, it was accepted in this case that the benchmark for members of the medical profession was the practice of their peers (in line with the first approach outlined above). Crucially, where medical practice was not uniform, it was *not* fatal to the defendant that some members of the profession would be opposed to the procedure or treatment employed. What mattered was whether the defendant could show that their actions were consistent with a body of responsible medical opinion. Some forty years later, in *Bolitho v City and Hackney Health Authority* (1997), the House of Lords accentuated the significance of the supportive opinion being 'responsible', this introducing some speculation about judges being willing to take a more interventionist approach; but, broadly speaking, the reference point for judgments of medical negligence continued to be professional medical practice. That said, in a landmark judgment by the Supreme Court in *Montgomery v Lanarkshire Health Board* (2015), the benchmark for informing patients as to their treatment options has moved decisively away from the professional medical perspective to that of the patient as a consumer of medical services (see, further, Chapter 25).

Unreasonableness as a ground for judicial review

The so-called 'Wednesbury' principle is one of the cornerstones of British administrative law. Deriving from *Associated Provincial Picture Houses Ltd v Wednesbury Corporation* (1948), the principle holds that a decision made by a public body will not be impugned on the ground that it is 'unreasonable' unless it is judged to be so unreasonable that no reasonable body could possibly have made such a decision. There is more than a little smoke and mirrors in this: we decide whether a public body has acted unreasonably by appealing to some unspecified reasonable body. Nevertheless, the underlying thinking suggests two key elements that give shape to our approach to the question of what is reasonable and what unreasonable.

First, the thinking is that there is a spectrum of reasonableness and a bandwidth within which people can 'reasonably' hold different views (compare Bingham, 2011: 64–65). In the *Wednesbury* case itself, the decision at issue, one made by the local authority, was that no child under the age of 15 should be admitted to local cinemas on Sundays. While the cinema owners took the view that this was unduly restrictive (not least because the restriction applied irrespective of whether the child was accompanied by an adult), others might have thought that the policy should be more restrictive (for example, that cinemas should not be open at all on Sundays). But, the point is that some such range of views will qualify as 'reasonable' (or, at any rate, 'not unreasonable') even though they are different views.

Secondly, the bandwidth of reasonableness comes to an end where the view in question is so unreasonable that no reasonable body or person could hold it. If a view or decision falls into this category, a court will step in to invalidate it, and the implication is that we should not tolerate it. People who hold competing or conflicting reasonable views can reasonably agree to disagree; but, where we encounter a view that is off the scale, we should not hesitate to reject it.

At this point, we should note that the general shape of thinking about reasonableness (a bandwidth of reasonableness where there might be different views but with outliers that are wholly unreasonable) also applies to our thinking about proportionality. For example, if the question is whether a citizen has employed reasonable or proportionate force in defending themselves against unlawful acts, then there is a bandwidth of reasonable or not unreasonable acts but, outside this bandwidth, we have acts that are, as some put it, 'grossly disproportionate' and themselves unlawful. Similarly, the bandwidth of reasonableness for the use of force by the police is considerable but, where the police act outside this bandwidth, in ways that are perceived by the local community to be inappropriate or wholly disproportionate, then we have the makings of serious disorder.

So far so good, but we still have a recurrent and persistent problem: which (reasonable) person or body serves as the reference point to test the reasonableness or unreasonableness of a view, and how do we test the reasonableness of the reference body or person?

If we settle on a particular community—whether Wednesbury, the West Midlands, or even Middle England—as our reference point for reasonableness, we can say that relative to standards of reasonableness that are recognised in that particular community, the view or decision or action is or is not reasonable, and is or is not within the bandwidth of tolerable difference. That is clear enough but it might not seem particularly compelling. Instead, might there be a 'cosmopolitan' reference point that reflects what is recognised as reasonable or wholly unreasonable in all (or nearly all) communities? For example, if the question had not been about the opening times of cinemas but about the licensing of slavery or torture, then maybe we could appeal to a cosmopolitan consensus to ground our view of what is reasonable and unreasonable. However, even with slavery or torture, this might be a narrow ledge because we know that, while it might be agreed that there are no circumstances in which practices of slavery or torture are reasonable, there is much less agreement about whether it is reasonable to tear down statues of local figures who were historically associated with practices of this kind.

Even if cosmopolitan standards gave us more critical power, we might still be concerned that they rest on recognition and acceptance in human communities. Can we not find standards and tests for what is wholly unreasonable in the fundamental 'terms and conditions' that are implicit in humans forming groups and communities and embarking on the enterprise of their governance? In other words, are there not prior commitments already implicit in our governance activities, irrespective of particular communities or groups; and, are these commitments not such that no human with any interest or stake in governance could reasonably revoke them (compare Sumption, 2019: 49–51; and Chapter 22)?

The margin of appreciation (and proportionality) in human rights law

Typically, if it is argued that the state is in breach of its human rights commitments, the first step will be to show that a particular human right is, as they say, 'engaged'. For example, it might be argued that the state is in breach of its commitment to respect privacy (under Article 8(1) of the ECHR). If this argument is accepted, it will be open to the state to defend its actions by reference to the grounds listed in Article 8(2). To bring itself within this Article, the state must show that its actions were in accordance with the law and that they were necessary in a democratic society 'in the interests of national security, public safety or the economic wellbeing of the country, for the prevention of disorder or crime, for the protection of health or morals, or for the protection of the rights and freedoms of others'. While the jurisprudence of human rights indicates that there is more to this than mere reasonableness, the qualifying requirements of necessity, proportionality and pressing social need, yield a margin of appreciation that is pretty flexible. Moreover, it is unclear where within the human rights community the European Court of Human Rights finds its reference point for such flexibility (Sedley, 2018: Ch 6).

One thing is clear. Where the states that are signed up to human rights take up a variety of positions on morally contested matters, the bandwidth of legality (as in *Wednesbury*) will be broad. However, if a particular state finds itself outside this bandwidth, it will be held to be in breach of its human rights commitments. In this context, the *Case of S. and Marper v The United Kingdom* (2009), the leading case in Europe on the taking (and retention) of DNA samples and the banking of DNA profiles for criminal justice purposes, is significant.

The background to the case is well-known. First, the technology of DNA fingerprinting and profiling was pioneered in the 1980s by Professor Alec Jeffreys at Leicester University. In principle, the technology could be applied for a range of purposes, such as paternity testing and identifying the victims of natural disasters. However, it was the prospect of using DNA profiling, both to eliminate and to identify suspects, in the criminal justice system that attracted huge interest. So, for example, when the police in Leicestershire were investigating two similar cases, one in 1983 and the other in 1986, where teenage girls had been raped and murdered, DNA profiling was used to eliminate a 17-year-old: although the suspect had admitted to one of the crimes, his DNA profile did not match the DNA recovered from the crime scenes. With their main suspect out of the picture, the police took DNA samples from 5,000 local men but they found no matches. However, the police learnt that one of the men, Colin Pitchfork, had paid a friend £200 to supply a false sample. Pitchfork was arrested; his DNA profile matched; and he confessed to the crimes.

Following the Pitchfork case and some other spectacular examples of near matches that led the police from minor offenders to serious offenders in the same family, advocates of crime control saw this technique as an important tool for the police and prosecutors; and the legislative framework was duly amended to authorise very extensive taking and retention of profiles. Even when legal proceedings were dropped or suspects were acquitted, the law authorised the retention of the profiles that had been taken. As a result, a DNA database with several million profiles soon was in place and, where DNA samples were retrieved from crime scenes, the database could be interrogated as an investigative tool (so that 'reasonable suspicion' could be cast on an individual, not by independent evidence, but by a 'match'). Precisely how much contribution to crime control was (or is) made by the profiles is hard to know. However, it was clear that the traditional rights of individuals were being subordinated to the promise of the new technology; and it was just a matter of time before the compatibility of the legislative provisions with human rights was raised in the courts.

The UK's legal provisions were duly challenged in the *Marper* case, where the Grand Chamber in Strasbourg held that the provisions were far too wide and disproportionate in their impact on privacy. The position taken by the court was not that taking and retaining DNA profiles would always be incompatible with human rights. However, the legislative powers drawn up in UK law were far more extensive than those in other European countries. The UK was an outlier; and, to this extent at least, individual human rights prevailed over the latest technology of crime control (Brownsword and Goodwin, 2012: Ch 4).

17

PROHIBITIONS, PERMISSIONS, AND REQUIREMENTS

Introduction

In this chapter, we introduce the signals that are given by legal rules, whether to prohibit x, or to require x, or to permit x. We can start with the then UK Prime Minister, Rishi Sunak, who in January 2023 was fined for not wearing a seat belt while travelling in the back of a car. He released the seat belt in order to face a camera and make a televised statement. There are some exemptions to the legal requirement that passengers in cars engage their seat belt—for example, exemptions for members of the emergency services or for medical reasons—but taking a photo opportunity is not one. The Prime Minister was in breach of the legal requirements. The rule relating to the wearing of seat belts is, of course, just one of many prohibitions and requirements that apply to the use of cars—for example, the prohibitions on using a mobile phone while driving, exceeding the speed limits, driving under the influence of drink or drugs, driving without due care and attention, and so on; and the requirement that the vehicle be taxed and insured, and the like. One thing that is not prohibited is smoking while driving; to that extent, smoking is legally permitted but, of course, in other places, smoking is prohibited. So it is that law's governance operates through *prohibitions*, *permissions* (where the permitted acts are neither prohibited nor required but at the option of the individual) and *requirements*.

Where those who are subject to law's governance fail to comply with a legal prohibition or requirement, they will be in breach of a duty. Enforcement action and penal sanctions might follow. Moreover, in some cases, there might also be compensatory claims made by parties who plead a breach of their rights—for example, if a motorist drives with undue care and attention

DOI: 10.4324/9781003507802-20

as a result of which a pedestrian is injured, the latter may claim that his or her rights have been infringed by the former's breach of duty. In these cases, there is a failure under both the criminal and the civil law; but there will also be many examples of claims (for example for breach of contract) where the breach of duty is not also a criminal offence but purely a civil wrong.

Operating in a Law 1.0 way, we can report that the legal position is that such and such an act is legally prohibited, or required, or permitted. However, this does not yet disclose the significance of compliance (with prohibitions or requirements) in law's governance and nor does it indicate how a legal permission can be glossed with incentives or disincentives as well as other kinds of governance pressure.

Compliance and non-compliance

Following on from our discussion of the regulatory environment in Chapter 14, we can now draw out the relationship between compliance (and non-compliance) with those legal rules that express prohibitions or requirements as opposed to conformity with technological governance.

In the year before he was fined for not wearing a seat belt while travelling in the back of a car, Rishi Sunak was fined for a violation of the Covid-19 social gathering regulations when he attended a birthday party for the then Prime Minister, Boris Johnson. At the time, there was far more concern about Johnson's non-compliance than Sunak's. For, not only did it seem as though Johnson was a serial violator of the Covid-19 rules, in *Miller 2*, he had also been reined in by the Supreme Court for non-compliance with UK constitutional laws. However we look at it, law's governance in the UK is less than perfect in achieving compliance with its requirements—and, what is more, it seems that, to some extent, there is a culture of non-compliance at the highest level.

Now, imagine a world of governance by technology where none of this would happen—indeed, where none of this could happen. In that world, vehicles (whether autonomous or human-controlled) simply would not operate unless and until passengers have engaged their seat belts and access to buildings would be denied (not by a police officer but by designed-in technology) where non-compliant acts are detected. Taking a bold leap, imagine, too, that technological management includes the 'coding' of persons. Here, newborns are chipped in such a way that, once they are adults, they are subject to a two-stage compliance control: first, where a high risk of non-compliance is detected, a notification is received and then, if the risk is not reduced, they are disabled. In such a technologically managed world, Sunak would have been warned that he should not release his seat belt (even for a photo-opportunity in his car) and that he should not attend an unlawful social gathering (even for a birthday celebration); and, in this world, any attempt to proceed notwithstanding these warnings would be futile. In this world, technological governance would ensure both perfect control and (if this is 'conformity') perfect conformity.

Comparing law's imperfect governance with governance by technology, we might be tempted to say, quite simply, that the latter performs better than the former; or, more cautiously, we might say that, *relative to the metric of compliance*, the latter performs better than the former. However, there are reasons to think that we should not say either of these things. We should not say the first thing because there is more to law's governance than compliance: to be sure, compliance matters but its significance has to be understood in the context of a governance enterprise that is human, relational, and respectful. Compliance is only meaningful where the context is governance by law because there is also the possibility of non-compliance. It is the fact that the opportunity for non-compliance is eschewed that is significant.

As for the second thing, I suggest that we should not say that either because it is not clear that the metric of compliance that we apply to law's governance is the same metric of compliance as that applied to technological governance. That said, if we take our lead from technological governance and its concept of compliance as conduct that 'conforms to' governance requirements, then it might well be the case that we find much less 'non-conforming' conduct in technologically managed environments than we do in environments that are subject only to law's governance. In which case, if we want to take the sting out of this by arguing that mere 'conformity' does not get to the essence of compliance and insisting that we should take our lead from the more complex concept of compliance that we associate with law's governance, then we need to be ready to defend the virtues of law's imperfect governance.

To put this in other words: let us grant that not everything that matters can be counted; and let us also grant that it does not follow that one regime or mode of governance is necessarily better than another where, in the former, we can count more acts of conformity than in the latter. Nevertheless, we still have to identify what it is about law's governance that, even if it cannot be counted, is something that matters.

Glossing permissions

Without thinking particularly radical thoughts, we might already sense that, in practice, not all legal permissions are the same; there are permissions and there are permissions. For example, there is a difference between an unregulated (unconditional) permission and a regulated (conditional) permission. Broadly speaking, I can take a walk or ride a bike to the beach without having to be certified and licensed as fit to do these things; but, if I want to drive a car to the beach, I need to satisfy several conditions before I can do this lawfully. Whereas the only thing holding me back from walking to the beach is my inclination or the adverse weather, the conditions that stand between me and being able to lawfully drive a car might be so demanding that I abandon any idea of doing so (formally permitted though it is).

When we turn to more radical thoughts, viewing a legal permission as just one feature of the larger regulatory environment, we might see that other modes of governance gloss that permission with all manner of disincentives and incentives. For example, public health policy might engage with lifestyles and personal preferences that are legally permitted by nudging people towards healthier diets, by advertising the risks of smoking and drinking, by generating social pressure for taking up vaccines and opportunities for screening, and even by imposing costs on those who are judged to have unhealthy lifestyles. At the same time, there might be various kinds of incentives for those who can demonstrate healthy lifestyles. The law might treat some act as optional but, in the bigger picture of governance, it is evident that there are permissions and permissions (compare Lessig's four regulatory modalities, or modes of governance, that we introduced in Chapter 4).

Finally, how should we translate law's prohibitions, requirements, and permissions into a technologically managed environment where agents are presented with two possibilities: 'can do' and 'cannot do'? 'Cannot do' is a straightforward prohibition; there is no possibility of non-compliance; and other governance signals are irrelevant. 'Can do' might imply either a requirement (where there is no option for non-compliance) or permission (where an alternative is available). In this latter case, even in a technologically managed environment, there might be occasions where what is in effect a permission is glossed with other governance signals.

18

RIGHTS, DUTIES, AND POWERS

Introduction

In the early years of the last century, the American jurist Wesley Newcomb Hohfeld (1964) noted that there is a good deal of ambiguity in the way that lawyers use the term 'right'—and, of course, in the present century, we frequently appeal to our 'rights'. Then as now, when we say that A has a right to do x relative to B, we might mean that the doing of x is permitted, that doing x is at A's option; and that A does no wrong to B. However, we might also talk about A having a right against B, meaning that A has a claim against B that B do, or not do, x. Here, the focus is on B's duties to A and on the possibility that B does a wrong to A. In the former case, A's right is merely permissive; in the latter case, A has a claim right.

Once we differentiate between A having a *claim right* in relation to B and A simply having a *permissive right* in relation to B, we might also wonder about the difference between legal rules that impose duties and those that confer powers. So, in HLA Hart's well-known conceptualisation of law (Hart, 1961), readers are told that the essence of law is found in the intersection of primary and secondary rules of law, the former being duty-imposing and the latter being power-conferring.

In a radical introduction to law, these conceptual questions might seem altogether too abstract and 'academic'. That is to say, we might think that, in the bigger picture of governance, it makes little practical difference whether the legal rules confer a mere permission, or a claim right, or a power. For, as we have already seen, in the bigger picture of governance, a mere permission might be glossed in various ways and, in technologically managed environments, governance does not run in the language of rights and duties.

DOI: 10.4324/9781003507802-21

Nevertheless, it is worth pursuing these conceptual distinctions to see, on the one hand, what insights they might yield but, on the other, what we might miss by focusing on them.

We can speak, first, to the loose usage of 'rights', the usage that troubled Hohfeld; and then, following a pathway through Hart's distinction between duty-imposing and power-conferring rules, we can see how this might divert attention from questions about both the warrant for law's governance and possibly conflicting forces in the larger field of governance.

Claim rights and permissive rights

When Sean Penn and Madonna married in the Summer of 1985, the couple went to extraordinary lengths to deter the paparazzi from covering their cliff top wedding in Malibu—by all accounts, Penn even fired his .45 gun at the helicopters circling overhead at the wedding location. Such was celebrity. But, to what extent were the parties—Penn and Madonna on one side and the paparazzi on the other—acting in line with their rights, and what kind of rights were involved?

Arguably, Penn and Madonna were exercising permissive (privacy) rights in trying to keep the paparazzi away from their wedding; but, equally, the paparazzi were also exercising permissive (press freedom) rights in trying to cover the event. To be sure, these permissive rights would have limits. For example, Penn might have exceeded the limits when he fired a handgun at the paparazzi (and this would have been a breach of duty) but not so in writing 'F ... Off' in the Malibu sand (as Penn also did). In general, this picture of bilateral permissive rights might fit quite well with the dealings between the press (trying, offensively, to obtain information) and those who are in the public eye (trying, defensively, to deny access). On this view, the super-rich who buy up a cluster of properties in order to shut out press intrusion do no wrong; but, equally, the press do no wrong in persisting with attempts to access information provided, of course, that they do not exceed the limits of the permission (as they would, for example, if they hacked into phones or the like).

That said, we might argue that Penn and Madonna's privacy was protected by a claim right to the effect that the press should not attempt to intrude on their wedding celebrations. While there might be some debate about the scope of this right—for example, whether the press would infringe the right if they published photographs of the wedding that had been sent to them by some unidentified third-party—we can take it that helicopters circling overhead would violate the right.

Of course, even with the protection of a claim right, there is no guarantee that personal privacy will be respected. For those who can afford to do so, it might be possible to take protective measures that keep the press at a safe distance, or in the event of an infringement of one's privacy to take legal action seeking compensation for the wrongdoing. However, for those who cannot afford either practical protection or litigation, the difference between permissive rights and claim rights is, alas, merely academic.

Powers and duties

In his conceptualisation of law, Hart (1961) differentiates between primary rules of law and secondary rules, the former imposing duties and the latter conferring powers. To elaborate a little, according to Hart, while the rules of, say, criminal law and tort law impose duties, the rules of, say, contract law and the law of wills are enabling (or empowering). While the rules of the latter are optional in the sense that there is no legal requirement that we enter contracts or make a will (the rules simply provide that, if we wish to make a legally binding contract or will, then this is what we should do), there is nothing optional about duty-imposing rules—if we fail to comply with our legal duties, the police might come knocking at our door or a writ will be served.

However, the key 'intersection', as Hart puts it, between law's primary rules and its secondary rules does not occur when duty-imposing criminal law meets with power-conferring contract law (as we saw that it might do when we discussed *Fisher v Bell* in Chapter 9). Rather, it is when the rules of constitutional law that authorise legislatures and courts to make and apply legal rules intersect with the rules, both duty-imposing and power-conferring rules, that are so made and applied. We can debate whether, in Hart's terms, these constitutional rules should be treated as duty-imposing primary or power-conferring secondary rules; but, wherever we stand on that question, it seems to miss the point that the constitutional rules are at a different level to the rules that are made by the authorised bodies in the required manner. In other words, Hart makes an important point by highlighting the intersection between the authorising constitutional rules and the rules that are then made in reliance on these authorising warrants; but, at this intersection, the contrast between duty-imposing and power-conferring rules seems to be less important.

Thus far, we have been, as it were, thinking in the Hartian box by taking it as read that law's governance can be represented as a 'pyramid' of rules formed by constitutional rules together with the rules that are made under the authorising warrants all of which form a legal system. Thinking in the box, we might also go along with Hart's claim that, at the apex of the pyramid, we have what he calls the 'rule of recognition' which serves to identify all the member rules of the system and, at least implicitly, to demand that the rules of the system are recognised and respected as such. In traditional jurisprudential circles, it is not the case that everyone does accept this claim. In fact, there is a huge literature debating precisely how we should understand the rule of recognition and whether it captures all the materials (such as legal principles) that we might want to treat as legally relevant. However, taking a radical perspective, the Hartian picture becomes problematic once we begin to think out from the internal structure of a legal system to the context in which the rule of recognition was instated or took shape. For the fact of the matter is that, in practice, legal systems do not normally present themselves as being optional and their historic origins will often be accompanied by violence and resistance. True, in international trade, contractors are free to choose which body of law shall govern their dealings (and, they will often choose English law or New York law); but, for the citizens of England or of the US, there is no option—they are bound by their national law. In this sense, whether its particular rules are duty-imposing or power-conferring, law's governance itself is not optional.

There are two major matters that an inward-looking focus on the distinction between duty-imposing and power-conferring rules turns its back on. One question concerns the claims made by those who rely on the authority of a particular legal system and who demand respect for its rules; and the other question concerns the forces exerted in the larger field of governance, in particular, whether all governance modalities are pulling and pushing in the same direction or whether there are oppositions, tensions, and resistance between them.

With regard to the first of these questions—as we noted in Chapter 6 and as we will discuss again in Chapter 31—in the early days of the Internet there was considerable resistance to the authority claimed by law's governance. Young people, especially, simply did not accept that the warrant for national law extended to online activities. On this view, national law had no mandate to colonise and govern the Internet; the rules of recognition for national law simply did not apply. So, what we see here is that there might be some resistance to the sovereign demands made on behalf of law's governance. The rule of recognition, in other words, might be deeply contested; and, even if the officials of the legal system treat the constitutional rules as binding, those who are governed might push back against the rules that are imposed on them.

As for the second question, there is the possibility that all inputs into the regulatory environment will be harmonious and non-conflictual. For example, when Lawrence Lessig (1999) talks about various regulatory modalities combining to channel behaviour towards the wearing of seat-belts, we have a picture of a field of governance in which law's rules are complemented by social pressure, market signals and technical coding. However, the picture might be very different, with resistance to law's rules being generated by social counter-cultures, by financial incentives, and by technological options that challenge effective legal control. Or, indeed, as with the governance of

Internet domain names, even if we are not dealing with outright resistance and rejection of the Internet Corporation for Assigned Names and Numbers (ICANN), the self-interest of key players might limit the willingness to cooperate (Weitzenboeck, 2014). Whatever else we might learn from our careful analysis of the distinction between primary (duty-imposing) and secondary (power-conferring) rules, it will not help us understand the challenges that confront law's governance, or the map of transnational governance and the importance of technical standards, and it will not assist us in developing and implementing a model of good governance.

19

CRIME AND PUNISHMENT, HARM, AND LIBERTY

Introduction

When a group draws up its basic code of conduct, it will want to identify what it regards as the most serious kind of wrongdoing. In the case of law's governance, this will be its code of criminal law, prioritising the interests of the members of the group in the protection of their life, their physical well-being, and their property. The list of core crimes, 'real' crime as some would have it, might not be long but it will represent the essence of the criminal law. With the industrialisation of societies and the application of potentially dangerous technologies (for example, transportation technologies) and machines, we find that a large number of regulatory crimes (concerning in particular health and safety and the environment) are added to the original list. More recently, we find that governments have responded to populist demands for new criminal offences resulting in a criminal code that critics would now see as bloated by a surplus of regulatory crimes and unnecessary offences.

Although the direction of travel might seem to be towards ever more criminalisation, there have been times, notably during the 1960s, when moves were being made towards decriminalisation, particularly of acts (such as suicide) that, even if many thought to be 'wrong', did not actually cause any direct harm to others. These were moves that concerned victimless crimes and a central argument in support of decriminalisation was that conduct should not be subject to the criminal law if it caused no harm to others. To be sure, some might find the conduct in question offensive but, if that sufficed for criminalisation (and punishment), how could we present ourselves as a community that valued liberty?

DOI: 10.4324/9781003507802-22

We can pick out some of the elements of these remarks by starting with two famous debates about decriminalisation, which will take us to questions about harm and liberty; and then we can speak to the concern that members of the community are left under-protected against dangerous people by the current approach to punishment.

Decriminalization

Our starting point is the well-known 1960s debate between Lord Devlin (1965) and HLA Hart (1963). Although the debate is about the proposed relaxation of the criminal law in relation to prostitution, and its possible relaxation in relation to homosexuality—with Devlin arguing for a conservative holding of the line and Hart advocating a liberal approach—the positions taken up by the protagonists are underwritten by the different assumptions that are made about the nature of social solidarity (Hart, 1967).

According to Devlin, because a community is held together by its moral bonds, it cannot afford to put any sphere of conduct (such as sexual preferences) beyond the reach of the criminal law. Where members of the community regard some conduct as intolerable, and where the conduct is already criminalised, then the reputation of the law would be damaged if the relevant restrictions were to be relaxed—or, if the conduct were not yet criminalised, the reputation of the law would be damaged if the case for criminalisation were not at least given serious consideration. By contrast, Hart, relying on the harm principle articulated by John Stuart Mill in his classic essay 'On Liberty' (1859), argues that conduct should not be criminalised unless it causes harm to others and, as a corollary, that paternalistic prohibition of supposedly self-harming conduct (particularly conduct that is supposedly morally self-harmful) does not pass muster. From a liberal perspective, where the criminal law represses sexual preferences that cause no harm to others, this does it no credit. Moreover, concerns of the kind expressed by Devlin that a relaxation of the criminal law might lead to a loosening of the social bonds or, even more dramatically, to a breakdown of society are misplaced in modern societies. By the 1960s, the UK no longer identified itself with Victorian values, and cutting some slack by relaxing historic restrictions on sexual conduct was not going to lead to social or economic disintegration.

If the liberal view prevailed in the first debate, it has not fared so well in the second debate, which is ongoing and concerns the possible relaxation of the law against assisted suicide. Formally, English law is clear on this matter, providing that 'A person who aids, abets, counsels or procures the suicide of another, or an attempt by another to commit suicide, shall be liable on conviction on indictment to imprisonment for a term not exceeding fourteen years'. However, the appropriateness of criminalising such conduct is hotly contested in principle, and in practice, there are difficulties about whether to prosecute doctors or family members who follow their conscience in assisting with the death of another (for example, by helping them travel from the UK to Dignitas in Zurich).

At one pole of this debate, we find conservative communitarians who oppose any relaxation in the law, and at the other, we have liberals who argue that individuals should be permitted to make their own choices about when to end their own lives (and, if their circumstances are such that they need assistance to action their choices, then those who assist should not be subject to criminal penalties). However, in at least three respects, there are wrinkles in this particular opposition. First, there are some who, in an ideal world, would take the liberal view but who hold back from doing so because they fear that, in a non-ideal world, it will not be possible to ensure that, in practice, assistance with dying is always freely requested. Secondly, although prosecutors can go some way to appeasing liberal critics of the law by exercising their discretion not to proceed, this is liable to upset not only the conservative constituency but also those who see no virtue in having a law that formally provides that assistance is a criminal offence while, at the same time, operating with an informal practice and policy of not prosecuting offenders. Thirdly, whatever legislative position is taken up now has to be compatible with a twenty-first century understanding of the UK's human rights' commitments.

While liberals have little chance of persuading conservative communitarians that they should switch to a more permissive position, they have good reason to engage with the concerns of those who argue that, in practice, we simply cannot guarantee that assisters always will be good Samaritans or that no one will try to take advantage of those who are vulnerable. Famously, this was the central objection expressed by Chief Justice Rehnquist in the leading US case of *Washington v Glucksburg* (1997); it is found, too, in the jurisprudence of the European Court of Human Rights, where national prohibitions against acts of assistance with suicide are protected by a margin of appreciation that gives particular weight to the potential vulnerability of the unwilling; and, in 2014, the judgments in the UK Supreme Court hearing of the joint appeals of Nicklinson, Lamb, and Martin, are full of references to this critical concern.

It was in this context that Lord Falconer's Assisted Dying Bill presented a procedure that was designed to give precisely the assurance that those who are vulnerable will not be tricked or coerced or otherwise pressurised into seeking assistance that they do not actually wish to have. At the core of the Bill was the requirement that the person who seeks assistance has a clear and settled intention to end their life. By restricting permissible assistance to cases where the person has been diagnosed as terminally ill and with a life expectation of no more than six months, the Bill invited the obvious criticism that it missed too many of the target cases; but, of course, this restriction increased the plausibility of the claim that only those persons who really do want to end their lives would be assisted. However, the key assurance in the Bill was given by the requirement that an independent doctor (together with the person's attending physician) should countersign the person's statutory form declaration but should do so only if satisfied that the person 'has a clear and settled intention to end their own life which has been reached voluntarily, on an informed basis and without coercion or duress'. When, in July 2014, the Falconer Bill was presented to the House of Lords for its second reading, there was a long and impassioned debate, drawing out all shades of opinion. However, with a strong signal from the Supreme Court in *Nicklinson* that a declaration of incompatibility was hanging over the legislative prohibition on assisted suicide unless Parliament took a hard look at the issues, it was no surprise that it was unanimously agreed that the Bill should proceed to the next stage. Nevertheless, when asked the real question just over a year later, the Commons, after another passionate debate, overwhelmingly rejected the Bill, voting 330–118 against relaxing the law.

Since those votes, there have been further attempts to change the law on assisted suicide and, at the time of writing, momentum for change is building as a result of a campaign led by Dame Esther Rantzen. Whether this latest attempt will succeed where previous attempts have failed remains to be seen; however, we can be sure that, so long as individuals feel that they should be free to make their own end-of-life choices, pressure for change will persist.

Harm

The Millian principle is apparently simple and, for liberals who want the law to permit individuals to make their own life choices, it is an attractive supporting pillar for their position. However, once we take a harder look at the harm principle, it crumbles. Indeed, its weakness is exposed as soon as we ask what exactly we mean by causing no 'harm' to others.

Consider, for example, the first of Isaac Asimov's well-known Laws of Robotics (https://en.wikipedia.org/wiki/Three_Laws_of_Robotics). According to this law, 'A robot may not injure a human being or, through inaction, allow a human being to come to harm'. What should we make of this law which prohibits both injurious action and harmful inaction? How should we read 'injure' (in the first limb of the rule) and how should we read 'harm' (in the second limb of the rule)? Is 'injury' co-extensive with 'harm'? If so, what exactly is covered? Is it simply physical and psychological injury or, more broadly, also damage to a human's property or financial loss or an invasion of personality interests? If not, and if 'harm' is broader than 'injury', is it not odd to read the rule as giving humans broader protection against inaction by robots than against action by robots?

But, unlike Asimov, Mill was not trying to lay down rules for robots. Rather, his concern was to lay down some limits for coercive governance whether legal or social. Crucially, if our lifestyle preferences do not harm others, or are purely self-regarding, then we should not be coerced into eschewing or abandoning such lifestyles. So, if we do not inflict physical or mental injury on others, should we say that we do them no harm (in the way, for example, that doctors believe that their first responsibility is to do no harm to their patients)? We might try to draw the line at this point but, in a property-owning community, this would seem to be unwise because coercion might be required to recover one's property or to protect it in the first place. For our purposes, the important question is not where we draw the line but the fact that where we do draw the line depends, not on the concept of harm as such, but on the background views that we have about where it would be appropriate or prudent to draw the line.

Devlin was reluctant to draw any kind of line because he believed that the community would be justified in reserving the right to employ coercion wherever it found conduct to be intolerable. Others want to reserve the right for cases where they think that conduct sets a bad example to others. For instance, while the ban on smoking in enclosed public places might be justified by pointing to the harm caused by passive smoking, in some open public spaces (like parks) there is also a ban on smoking but now the justification is that smokers set a bad example to others, especially children, who might be harmed by supposing that it is 'cool' to smoke.

For those who debate these matters on the moral high ground, as is the case with Hart and Devlin, their view of 'harm' takes its content from the background theories on which they are drawing, whether liberal or communitarian, whether focused on the rights and liberties of individuals or their duties. Different theories generate different takes on what is 'harmful' and, unless we can demonstrate that our favoured background theory is superior to its rivals, our reading of 'harm' to others will have no special credentials.

Liberty

In his debate with Devlin, Hart seems to make a telling point when he argues that we cannot justify criminalising some act merely because some members of the community are offended by it; if it were otherwise, says Hart, liberty would mean nothing. However, like the concept of harm, the concept of liberty is much contested. In Hart's liberal way of thinking, citizens will value a 'negative' kind of liberty in the sense that the state leaves them alone to lead their own lives and to make their own choices so long as these do not impinge in unacceptable ways on others. Similarly, governments that favour negative liberty would be likely to express a reluctance to impose restrictions on their citizens during a pandemic. By contrast, some might argue for a more 'positive' kind of liberty in which the state steers citizens towards an officially approved lifestyle.

When we translate these different versions of liberty into law's governance, we will expect to find that, where negative liberty prevails, the rules are largely permissive but, where positive liberty prevails, then the rules focus on what is prohibited and what is required. However, recalling a radical perspective, we know that whatever the rules might say they will leave open the practical possibility of non-compliance. This being so, even if the legal rules are consistent with negative liberty, in practice, citizens might not be in a position to take up their options; and, conversely, even if the rules reflect a culture of positive liberty, some citizens might rebel against the state's directives. And, the radical perspective also underlines the fact that, whether the law reflects negative or positive liberty, and whether it is expressed as permissions or prohibitions/requirements, citizens might find that the state manages the environments in which they act in such a way that they are precluded from pursuing their preferred option or doing other than what the state dictates.

To illustrate this point, recall again the two dimensions of any regulated space: the coding of law's governance, the rules and regulations, all of which reflect a certain view of liberty; and the architecture and design of the space which govern the practical possibilities for humans who act in the space. Think, for example, about the regulated space of the concourse area at the renovated St Pancras railway station. Here, there are a couple of upright pianos. There seem to be no restrictions on who can play or what can be played; and, most days, a diverse range of piano music can be heard being played by a motley set of players. In what is already a bustling place of many sounds, the pianists add to the metropolitan mix.

Suppose, though, that a significant number of people who travel through St Pancras would prefer the volume to be turned down somewhat. They complain that the pianists add to the sounds of the station but not in a good way. Responding to such complaints, the station managers consider, first, whether some rules might be introduced to regulate the playing of the pianos (for example, restricting the times when the pianos may be played) and, secondly, whether some non-rule regulatory measures might be taken (for example, removing one or more of the pianos).

Now, humans have certain capabilities which, given an appropriate space or place, they can exercise. For example, in the station concourse, they can walk and talk; and, if a piano is free, they can sit and play some music. So far, so unregulated. However, if these activities are to be regulated by rules, the restrictions imposed by the rules overlay the particular space (or, the particular sphere of possibility). The focus for the rules is on what is regulated, not on the capabilities of humans and not on what *can* be done in the regulated space. By contrast, where technological measures are employed, the focus is on re-sculpting human capabilities or the features of the regulatory space (as by removing the pianos) precisely in order to regulate what can and cannot be done.

This difference in focus is one of the key things that sets Law 3.0 apart from Law 1.0 and Law 2.0, both of which are focused on applying or making changes to the regulatory code rather than making changes to the regulatory space, or the sphere of possibility, itself. Moreover, this difference is extremely important for our appreciation of how Law 3.0's technological measures can impact on our individual liberty (Brownsword, 2017a).

As we have said, much thinking about liberty values a rule framework that gives us options—for example, a rule that makes it entirely optional whether one plays one of the pianos at St Pancras station. Given this rule, those who opt to play do no wrong to anyone; but, equally, those who opt not to play, do no wrong. According to the rules, playing is optional; there is a liberty to play or not to play. However, this view of liberty is somewhat limited because it does not speak to whether the option is actually available in practice. According to the rule, playing a piano at St Pancras station is optional whether or not there are pianos actually standing in the concourse. Taking a limited view, there would be neither more nor less liberty to play a piano at the station irrespective of whether there were pianos available to be played, irrespective of whether pianos were being installed or being removed.

While, in a Law 1.0 or a Law 2.0 conversation, questions about liberty focus on the relevant rules and whether or not conduct is optional, in a Law 3.0 conversation, questions about liberty need also to focus on whether regulators are restricting (or expanding) the practical options that we have. Indeed, the more that regulators rely on technological measures, the more that it will be the impact on our practical liberty that needs to be monitored. In rule-governed situations, it will be important to ask whether the rules treat some conduct as optional; but, in situations where technological measures are employed, the important question will be whether that same conduct is something that in practice is actually at our option—in other words, is this something that we actually can choose to do or not to do?

When the management removes the pianos from the concourse at St Pancras railway station, we know that the world has changed. While whatever the rules provide about piano-playing at the station might not have changed, playing a piano there is no longer a practical option. To this extent, our liberty, particularly the liberty of prospective piano players, has been diminished. With Law 3.0, the risk is not so much that our paper liberties might be diminished by visible and well-advertised changes to the rules but that our practical liberties might be much less visibly reduced by the overnight removal of the pianos. This is not to say that the expansion or contraction of our paper (rule-based) liberties is no longer relevant. Rather, it is to say that, with the coming of Law 3.0, we should be alert to monitor and debate the impact on our practical liberty of the increasingly technological mediation of our transactions and interactions coupled with the use of technological management for regulatory purposes.

In sum, in Law 3.0, if we value our liberty, we should pay more attention to what we can and cannot do and be somewhat less concerned about what the rules say we ought and ought not to do.

Punishment and under-protection

Some dangerous people (like suicide bombers) will not survive the commission of their crimes; and, others (like the 'Moors murderers', Ian Brady and Myra Hindley) will never be released back into the community. However, some dangerous people—people like the London taxi driver, John Worboys, who, in 2009, was convicted of 19 offences including one count of rape, five sexual assaults, one attempted assault and 12 drugging charges (Rozenberg, 2020: 59–65)—might one day be released back into the community. Worboys was given an indeterminate custodial sentence (for the sake of public protection) with at least eight years to be served in prison. Following Worboys's conviction, the police received many other complaints from women who alleged that they had been drugged and assaulted by him. In January 2018, when the Parole Board decided that Worboys should be released, there was a wave of protest which led to a successful challenge in the High Court. In November 2018, the Parole Board duly changed its mind, concluding in effect that Worboys—now notorious as the 'black cab rapist'—was too dangerous to be released.

This vignette captures a dilemma that might arise, and not infrequently does arise, where offenders who have served a specified term in prison and who are due for release are still considered to be 'dangerous'—whether presenting a risk to a particular individual, or to a particular group or class of individuals, or to persons generally. If the offender is released and quickly re-offends, victims will rightly argue that they have been under-protected by the State. In cases such as that of Worboys—and, similarly, that of Usman Khan who, in November 2019, killed Jack Merritt and Saskia Jones at a prisoner rehabilitation conference at Fishmongers' Hall in London—victims (actual and prospective) will complain that the system is letting them down. If, however, the offender is not released, and if in fact there would have been no further offending, no future victims, then an injustice is done to the offender. Those who campaign for the convicted and their rights will argue that the State should take the rights of those who are due for release from prison more seriously. However, in practice, because we will not know whether offenders who are not released would have re-offended (we will not know whether they are false positives), and because the popular media will ensure that we do know that an offender whose release is controversial has re-offended (we know whether they are false negatives), there is a strong pressure to keep supposedly dangerous offenders locked up.

While the public might be reassured that, in any case where there is doubt about the matter, a supposedly dangerous offender will not be released back into the community, the reassurance would be all the greater if those who are judged to have dangerous behavioural characteristics were prevented from committing crimes in the first place. The thought that proactive prevention is better than reactive punishment is a matter to be taken up in Chapter 21.

20

PROPERTY

Introduction

In the two mistake of identity cases—*Phillips v Brooks* and *Ingram v Little*—that we discussed at some length in Chapter 5, the claim made by the original sellers was essentially that the downstream buyers were in possession of their, the sellers', property. The jeweller, in *Phillips v Brooks*, claimed that the ring was still his property; and, the Bournemouth ladies, in *Ingram v Little*, claimed that the car was still their property. No one doubted that items such as jewellery and cars are capable of being property objects and that, as such, their owners had the right to control who had possession of their property as well as to sell it. The only question was whether, following the deception, the owners were the original sellers (who certainly were the owners of the goods prior to the sale to the fraudster) or the downstream purchasers (who were now in possession of the goods and who also believed that they were the owners).

These cases contrast with the more recent case of *Moore v Regents of University of California* (1990) where the central question was whether a surgically removed spleen together with samples of blood and the like should be treated as property objects in the same way that jewellery and cars are property objects. If they should be so treated, then further questions arose as to who held the relevant property rights and what precisely those rights covered.

Again, these cases contrast with current debates about the status of non-fungible tokens (NFTs). These unique digital tokens might relate to an item that we would recognise as a property object but is a digital token itself, which can be traded, to be recognised as a property object? To this extent,

DOI: 10.4324/9781003507802-23

NFTs raise a property question that is like the central question in *Moore*; but, the epicentre of debates about the status of NFTs is whether and how they might be fitted within traditional categorisations of property as 'tangible' or 'intangible' (or 'moveables' and 'immoveables'); and, whether, if they cannot be fitted in, then a new third category of property should be recognised to accommodate digital assets such as NFTs.

In the light of these short remarks, it is apparent that traditional property law thinking is disrupted by new technologies which raise questions about what counts as a property object, who has property rights over these novel items, what those rights are, and whether novel objects can be accommodated within traditional classifications of property as tangible or intangible.

What can count as a property object and who can have property rights?

The John Moore case arose in California in the mid-1970s. Moore was a patient at the UCLA Medical Center, where he was diagnosed with leukemia. Moore's doctors lawfully removed his spleen and took various other samples. Subsequently, his physicians used the tissue and samples for their research in developing a cell-line that was commercially valuable and which was patented. Following his treatment at the hospital, Moore survived for some 25 years but, for many of these years, he was embroiled in a lawsuit against the Regents of the University of California in which he claimed that the physicians had, in effect, misappropriated his property and that he should be entitled to a share of the profits generated by the cell-line and its protective patent. Standing in the way of Moore's claim, the central question was whether the detached body parts and samples should be treated as property objects and whether Moore should be treated as the proprietor.

In both the common law and the civilian legal worlds there is an historic reluctance to recognise that a human body should be treated as a property object, whether because this would seem to condone slavery (where we have slave owners and slaves whose bodies are the property of the owners) or because commodifying or commercialising the human body does not comport with human dignity. Either way, the human body is not to be treated as a mere 'thing'. However, in the Moore case, the question was not whether the whole body of a living human should be recognised as a property object, it was about the status of detached body parts (which, once upon a time, would have been disposed of as surgical waste but which now had some value to medical researchers). Further, from Moore's point of view, it was not a matter of whether A should have property rights over B but whether A or B should be recognised as having property rights over body parts of which Moore was the source.

The majority of the Californian judges hearing the Moore case, reflecting this traditional reluctance to recognise human bodies as property objects, ruled against him on this point. However, it is generally accepted that parties who exercise some skill in relation to detached body parts can have rights over what are then treated as property objects; and, in *Moore*, the research led to the grant of patents (which are intellectual property rights).

A settlement between the parties was reached in *Moore* but, from a jurisprudential point of view, the case left a good deal of unfinished business. First, there is the question of whether the law meets its own traditional criteria of coherence in denying the source of the tissue proprietary rights but, at the same time, recognising that others can have proprietary rights in the tissue. Secondly, there is the question of whether, as a matter of principle or policy, we can justify the research community having property rights in tissue but denying any proprietary interest to the source or to research participants. The debate rumbles on but, in England, there have been moves to recognise that those who entrust their sperm or eggs or embryos to clinics for safe keeping (with a view to later use for reproductive purposes) should not be denied legal redress simply because of the property question (see, e.g., *Yearworth v North Bristol NHS Trust* (2009)).

Proprietary rights as a bundle of rights

If we recognise that an object such as detached body parts, or a digital token or file, or even personal data itself, can be treated as property, then there is still a discussion to be had about the range of rights held by the proprietor. Treating proprietary rights as a bundle of rights, we might recognise the proprietor as having full-blooded ownership (to control, to license, to sell, and so on) or as having a more restricted set of rights from the bundle. If the right is to control access to the property object, the proprietor can grant or deny access: if access is granted, it is on the terms specified by the proprietor; and, if access is denied, it is not incumbent on the proprietor to give good reasons—the proprietor's veto on access or use is entirely at his or her will. Moreover, the proprietor's control rights are infringed if the property object is accessed without permission and this is so even if no damage is suffered. So, if we are treated as proprietors of our personal data, its use by data processors without our consent constitutes a wrong regardless of whether we suffer any damage as a result of the processing.

Returning to *Moore*, the claim was not that access to the body parts would have been denied; rather the claim was that Moore should be paid his share of the commercial gain that was made. However, in other cases after *Moore*, the sources of tissue were arguing that it was their control right that had been infringed; they were asserting the right to veto certain uses of the tissue (or the patenting of the research products). Accordingly, to the extent that the objection to treating body parts as property is that it facilitates commercialisation of the human body, it might be possible to assuage this concern by taking the commercialisation stick out of the particular bundle of property rights.

Do novel property objects fit in traditional classifications of property?

English law starts by differentiating between 'real property' (land and real estate) and 'personal property' (other 'things'); and, then, it classifies these 'other things' as either 'things in possession' (tangible things) or as 'things in action' (these being legal rights or claims that are enforceable by action). Crucially, in a jurisprudence that dates back to the Victorian years, the orthodox view in English law has been that there is no third category of personal property (and property rights) that lies between things in possession and things in action. However, in recent years that view has been challenged as courts in different common law jurisdictions have been willing to entertain the idea that digital assets might fall into a third category of personal property (see, Law Commission, 2023, 3.38–3.48). Endorsing this judicial development of the law, the Law Commission for England and Wales has recommended that there should now be a statutory formalisation of this evolving common law position, confirming and supporting that 'being neither a thing in possession nor a thing in action does not prevent a digital asset from being capable of being a thing to which personal property rights can relate' (Law Commission, 2023, para 2.17).

From a radical perspective, it is evident that Law 2.0 thinking will be much more likely than Law 1.0 thinking to break free from traditional classifications but also to do so for policy-based reasons. Having escaped the Law 1.0 box, we can ask not only whether traditional classifications in personal property law are fit for purpose but also whether the classifications in intellectual property serve relevant policies (as is the case with debates about the status of AI as an 'inventor' or as an 'originator' of creative work) and, going beyond property questions, we can ask whether there should be special classes of governance (with their own bespoke rules) for e-scooters, robots, virtual persons, drones, and so on.

21

PRECAUTION AND PREVENTION

Introduction

Shortly before Christmas 2018, an unauthorised drone was sighted at Gatwick airport. As a precautionary measure, all flights were suspended and, for two days, the airport was closed. With thousands of passengers inconvenienced, this was headline news and a major media event.

There were two strands to the media coverage. One strand was about the plight of the passengers, about packed terminal buildings, and about the disruption caused to holiday plans and to family get-togethers. From a governance perspective, the story here was about the need to take precautionary measures, inconvenience to passengers notwithstanding, when there were serious safety concerns. The other strand was about the governance steps that should be taken to prevent a re-occurrence of the incident, whether the adoption of new rules for drone use or technical measures to keep drones well away from airports.

In this chapter, we can say a few words about these two strands of governance thinking: first precautionary reasoning and then a preventive approach (whether prevention by rules or by technological measures).

Precautionary reasoning

At Gatwick, although there was a good deal of frustration amongst people who did not know whether they would be able to get away for Christmas and who, meanwhile, were marking time in over-crowded terminal buildings, it was generally accepted that the precautionary measures that were taken were appropriate. If aircraft had continued to fly and if a plane had

DOI: 10.4324/9781003507802-24

been brought down by the drone, we can be sure that there would have been widespread criticism of the failure to take the safety concerns seriously. Indeed, in these circumstances, we can imagine that one of the headline recommendations of an after-the-event inquiry into the plane crash would be that a precautionary approach should be taken, frustration and inconvenience notwithstanding.

We might also recall the extensive and extended disruption to air travel caused in 2010 by the volcanic eruption at Eyjafjallajökull in Iceland (this eruption discharging clouds of ash into the atmosphere) (https://en.wikipedia.org/wiki/2010_eruptions_of_Eyjafjallaj%C3%B6kull). Millions of passengers were inconvenienced by the precautionary measures that were taken but, again, as at Gatwick, there were relatively few critical voices. Accordingly, we might think that where there are serious safety concerns—even if there is a degree of uncertainty about just how risky the conditions are—a precautionary approach to governance will meet with little resistance. However, to the contrary: frequently, those who advocate precautionary governance will experience severe resistance.

Often, precaution is advocated in a context where its opponents view it as irrational or disproportionate. In particular, opponents will argue that, as a result of one-sided precautionary governance, beneficial innovation will be delayed or, worse, will not materialise. The message is that precaution has a price and that those who have governance responsibilities need to consider the costs of precaution before striking the right balance between the harms that we hope to avoid by precaution and the harms (or loss of benefit) that we suffer as a result of precautionary restriction.

Rio and resistance

In our over-heating world, climate change is rarely out of the news and the international community's failure to meet targets for the reduction of carbon emissions is typically part of the story. In this context, we should recall that the focus of Principle 15 of the Rio Declaration on Environment and Development in 1992—which, arguably, is the foremost articulation of a precautionary approach—is on 'threats of serious or irreversible damage' to the *environment* (see, https://en.wikipedia.org/wiki/Rio_Declaration_on_Environment_and_Development). Here, the balance of costs and benefits is clear: unless the environment is sustainable, human life on Earth is not sustainable.

So much for precaution and concerns about the environment. However, emerging technologies give rise to many kinds of concern—not only threats to the environment but also threats to human health and safety, human rights, and human dignity, and so on; and, as Principle 15 recognises, there might be considerable uncertainty about the nature of the threats as well as the likelihood of their eventuating. In this context, we should expect regulators to apply precaution in a way that is proportionate, responsible, and rational.

Objectors protest, however, that precaution tends to operate as a licence for irrational and irresponsible regulatory intervention—irrational because precaution focuses in a one-eyed way on the need to avoid a particular set of adverse consequences and irresponsible because the adverse consequences of making a precautionary intervention are ignored (see, e.g., Sunstein, 2005). Moreover, with the benefit of hindsight, regulators might realise that their intervention was unnecessary, in which case it was all cost and no benefit.

In the light of this, we might accept that some precautionary bets will be well-placed and others will not. If our precaution is assessed bet by bet, product by product, case by case, it will be constantly on the back foot. Rather, we should judge a precautionary approach over the long run. The real question is how much precaution we should invest in systematic ex ante regulatory checks.

Ex ante regulatory checks

In favour of systematic precaution, we might cite the experience of lightly regulated drugs prior to, and including, the catastrophic use of Thalidomide. Here, we commonly contrast the precautionary regulatory culture of the EU with the proactionary culture of the US; and, post-Brexit, we might expect the regulatory culture in the UK to be 'pro-innovation' in a way that falls somewhere between precaution and proaction (Department for Science, Innovation and Technology, 2023). In the EU, regulators insist on extensive checking for product safety, for risks to human health and the environment, and so on. The safety net is not perfect but ex post legal firefighting is a matter of regret. By contrast, in the US, a particularly aggressive form of ex post private law (mass tort claims in particular) is a feature of the general regulatory balance.

The Internet might be seen as a test case for the choice between precaution and proaction. Arguably, we would still be waiting for the Internet if it had been subjected to precautionary risk assessment and management. On the other hand, a lack of anticipation and precaution means that we are only now seeing the downsides. As Max Fisher (2022: 3) puts it, what we now have is the invisible hand of social media shaping 'the bounds of acceptable politics and speech for [billons of] users worldwide'; and, at the same time, a 'combination of ideology, greed, and the technological opacity of complex machine-learning blinds executives from seeing their creations in their entirety. The machines are, in the ways that matter, essentially ungoverned' (340).

Currently, there is a good deal of enthusiasm for so-called 'regulatory sandboxes' where the usual regulatory requirements can be relaxed somewhat in order to see how new products perform. While the early experience with financial products (fintech) is positive, it remains to be seen how sandboxes might contribute to governance in other domains (e.g., in health); but, whichever approach we adopt, proactionary or precautionary, it will leave some members of the community discontent—the tilt of regulatory deals, like their substance, will be seen as too much towards innovation or too much towards risk management.

Prevention

Traditionally, law's governance is reactive: the rules are declared; and, where there are breaches of the rules, then various kinds of legal processes might be initiated. First, there is wrongdoing, and then a reaction might be triggered, whether a private law claim or a criminal justice response. However, in principle, the law might be more preventive in its approach and this is where we can pick up the second strand of the Gatwick story.

Responding to the rogue drone at Gatwick, the principal question was how a repetition of the incident could be prevented. Representatives of the pilots' association told television interviewers that they had been saying for some time that drones presented a real danger to aircraft and that the exclusion zones around airfields (set by the current legal rules) needed to be extended. In due course, the government responded by announcing that the police would be given new powers to tackle illegal drone use, and that the drone no-fly zone would be extended to three miles around airports.

While the revised rules might reduce the risk of drones accidentally interfering with aircraft, they (like all rules) could still be broken, and they could not guarantee that the operation of the airport would be free from drone disruption in the future. Taking a more preventive approach, it might be suggested that governance should invest in intelligence gathering so that potential rogue drone operators could be identified and monitored. To this extent, such a strategy would be to put illegal drone use in the same category as terrorism. But why stop there?

Even if it is fanciful to imagine resort to 'precogs' as in Steven Spielberg's film *Minority Report* (https://en.wikipedia.org/wiki/Minority_Report_(film)), why not invest in smarter risk management? Or, as some suggested at the time of the Gatwick drone, the focus should be on developing a technological solution, ideally one that would render it impossible in practice for a drone to be flown near an airport (or, failing that, a technology for disabling and safely bringing down unauthorised drones). Again, why not? If wrongdoing is to be prevented, why not invest in smarter Law 3.0 governance of this kind?

So far as private law is concerned, prevention tends to be the exception rather than the rule. To be sure, where breaches of private law rules are anticipated, applications can be made for injunctions to be issued against those who might otherwise cause harm or damage; and, in the context of IP disputes, Anton Piller and Mareva orders can be made where there is a serious risk that a defendant might compromise evidence that would be relevant at a trial, or remove assets that would otherwise be available to satisfy a judgment award. Nevertheless, there is a hesitation to restrain conduct in advance of it being established that the alleged legal wrong has taken place. Arguably, just as *precautionary* measures should be taken only when their potential benefits but also their costs have been assessed, *preventive* measures should be taken in a way that gives proper consideration to both their benefits and their costs.

There is also more than a little hesitation about the use of preventive strategies in the criminal law. In particular, there are concerns that preventive orders might operate without the usual procedural constraints that are demanded by respect for human rights (see, Ashworth and Zedner, 2014) and that new preventive tools might be utilised uncritically simply because they are available (see, Harcourt, 2007). Before we think radical thoughts about the prevention and control of crime, we need to ask ourselves whether the practices of preventive and punitive justice are relevantly similar such that the former should be modelled on the (liberal) principles that guide the latter? In particular, we need to ask whether false positives and presumptions of innocence in relation to the latter are translatable to the former. Moreover, we also need to ask whether prevention that is undertaken as a regulatory exercise in risk management is comparable to punitive detention, denunciation, and stigmatisation.

False positives

To deal with the first point, we might concede that there is an apparent lack of symmetry between agents who are accused of having committed a crime and agents who are assessed as possible future offenders. In both cases, we can conceive of there being both true and false positives; and, indeed, we can be concerned that errors are not made. However, it is only in the context of an agent being accused of having committed a crime that we have an actual crime against which to review whether a person convicted of the offence is actually a false positive and whether a person acquitted of the offence is actually a false negative. By contrast, in the context of prevention, while we can test whether a person against whom no preventive measures are taken is a false negative (by checking whether they do then commit the offence), we cannot check whether a person against whom preventive measures are taken is a false positive (because there is no relevant actuality to check).

Acknowledging this difficulty, it is important that we do not draw the wrong conclusion. What we should not conclude is that we need not be concerned about false positives in the context of prevention. To the contrary, because there is no practical way of demonstrating that an error has been made, that the person who is prevented is a false positive, what we should conclude is that there is all the more reason for taking every possible precaution against an error being made.

Risk management

Turning to the second question, how plausible is it to treat preventive measures as an exercise in risk management? In *United States v Salerno and Cafaro* (1987), one of the questions was whether detention under the Bail Reform Act 1984 should be treated as a punitive or as a preventive 'regulatory' measure. The majority concluded that such detention fell on the regulatory side of the line and that preventing danger to the community was a legitimate regulatory goal. However, the minority Justices were not convinced: the constraints of criminal justice were not to be side-lined so easily. Thus,

> Let us apply the majority's reasoning to a similar, hypothetical case. After investigation, Congress determines (not unrealistically) that a large proportion of violent crime is perpetrated by persons who are unemployed. It also determines, equally reasonably, that much violent crime is committed at night. From amongst the panoply of 'potential solutions', Congress chooses a statute which permits, after judicial proceedings, the imposition of a dusk-to-dawn curfew on anyone who is unemployed. Since this is not a measure enacted for the purpose of punishing the unemployed, and since the majority finds that preventing danger to the community is a legitimate regulatory goal, the curfew statute would, according to the majority's analysis, be a mere 'regulatory' detention statute, entirely compatible with the substantive components of the Due Process Clause.
> The absurdity of this conclusion arises, of course, from the majority's cramped concept of substantive due process. The majority proceeds as though the only substantive right protected by the Due Process Clause is a right to be free from punishment before conviction. The majority's technique for infringing this right is simple: merely redefine any measure which is claimed to be punishment as 'regulation,' and, magically, the Constitution no longer prohibits its imposition.
>
> *(760)*

So, heeding the minority's reservations, we should not be taken in by a regulatory sleight-of-hand that seeks to evade important community values. For example, while we all understand that no adverse moral judgment should be made about an agent who is compulsorily detained for the reason that he is an innocent carrier of a dangerous disease, we might view preventive measures taken against those who are predicted to commit a crime as quite another matter. Adverse judgments of this kind tend to stick; and, it bears emphasising that there is limited practical opportunity for those who are false positives to show that an error has been made. In line with the thinking of the minority Justices in *Salerno and Cafaro*, we might well conclude that merely labelling the preventive practice as an exercise in risk management does not ease the injustice of wrongly labelling the person as a future offender.

Here, as elsewhere in our discussion of law's concepts, we find that the way in which our concepts are specified is not neutral; our conceptual framing—of harm, of liberty, of precaution and prevention, and so on—will reflect particular values. It is time to address law's governance and its values directly.

PART 4
Values

22

FUNDAMENTAL VALUES

The conditions of possibility

Introduction

According to the renowned Italian-American physicist, Enrico Fermi, it is paradoxical that, on the one hand, it seems highly unlikely that we humans are the only intelligent life that exists in the vastness of our universe and yet, on the other, we have no evidence that there is such life elsewhere (https://en.wikipedia.org/wiki/Fermi_paradox). How so? One day, while having lunch with colleagues at Stanford, Fermi came up with a theory. He speculated that the answer might be that, before intelligent life develops the technological sophistication that is required to connect distant civilisations, it self-destructs. Whatever we might make of the paradox and Fermi's speculation, we can see that, during the present century, humans on planet Earth will need to recognise and act on three imperatives if they are not to self-destruct.

Three imperatives

The three imperatives are as follows: first, humans must protect the global commons, respecting the planetary boundaries and its resources lest human existence on Earth is no longer sustainable (Rockstrom, 2009); secondly, humans must observe the conditions for peaceful co-existence, both between humans in a particular community and between communities; and, thirdly, humans must respect the conditions that support their agency and autonomy. Anyone who doubts what unregulated greenhouse gas emissions might do to the Earth should take a look at Venus (Grayling, 2022: Ch 1); and, anyone who doubts the catastrophic effects of the compromising of the conditions

DOI: 10.4324/9781003507802-26

for human agency should take a look at the dystopias imagined by novelists such as Huxley and Orwell.

Ideally, humans who intend to colonise Earth would sign up to these imperatives before they have begun the process of forming their own communities and before they have invested in their own interests. However, the challenge now is much more difficult because, at all levels, too many humans have invested in current arrangements. Even so, we can find echoes of these imperatives in several of the 17 UN Sustainable Development Goals (https://sdgs.un.org/goals)—for example in Goals 13–16 (concerning, respectively, climate action, life below water, life on land, and peace, justice, and strong institutions). However, while UN support for these goals is of great practical importance, the point of principle is that it would be simply incoherent for any human to reject the imperatives. For instance, if any human were to propose that it should be permissible to deplete the global planetary resources at will and to undermine the possibility of communities forming around their own projects and developing in their own way, then this should be rejected as being so unreasonable that no reasonable human could hold such a view.

That said, the world does not stand still, and once we try to firm up the demands made by these imperatives, there will be scope for disagreement. For example, we can give a general indication of the requirements of the first imperative by saying that governance should always be compatible with the protection, preservation, and promotion of the natural ecosystem for human life. This, we might suggest, entails that the physical well-being of humans must be secured; that humans should have the benefit of clean air, food, water, and shelter; that they should be protected against contagious diseases, and that, if they are sick, then they should have access to whatever medical treatment is available. While this might be intended as a minimum set of conditions, in our technological time, we might wonder whether it is perhaps under-inclusive—for example, in a high-tech setting, should these conditions not also include access to, say, a broadband connection (see, e.g., Sun, 2022)? Even without expanding the minimum set, there is a question about which baseline precisely constitutes the minimum. If we assume that the baseline is set at a level where many humans and some communities are above the line, there will still be some who are below the line. If so, how are the latter to be brought to a position at or above the baseline? Certainly, governance in the above-baseline communities should do nothing to make the position worse, but do they also bear the burden of rectifying the situation? Again, it is all very well agreeing that there should be access to medicines, but drugs produced by the pharmaceutical companies do not come out of nowhere, and, in international human rights law, there is a history of difficult negotiation around the commercial interests of the medicines industry in tension with the interest in access (Plomer, 2015).

Similarly, we can anticipate some contestation around the imperative that demands peaceful co-existence between communities. To the extent that we treat the paradigmatic violation of this imperative as the initiation of kinetic military action, there might be some disagreement about where non-kinetic interference sits. For example, nation states might claim to be acting in line with this imperative because they are not engaging in 'aggressive' acts while, at the same time, they engage in various kinds of hybrid and cybrid threats, disabling critical infrastructures and destabilising communities (Freedman, 2017). There is also much room for discussion about the nature of human agency and its supporting conditions (concerning human self-development and then for engagement in purposeful self-direction whether for oneself, with others, or in groups and communities). In what ways, for example, might large-scale surveillance practices interfere with the conditions for agency (Zuboff, 2019)?

Neutrality

It is vital to understand that the imperatives are not focused on the question of what kind of human community we might want to be; the imperatives and the essential conditions are focused on the possibility of human community itself. Possibility is prior to the articulation of particular communities. As between one human community and another, the essential conditions are neutral.

What this means is that the imperatives should go no further than the conditions of possibility. They must remain neutral between particular humans, particular communities, particular projects, particular views of what is prudent or moral, and so on; these are imperatives that are foundational for the possibility of human community but, other than insisting that the foundational conditions themselves are respected, they are strictly impartial between particular humans, particular articulations of community, and particular preferences, positions, and policies. In other words, we should not expect the imperatives to indicate a blueprint for a particular human community.

Provided the conditions as specified are faithful to the idea of neutrality, no human can coherently oppose the principle that our governance should respect those conditions. Whether we say that it would be incoherent for a human to contest the prudence of observing the conditions or to deny that the principle (being categorically binding and overriding) expresses moral rights and responsibilities, scarcely matters. There is no denying the imperatives—provided that they do not overreach and depart from neutrality.

Non-ideal conditions

Over and above the imperatives, and given the non-ideal conditions in which we now seek to establish them, two practical measures need to be adopted. One measure concerns precaution and the other relates to stewardship.

First, because self-interest is so much entrenched in both domestic and international relations, a precautionary buffer should be adopted. As we saw in the previous chapter, this means that if there is any reasonable doubt about whether an imperative is being violated by some act or practice, it should be restricted or even cease. To those who protest at this inconvenience, we can concede that, after the event, we might find that our precaution was unnecessary. But, we have to act on what we know at the time, and if the choice at the time is between a possible catastrophe and a possible loss of utility, then it is better to be precautionary than sorry.

Secondly, because the most dangerous violations of the imperatives are likely to occur on the international stage, global regulatory stewards need to be authorised to maintain respect for the imperatives. Granted, the idea that the global powers would support such an initiative might be wishful thinking; but, when even the most powerful nations are threatened by a breakdown in the conditions for governance, who knows, we might be surprised.

The Archimedean vantage point

Finally, it bears repetition that, while the foundational imperatives might not be extensive, any views or actions, any positions or policies, that are incompatible with these constitutive commitments—which are the key to the viability of human communities (Fairfield, 2021: 143; Yeung, 2019: 42)—must be rejected as so unreasonable that no reasonable human could possibly entertain them. To be sure, a Devil's Advocate or a Cartesian demon might contend that they see no reason to respect the imperatives; but, this is an admission that those who so contend are not humans rather than an argument against the coherence—the compelling coherence—of human recognition of the binding nature of these imperatives.

It follows that the answer to our question about foundations for our concepts and values is found with the imperatives. This is where we have our Archimedean vantage point.

23

COMMUNITY VALUES

Human rights and human dignity

Introduction

It is for the members of each community to identify the fundamental values of their particular community, to articulate the values that make the community the particular and distinctive community that it is. Members should ask: What is it that we in our community stand for? For modern nation states, it is the constitution that typically gives expression to the fundamental values of the community; and what we will often find in such communities is a constitutional commitment to (some permutation of) human rights and human dignity. For example, in its opening section, the South African Constitution declares that the Republic is founded on 'Human dignity, the achievement of equality and the advancement of human rights and freedoms', these values then being elaborated in a Bill of Rights that runs through sections 7-39 of the Constitution. Similarly, Article 1 of the German Basic Law provides:

(1) Human dignity shall be inviolable. To respect and protect it shall be the duty of all state authority.
(2) The German people therefore acknowledge inviolable and inalienable human rights as the basis of every community, of peace and of justice in the world.
(3) The following basic rights [which are set out in subsequent sections] shall bind the legislature, the executive and the judiciary as directly applicable law.

DOI: 10.4324/9781003507802-27

The members states of the EU echo the same kind of constitutive values in the Charter of Fundamental Rights, Article 1 of which provides: 'Human dignity is inviolable. It must be respected and protected'. This is followed, in Article 2, by recognition of the most important of human rights, the right to life. Even in such a small sample, we find an apparently shared commitment to human dignity and human rights. But, of course, there is a certain amount of devil in the detail of which human rights are recognized, how particular human rights are interpreted, and how the concept of human dignity is conceived.

Human rights and human dignity

Recalling the protests of the students outside the European Patent Office (see Chapter 6), their principal objection—advanced in the name of respect for human dignity—was to patents being granted on living things; and, inside the EPO, it was in the name of human dignity that genetic modification was condemned. On the other side, those who argued in favour of a liberal interpretation of patentability, might have rested their case on the utility of supporting medical research and development that promised to relieve human suffering; but, equally, they could have proposed a human right to undertake beneficial research which itself rested on respect for human dignity. In a sense, this is not too surprising, because we have understood for some time that respect for human dignity can be pleaded on both sides of debates (such as the debate between those who oppose euthanasia or assisted suicide in the name of the sanctity of human life and human dignity and those who support individual end-of-life choice also in the name of human dignity); and, we have also known that these competing conceptions of human dignity rest on either a conservative dignitarian view or a liberal ethics. In short, constitutional commitments to human dignity might reflect a conception of 'human dignity as constraint' (the conservative view) or 'human dignity as empowerment' (the liberal, rights-accentuating, view) (Beyleveld and Brownsword, 2001).

Community values and emerging technologies

That said, emerging technologies have drawn out more conspicuously these different conceptions of human dignity as well as sharpening the profile of the field of values in which they are debated. Put simply, we now find a group of views (including the conservative dignitarian view) that stand on 'duties'; we have views (including the liberal view of dignity) that stand on 'rights'; and we have views that stand on promoting some desired state of affairs, or good, of which utilitarian views are the most prominent.

So, in debates about the governance of biotechnologies, we have the duty-based perspective condemning any practice, process or product—human reproductive cloning, therapeutic cloning, and stem cell research using human embryos being prime examples—which it judges to compromise human dignity (see Caulfield and Brownsword, 2006). Such condemnation (by reference to human dignity) operates as a 'conversation stopper'. Against this kind of view, we have the rights-based perspective arguing that humans have a right to enjoy the benefits of new technologies which, for governance purposes, means that the technologies should be permitted but that their use and application should be subject to the consent of rights-holders. Completing the debate, we have utility-based views which are often implicitly pleaded by those who promote new technologies and who are keen to capitalise on their potential benefits.

Where technologies largely give rise to concerns about the health and safety of users and others, the conservative dignitarian voice might be more muted. Here, it will generally be for the utilitarians to persuade themselves that, while there might be some downsides to a technology, the upside gains mean that overall there is a net benefit and, having done that, to assuage the concerns voiced by those who speak from a rights-based perspective—for example, concerns about having unrestricted access to AI tools or performance-enhancing drugs which might bring with them what is seen as an unfair advantage in competitive situations.

Imagine, for example, that a community has at its disposal the kind of bioengineering technologies that we associate with the synthetic beings (the replicants) in 'Blade Runner' (https://en.wikipedia.org/wiki/Blade_Runner). How might a community's fundamental values bear on governance of such technologies? If health and safety is the only question, then the governance discussions will reflect utilitarian judgments. However, if the presence of replicants in the community presents threats to the recognized human rights, then the governance debate will be more complex. The fact that the application of the technologies will be beneficial overall will not carry the day; it will also need to be compatible with respect for human rights. If the question about compatibility is answered satisfactorily, then it will be something like the conservative dignitarian view that will offer the last line of resistance. Advocates of such a view might say that the application of these technologies offends human dignity by going beyond what is natural for humans or by 'commodifying' humans (treating them as beings with so many functional parts) or simply by saying (in a conversation-stopping way) that, if we cannot see what is wrong with creating replicants, there is something wrong with us.

If there is significant support for each of the perspectives that we find in these debates, how is law's governance to find an acceptable position? Given that we are focusing on the constitutive values of the community, we have to treat these values as being privileged: for members of the community, they will matter more than non-constitutive, non-fundamental values. This means that any values that have a clear foothold in the constitution will take priority over values that do not. So, where communities commit to human dignity and human rights rather than utilitarian values, then it is the former that take priority over the latter. However, this still leaves a major problem where there are competing conceptions of human dignity in play or where it is argued that certain human rights (such as privacy, which we discuss in the next chapter), although not explicitly recognized, are nevertheless implicit in the constitution. If disputes about such matters are to be resolved peacefully, then they will be referred to the courts and, potentially, this puts the judges at odds with the politicians, and sometimes the people, who want to do one thing but find that the courts are putting constitutional obstacles in the way.

24
PRIVACY

Introduction

When communities commit themselves to respect for human rights and human dignity, they will often also commit themselves to privacy. In our information societies, one way of characterising privacy is to say that it sets limits to the right to know. So understood, privacy is not anchored to those particular places and spaces (such as one's home) where we expect to be left alone and not be observed; for, even in public places, privacy sets limits to information gathering that might be sensitive in relation to our reputation or image, or to our sense of identity, and the like. To the extent that these limits are set not just by reference to our personal expectation of privacy but by expectations that are reasonable relative to community standards, law's governance will need to be flexible and responsive to the shifting sands of community expectation.

It might be argued, however, that privacy goes deeper than any of this and that, in some respects, it engages the conditions of possibility, particularly the agency conditions, that we introduced in Chapter 22. On this view, the extent of privacy protection is not something to be negotiated within each human community but a non-negotiable condition for the viability of human communities. Even if there is some uncertainty about when information gathering engages these essential pre-conditions, we should govern in a spirit of precaution; in this spirit, we should take a hard look at excessive surveillance by nation states or by private enterprises that themselves have resources that often exceed those of nation states. Accordingly, when the European Court of Human Rights (in the *Marper* case) judged that the UK's legal position on the taking, making, and retaining of DNA profiles was

DOI: 10.4324/9781003507802-28

incompatible with the Convention right to private and family life, it might have been protecting more than the reasonable expectations of Europeans; and, when Shoshana Zuboff criticises the data-collecting practices of the 'surveillance capitalists' (Zuboff, 2019: 155–157)—practices which open the way not just to predicting the preferences of consumers and citizens but actually to shaping them—she might be making a point about more than the reasonable expectations of those who live in Western democracies.

As is already evident in these remarks, the information-gathering potential of new technologies (particularly, biotechnologies, information and communication technologies, AI, and neurotechnologies) provokes multiple concerns, many of which find their legal expression in claims relating to privacy (Brownsword, 2012). On the one side, we will have the police and criminal justice agencies pleading an interest in controlling crime and convicting offenders, or the public health agencies pleading the need to monitor the spread of a disease, or insurers (or employers) pleading the right to access genetic information in order to risk assess their applicants (or prospective employees), or the press pleading the public interest in some story; but, on the other side, there will be a push-back from those who think that the privacy line has been crossed. In this sense, privacy is contested on many fronts and in many domains. Indeed, many now subscribe to a school of thinking that treats context as central to governance that seeks to draw the line between what is covered by privacy and what is not.

In what follows, we can speak to the life and times of privacy by recalling the birth of an explicit privacy right (provoked by developments in photographic technology); and, then, echoing some aspects of our discussion in Chapter 18, we can comment briefly on the reported death of privacy—or, if those reports are exaggerated, at least the downgrading of privacy.

The birth of privacy

Although the Constitution of the US does not explicitly recognise a right to privacy, in modern times it has become an important feature of the Supreme Court's jurisprudence (Henkin, 1974). Similarly, although the historic common law does not explicitly recognise a right to privacy, it has become a major feature of modern jurisprudence.

To focus on the common law development, we can trace the birth of a privacy right to a late nineteenth-century law review article. This article, by Samuel Warren and Louis Brandeis (1890), poses a textbook Law 1.0 question to which they responded by arguing for recognition of a right to privacy. The question, in their own words, was 'whether the existing law affords a principle which can be properly invoked to protect the privacy of the individual; and, if it does, what the nature and extent of such protection is'; and, their response was that, thanks to 'the beautiful capacity for growth which characterises the common law', such a principle could be found and, moreover, it could be relied upon 'to afford the requisite protection, without the interposition of the legislature' (all at 193). The reason why the question needed to be asked (as the authors judged it) was the unacceptable use of cameras which had led to the 'unauthorised circulation of portraits of private persons' (193). In some contexts, it was not practical to take photographs without the consent of the parties who would sit for the photographer; here, the interest of the individual in their privacy could be protected either by contract law or by the law of confidentiality. However, because it was now possible to take photographs surreptitiously, the answer needed to be based in tort law. Even though the unauthorised taking and circulation of photographs did not cause any injury or damage to a person or their property (and, to this extent, no harm was done), Warren and Brandeis argued that a right to privacy was already implicit in the general principles of law relating to the protection of the interest in personality and the right to be let alone. The precise way in which the jurisprudence of the privacy right was to be developed would be left to the courts (see Prosser, 1960).

What we might make of the recognition and then the judicial development of the right to privacy in the US jurisprudence, both constitutional and private law, will depend very much on where we stand politically and ethically in the community. Similarly, what we make of privacy and its particular protections elsewhere in the common law and the civilian world will depend on the traditions of our community and whatever consensus forms about the limits to information gathering in our technologically disrupted communities. Even if there is a broad consensus that persons who are public figures (whether as politicians, as 'royalty', or as celebrities) cannot expect the same level of protection that privacy affords to persons whose lives are not already public in this way, precisely where information gathering and dissemination crosses the line of acceptability might be contested and unclear regardless of whether the person is already a public figure.

The death of privacy

In the early days of the Internet, I recall being surprised by the carefree attitude that some people seemed to have towards disclosing their personal data in online environments. For them, privacy simply did not seem to be an issue; they said that they had nothing to hide—and, indeed, it seemed that many people worldwide either did not care about privacy or were prepared to trade their personal data for various online benefits. On such evidence, the message from Silicon Valley was captured by Scott McNealy, the CEO of Sun Microsystems, when he famously announced that 'Privacy is dead—get over it'. Was he right? Is privacy (or the right to privacy) being eroded in our information societies? As a corollary, at any rate in Europe, the tech companies might add that Europeans accept the fair dealing principles of data protection law as sufficient protection for their privacy interests. However, it is quite a leap from a privacy right that protects our interest in controlling who has access to our personal data to data protection laws that remove that privacy control and instead, set out a regime of principles for the fair and transparent collection and processing of personal data.

Given that privacy speaks to a range of human interests as well as operating with a variable standard of 'reasonable expectation', we should be slow to conclude that there really is no life left in privacy. Those who are prepared to trade their privacy protection for some consumer benefits might change their minds; and, even those who no longer care about privacy in online consumer and social environments might still value privacy in some offline contexts. That said, we all know that, when confronted with online sites, there is a widespread tendency simply to click through the consent buttons that signal acceptance of a website's terms and conditions, including their terms and conditions relating to the human interest in privacy and fair collection and processing of personal data. From this, we might infer that online users value their privacy less than they once might have done. More importantly, the routine way in which humans click their consent prefigures a tendency to go with the technological flow. If so, then it is not only the significance of privacy that is being transformed but also the significance of consent.

We will take up the value of consent in the next chapter; but, before we leave privacy, we can say a few words about its possible downgrading. Arguably, privacy has been downgraded by data protection laws that are now at the centre of governance in the EU. In their initial articulation, data protection laws stood very explicitly on privacy as the fundamental value. However, the direction of travel in subsequent thinking has been towards an acceptable balance of interests between data processors and data subjects. This merits further consideration but, here, picking up a thread of Chapter 18, we can focus on the possible downgrading of privacy *as a claim right*.

Applying the distinction between claim rights and permissive rights, we can trace the erosion of privacy by pursuing three questions: first, whether the core interest in controlling access is treated as a claim right or as a permissive right; secondly, whether there has been any relaxation of whatever restrictions there are limiting the (offensive) permission to try to access and use privacy-protected information; and, thirdly, whether there have been any changes in relation to the defensive means that may be deployed pursuant to the privilege of protecting one's privacy. Where the core claim right has been downgraded to a mere permission, that is not quite the death of privacy but it is a watershed moment. For example, whereas I once might have argued that online search engines have a duty not to try to profile me, the best that I can argue now is a privacy permission to try to avoid the profilers or to frustrate and confuse them by employing various kinds of obfuscations and misleading searches. By contrast, where the ground rules have changed in relation to the exercise of the permission in a way that favours the offensive interests, then that is also significant but, symbolically, not a watershed.

Of course, whether privacy has or has not been downgraded on paper, in practice, it will be the privileged and propertied who are able to exclude unauthorised intrusion. It will be the super-rich who can take practical measures to shut out unwelcome intrusion and who will do no wrong thereby; and, to the extent that privacy is still recognised as a claim right, and where there are breaches of duty, it will be the super-rich who will be able to afford the services of expensive lawyers and who will have the option of litigating their claims.

Similarly, the practicalities limit the options of ordinary people where the ground rules relating to permissive rights change. The actuality might be that it is simply more difficult to keep information to oneself (Brownsword, 2017a). For example, the use of remote surveillance technologies, just like the practice of 'googling' someone, can reveal all sorts of information about a person the disclosure of which has not been authorised as such. However, to some extent, this is simply a fact of life in the information society. Accordingly, if privacy is not to be eroded, this will take more than well-intended legal interventions; it will also need social norms that underline the importance of respect for privacy.

A radical thought

If we can make places, products, and processes safer by design, then a radical thought is that there might be a technological solution to our concerns about privacy infringements. As Woodrow Hartzog has argued, 'the design of popular technologies is critical to privacy, and the law should take it more seriously' (Hartzog 2018: 7). If we agree that privacy should be designed-in as if it were a claim right, then presumably denial of access would be set as the default: as with a door that automatically locks when it is closed, it would require a positive act by the protected party to unlock the door. However, if we treat privacy as merely a permissive right, then the default would not be set for denial of access and it would require action—whether drawing the curtains or resorting to cryptography—to protect one's privacy.

So far so good, but we should not underestimate the challenges to be faced by trying to implement a Law 3.0 approach to the governance of privacy.

First, how much support will there be for privacy by design (Bygrave, 2017)? Will it be possible to recruit the necessary legal and technical experts as well as stakeholders and community representatives to undertake governance of this kind? Will they be able to agree on the design specification and have the skill to implement it?

Secondly, where the governance question of who should have access to what information in what circumstances hinges on what members of the community judge to be 'reasonable', there are likely to be many shades of opinion. As we said in Chapter 16, on many questions, there is likely to be more than one view, each of which is reasonable (or not clearly unreasonable). Members of the community might reasonably disagree on the position to be designed in. How is this to be handled? Similarly, how do we design-in answers to questions about the weight and significance of the 'public interest' in overriding privacy? Do we need to retain human oversight or more for those cases where the designed-in solution is reasonable but not the only reasonable view?

Thirdly, as the practice of designing-in privacy protection spreads, this might have some impact on what members of the community judge can be reasonably expected. However, it would be too optimistic to expect the community's views to stabilise. Members will continue to have their own views about what is a reasonable level of protection of privacy and, as with all regulatory endeavours, there will be a challenge in keeping the design connected to the shifting patterns of community judgments. For example, what should we do about a technical fix for privacy that has a predictable effect and reflects a governance position that is not unreasonable but which now seems to be out of touch with public opinion? Should we impose 'sunset clauses' on designs to ensure that they are reviewed and revised from time to time?

On the face of it, we should not be lured into thinking that a technological approach to governance will necessarily translate into a once-and-for-all fix. At least, in the case of 'privacy by design', it seems that constant updates will be needed, that design positions taken (and features embedded) will need to be treated as provisional, and that the project will prove to be a constant work in progress. But, then, if governance by design is to be fit for purpose, should we expect it to be anything other than this?

25

CONSENT

Introduction

In the landscape of law's governance, consent is a familiar feature. Where legal rules impose prohibitions, it might also be provided that any attempt to bargain around the restrictions or responsibilities will be of no effect; but, in many cases, the prohibition may be lifted where the protected party consents; and, where legal rules concern transactions or agreements, consent will be a feature of the governance. Moreover, where regulatory deals are being made for the governance of emerging technologies, the inclusion of conditions relating to consent might well be critical in securing the acceptability of the regulatory package. In this context, we might be troubled that, with consent being 'instrumentalised' for the sake of the regulatory deal, it loses its essential ethical and justificatory features. However, before we get to this point, we need to have a view about the place of consent within ethics.

Consent as a justification

In ethical thinking, there are two kinds of justification: one is general and the other is limited and personal. Suppose that we want to justify our act x. If we appeal to a general justification, we will argue that doing x is the right thing to do regardless of who might have consented to it or who might object to it. If we appeal to a limited justification, we will argue that we do no wrong by doing x relative to C who has consented to the doing of x. In other words, the limited justification, based here on C's consent, is to the effect that no wrong is done to C (or C is precluded by consent from alleging

DOI: 10.4324/9781003507802-29

wrongdoing); but, C's consent (unlike a general justificatory argument) will not justify the doing of x relative to any non-consenting parties.

By way of illustration, let us suppose that C consents to a medical procedure which involves transplanting an organ from a genetically modified pig. How might the members of the medical team justify their act of xenotransplantation (in this case, a pig to human transplantation) which many might view as creating a risk of bringing across to humans non-human animal diseases? Relying on the limited justification that draws on C's consent, they can say that they do no wrong to C; and, to the extent that the objection is that C might be harmed by the procedure, this limited justification is fine. However, what if the objection is broader than this? What if it is the risk to non-consenting humans that is the issue? Here, the limited justification is of no avail and the team will need a general justificatory argument, possibly along the utilitarian lines that, all things considered, humans will benefit more than they lose by xenotransplantations.

While it is important to understand the limited nature of a consent-based justification, we need to see how consent fits into the general pattern of ethical debate because there will be some ethical views that will argue that, even if C consents to x, it will still be wrong to do x. In other words, even where the limited justification seems to hold, there will be ethics that condemn the authorised action as wrong.

Consent and the pattern of ethical debate

In Chapter 23, it has already been suggested that the pattern of ethical debate is essentially three-sided, with ethical views being based on rights, or duties, or the pursuit of some 'good' (such as utility or the general welfare). Given this pattern, the key take-away in the present chapter is that consent fits most naturally with rights-based ethical views.

Where a community takes a rights-based perspective, the consent of rights-holders will play a key role in negotiating the relationship between members of the community. As we saw in the last chapter, it was the *unauthorised* taking and circulation of photographs—in other words, the taking and circulation of photographs without the consent of the person—that provoked Warren and Brandeis to argue for a privacy right. There was no objection to rights-holders giving their consent to acts which would otherwise infringe their privacy.

This contrasts with the view that we find in duty-based conservative dignitarian quarters where it is not consent (or a lack of consent) that matters so much as whether the act in question compromises human dignity. Accordingly, where an act is judged to compromise human dignity, it is categorically wrong; and, the fact that others would consent (or have consented) to the act in question makes no difference. In other words, the idea that one agent, A, may authorise an act by another agent, B, which would compromise human dignity is simply not entertained. In the illustrative case of xenotransplantation, if the genetic modification of pigs or the transfer of pig organs to humans is judged to compromise human dignity, the procedure is ethically wrong; and, it matters not at all that the patient has consented or, indeed, that everyone in the world consents; the act is wrong … simply wrong, period. Similarly, before we applaud pioneering human-to-human transplants of hearts or wombs or whatever, we should pause. As Janice Turner has recently reminded *Times*' readers, 'The womb comes attached to a woman: it is not an interchangeable Lego part, a crop to be harvested, or a vessel sold to the highest bidder for rent or sale' (Turner, 2023: 23).

For those who think in a utilitarian way, consent is of no special significance in itself; and, utilitarians will view the need for consent as a kind of transaction cost. However, if the consequences of acting without consent impact negatively on overall utility, then there might be an argument for acting with consent. Thus, particularly in regulatory contexts, utilitarians might build a deal around consent even though, from a rights perspective, there is no prima facie violation of a right and no need for an authorising consent. For example, following a number of scandals around the turn of the century, when hospitals retained the organs of young (deceased) children without the consent of the families, a new regulatory deal (the Human Tissue Act, 2004) was done in which the legality of organ retention would depend on consent. This probably made sense from a utilitarian perspective but, from a rights perspective, it might have been viewed as inappropriate and unnecessary; and, from a dignitarian perspective, if organ retention was ethically wrong, then obtaining consent from the families would not make things right.

It follows that the headline debate in relation to consent is between the rights-based perspective that takes consent very seriously and those other perspectives in which consent is either not relevant at all or only contingently something that matters (Beyleveld and Brownsword, 2007: Ch 1). That said, many of the governance questions about consent do occur *within* the right-based perspective. In such rights-based deliberations, it is assumed that a 'consent' will only be valid where it is given freely and on an informed basis, where it is signalled clearly, and where it is given by a competent agent. However, each of these elements invites debate. When is consent given freely? When is consent informed? When is consent clearly signalled? And, when is an agent competent to give consent?

When is consent given freely?

If B forces (coerces) A to give consent, then this will not count as a valid consent; A's 'authorisation' has not been given freely. So much for the easy case.

What should we make, though, of cases where the pressure applied by B is not forcible? For example, what if B will apply economic sanctions if A does not consent? Where on the spectrum of pressure that impacts negatively on A do we draw the line?

If we manage to reach agreement about which kinds of negative pressure will preclude treating A's consent as freely given, we still have several questions to answer. First, where there is no pressure as such applied by B, but the circumstances in which A is invited to consent constitute a kind of duress, what do we make of A's supposed consent? For example, if A is a convicted sex offender who chooses to be castrated rather than to serve a long prison sentence, would we say that A has freely agreed, that A has consented to the treatment option? Secondly, what if the pressure applied by B is entirely positive in the sense that B is offering an inducement to A? Here, we might argue that there is no problem with a small inducement but that larger inducements can distort A's judgment in a way that is problematic. Whether or not the problem is then rightly characterised as being one of A's 'consent' no longer being free might also be a matter to consider. Thirdly, there are also questions to be asked where there is no pressure at all from B, neither positive nor negative, but the fact of the matter is that B exerts undue influence over A's decision-making (even though B makes every effort to encourage A to make their own decision). Once again, we might think twice before characterising this as a case in which A's consent is not given freely but A's lack of self-reliance will trouble those who take consent seriously.

When is consent informed?

If B obtains A's 'consent' by fraudulent means, this is a clear case in which we should not recognise A's authorisation as valid. A consent obtained by disinformation is not valid. Again, though, once we look beyond this easy case, we face difficult questions about cases where B unintentionally misinforms A, or where B does not disclose something that is material to A, or where B's conduct is beyond reproach but there are facts which would impact on A's decision but of which he is unaware (Beyleveld and Brownsword, 2007: 170–183).

In relation to the question of disclosure and informed consent, a considerable body of medical law jurisprudence has developed in a way that takes a patient-centred approach rather than a more traditional paternalistic physician-centred approach. To the extent that the former approach presupposes a rights-based view, the direction of travel here is from views that prioritise what physicians judge to be in the best interest of patients to a view that prioritises patient consent. As a corollary, the traditional idea that, in line with the so-called 'therapeutic privilege', physicians may legitimately withhold information (e.g., about the risks or side effects of a procedure) that they think is not in the interest of patients to know, is to be read very restrictively.

When is consent clearly signalled?

If we take consent seriously, we want to be confident that (i) the question of consent is plainly put to the would-be consenting agent and (ii) that, if the agent wishes to consent, then the authorisation is clearly signalled.

So far as the first requirement is concerned, it is, of course, important that the agent is asked very plainly and clearly whether or not they wish to consent. However, many would argue that the putting of the question has to be part of a process, that consenting is relational. Accordingly, it will not do to spring the question out of nowhere and, in some cases, it is not enough to put the question just once—for example, if the agent is being asked to consent to a non-resuscitation order, or to the withdrawal of life support, or to assistance with suicide, or the like, then (so it might be argued) we need to be sure that the agent really does know their own mind.

With regard to the second requirement, to avoid any misinterpretation of the agent's wishes, consent should be by opt-in. If we are being asked to tick a box, we need to place a tick in the box, not to be presented with a pre-ticked box which we can untick if we so choose. But, some will protest, signalling by opt-out will generate more consents than consent only by opt-in, and the consents in question might well be to acts which, in the long run, are clearly of benefit either to the agent personally (such as joining a pension scheme that is offered by your employer) or to others (such as agreeing to be an organ donor). Underlying this objection is the thought that requiring but not then obtaining consent can lead to so much disbenefit. However, this is largely a utilitarian thought, not a thought that has priority where our main concern is to take rights, consent, and individual choice seriously. If we are to respect individuals, we should not nudge them towards utility-maximising outcomes and we should not rely on opt-out instead of consent by opt-in.

When is an agent competent to give consent?

There is no easy way to govern the line between a mature rights-holder who is fully competent to consent and an immature still-developing rights-holder who is not yet fully competent to consent. If we try to govern with a bright-line rule that sets an age at which children mature into fully competent adults, or if the law sets a series of ages at which children are treated as being competent to consent for various purposes, there will always be cases that challenge the scheme. For example, if we set the age of 16 as the threshold for full competence, what do we say about a 15-year-old who already seems to know her own mind and displays the competence of an adult? Do we say that her consent should not be recognised? In the landmark English decision of *Gillick v West Norfolk and Wisbech Area Health Authority* (1985), the House of Lords said that the relevant test for valid consent was not so much the age of the person as whether (as Lord Scarman put it, at 422) there was evidence of 'a sufficient understanding and intelligence to be capable to making up [their] own mind on the matter' or (as Lord Fraser said, at 409) the person was 'capable of understanding what is proposed, and of expressing his or her own wishes'. While this might seem somewhat circular, a person being treated as legally competent to consent when they seem to be competent to consent, we still might prefer the flexibility of this kind of approach to the rigidity of an age-eligible rule.

In *Gillick*, the 15-year-old was in good health and her consent was in relation to the receipt of advice from a doctor about the use of contraceptives. But, if so-called 'Gillick competence' is the test for the validity of consents given by 15-year-olds, should it also be the test for the validity of a *refusal* of consent where doctors are wishing to administer a potentially life-saving blood transfusion to a teenager who objects to the procedure? Even if the teenager seems very clear about the implications of not having the procedure, many will understand the best intentions of doctors who undertake the procedure, the lack of consent notwithstanding, and we should not be altogether surprised if lawyers argue that, on these facts, the young person's understanding really was not sufficient.

Where an infant or child is nowhere near Gillick competence, their parents will act as proxies, striving to serve the best interests of the child. In medical settings, this is unproblematic so long as the parents' view aligns with the view of the medical professionals as to what is in the best interests of the child. However, where the medical view and the parental view do not align, we can have a major tension—whether because the medical view is that a procedure is essential but the parents withhold their consent (as in the famous case of the conjoined twins, Jodie and Mary, *Re A (Children)* (2000), which we will revisit in the next chapter) or because the medical view is that further treatment is futile but the parents do not wish to accept that no more can be done (for example, as in Jaymee Bowen's case, *Re B, R v Cambridge Health Authority* (1995)).

Finally, what about those cases where a parent is asked to give their proxy consent on behalf of an adult child who is either (a) no longer competent or (b) of low IQ and who has never achieved Gillick competence? In the former scenario, the general view amongst rights-theorists is that the parent should try to put themselves in the position of their once competent son or daughter and ask what they would have wanted in the circumstances. To the extent that the parent is able to do this, they make a 'substituted judgment' on behalf of their son or daughter; and they give or they withhold their consent accordingly. However, in the latter scenario, there is no substituted judgment to be made; it is for the parent to judge what is in the best interests of their son or daughter. This can put a considerable strain on a parent's loyalties as we see in the Kentucky case of *Strunk v Strunk* (1969) where a mother consented to the transplantation of a kidney from her mentally incompetent 27-year-old son Jerry to her fully competent 28-year-old son Tommy. This was a life-saving procedure which was undoubtedly of benefit to Tommy but the court also held that the transplantation was in the best interest of *Jerry*. On the face of it, this strains the idea of best interests because this was a risky procedure from which Jerry apparently would gain no benefit. At best, it might be suggested that Jerry would benefit from the survival and continuing affiliation of Tommy and that he would feel bad about it if he had not helped to save Tommy's life when he was in a position to do so. In other words, we might be able to find an all things considered kind of justification for going ahead with the transplantation but it would no longer be anchored to rights-thinking and consent.

26
JUSTICE

Introduction

According to the standard introduction to law, it is the idea of legality—that is, the impartial administration of the community's rules of law—coupled with the principle of treating like cases alike that holds the key to justice. Philosophers and politicians may debate the justice of social arrangements—some arguing that limited resources should be distributed equally, or on the basis of need or desert, and so on; but, for lawyers, justice is simply 'justice in accordance with the law', which is to say that the legal rules have been applied. Or, to put this in other words, for lawyers, justice is a matter of entitlement, a matter of legal rights being vindicated and legal obligations enforced (all as per the rules and the precedents).

To this, we need to add some qualifying remarks concerning the facts. When cases come before a court, whether they are criminal cases or private law claims, there might be some arguments around preliminary points of law. *Donoghue v Stevenson*, which we have mentioned in several of the earlier chapters, was one such case. In general, though, a finding of the facts needs to be made. The rules are then applied to the facts as found. But, the facts do not find themselves and the just administration of the legal rules presupposes that the facts have been correctly found. Where errors occur in the fact finding, even if the rules have been correctly applied, there will be a miscarriage of justice. For example, there were some particularly serious miscarriages of justice in the long-running (and, recently, extensively publicised) dispute between the Post Office and hundreds of sub-postmasters and sub-postmistresses with regard to shortfalls shown by the Horizon point of sale and accounting system that sub-postmasters were required to use.

DOI: 10.4324/9781003507802-30

While the former insisted that the shortfalls must have arisen from mistakes or dishonesty by sub-postmasters, the latter argued that the system suffered from technical flaws which led (erroneously) to shortfalls being shown. In many cases, the Post Office's version of the facts was preferred but, actually, the sub-postmasters and sub-postmistresses were right: it was the technology that was the problem and it was a problem compounded by the Post Office's determination to shift all responsibility to those to whom it had given no choice other than to use the system. In the wake of the injustice arising from the dispute, the Post Office entered into a multi-million pound settlement of the civil claims; a public inquiry was set up in February 2022 to examine the wrongful conviction of hundreds of sub-postmasters and sub-postmistresses; following a television documentary featuring the case early in 2024, there was a huge public outcry leading to pressure being put on the government to take steps to quash all the convictions and to accelerate the compensatory payments to the victims; and, in March 2024, the government responded by introducing the Post Office (Horizon System) Offences Bill with a view to clearing the names of those hundreds of people whose lives have been ruined by what is now a national scandal (see Gov.UK Press Release, 2024).

So, it is not enough that the rules are applied; the facts must also be found accurately. However, even if these requirements are satisfied, some might argue that this is still not sufficient for justice. We also need to ask whether our procedural rules are themselves just, whether the rules of law that are applied are themselves just, and whether the outcomes that are generated by the rules in individual cases are just. This is a substantial agenda and, in each case, we are pushed into thinking outside the box because we are looking for our criteria of justice outside the law's own governance framework.

In the case of the procedural rules, especially the rules that govern the admissibility of evidence in criminal proceedings, our view about the justice of the rules will hinge on whether we incline towards a liberal view that centres on due process or a view that prioritises crime control. While those who take the former view will deplore what they regard as traps or unfair procedures (such as obtaining a confession by trick or oppression, or obtaining evidence without the cover of a judicial warrant), those who take the latter approach will despair of those cases where manifestly guilty persons escape conviction on a procedural technicality. Similarly, our assessment of the justice of the substantive rules of law will depend on our philosophical or political position. As for the question of whether the outcomes in particular cases are just, as we saw in our earlier discussion of hard cases (see Chapter 10), while some lawyers will want to stick with the justice of applying the legal rules others will tap into the sense that there has to be some adjustment where the application of the rules looks manifestly unjust.

In what follows, we can say a bit more about the reluctance of the courts to look beyond the consistent application of the legal rules for their guidance on justice, and then we can open up the radical question of how technological forms of governance might align with our human views on justice.

Courts, judges, and justice

In the previous chapter, we mentioned the case of the conjoined twins, Jodie and Mary (in *Re A (Children)* [2000] 4 All ER 961). The question for the court was whether the girls could be lawfully separated. The dilemma was that, if the girls, who were joined at the lower abdomen, were to be surgically separated, this would result in the death of Mary, whose lungs and heart were too deficient to oxygenate and pump blood through her body. Had Mary been born a singleton, she would not have been viable; and, she was alive only because a common artery enabled her sister, who was stronger, to circulate life-sustaining oxygenated blood for both of them. Separation would require the clamping and then the severing of that common artery leading to Mary's death. Without the separation, it was expected that both girls would die within three to six months, because Jodie's heart would fail. The parents, who were from a devout Roman Catholic community in the Mediterranean, had brought the girls to a hospital in England but they could not bring themselves to consent to the operation. It was the hospital that sought a declaration that the operation could be lawfully carried out.

While the medical instinct was to undertake the surgery and at least save one of the girls, the judges who heard the case found themselves uncomfortable about any of the decisions available to them. How was it possible in such a tragic case to reach a just decision? As Lord Justice Ward put it:

> In the past decade an increasing number of cases have come before the courts where the decision whether or not to permit or to refuse medical treatment can be a matter of life and death for the patient. I have been involved in a number of them. They are always anxious decisions to make but they are invariably eventually made with the conviction that there is only one right answer and that the court has given it.
>
> In this case the right answer is not at all as easy to find. I freely confess to having found it exceptionally difficult to decide – difficult because of the scale of the tragedy for the parents and the twins, difficult for the seemingly irreconcilable conflicts of moral and ethical values and difficult because the search for settled legal principle has been especially arduous and conducted under real pressure of time.
>
> The problems we have faced have gripped the public interest and the case has received intense coverage in the media. Everyone seems to have a view of the proper outcome. I am very well aware of the inevitability that

> our answer will be applauded by some but that as many will be offended by it …
>
> It is, however, important to stress the obvious. This court is a court of law, not of morals, and our task has been to find, and our duty is then to apply the relevant principles of law to the situation before us—a situation which is quite unique.
>
> *(968–969)*

In the event, the three members of the Court of Appeal, each applying a different justificatory argument, agreed that the relevant legal principles supported the view that it would be lawful to carry out the procedure. The doctors duly separated the girls; Mary died; Jodie survived; and justice was done in accordance with the law (or, more accurately, in accordance with three different readings of the relevant legal principles).

In another tragic case, that of Tony Bland, who was one of the victims of the disastrous crush at the Hillsborough football stadium in April 1989, the courts found themselves similarly challenged (*Airedale NHS Trust v Bland* (1993)). Although the young man did not die immediately, he did not recover consciousness and, for several years after the disaster, he lay in hospital in a persistent vegetative state. With no hope of recovery, the question arose whether it would be right to take him off the life support systems and let him die. What was the just decision? In the Court of Appeal, Lord Justice Hoffmann emphasised the importance of law aligning with moral values. Thus:

> This case has caused a great deal of public concern. People are worried, perhaps not so much about this particular case, but about where it may lead. Is the court to assume the role of God and decide who should live and who should die? Is Anthony Bland to die because the quality of his life is so miserable? Does this mean that the court would approve the euthanasia of seriously handicapped people? And what about the manner of his death? Can it ever be right to cause the death of a human being by deliberately depriving him of food? This is not an area in which any difference can be allowed to exist between what is legal and what is morally right. The decision of the court should be able to carry conviction with the ordinary person as being based not merely on legal precedent but also upon acceptable ethical values.
>
> *(851)*

In the event, all nine judges who heard the *Bland* case (that is, the judge at first instance, the three members of the Court of Appeal, and then, on final appeal, the five members of the House of Lords' panel) agreed that it would be lawful to withdraw the feeding and hydration. As in the case of the conjoined twins, it probably would not have made any difference to the outcome of the *Bland* case whether the court did or did not take account of the ethics of withdrawing life support but, in this instance, Lord Justice Hoffmann clearly thought that the decision of the court would be better received if it was presented as being in line with the ethical convictions of the community. The feeding and hydration were duly withdrawn; this was judged to be in the best interests of Tony Bland who could then die with dignity; Tony died; and justice was done in accordance with both the law and acceptable ethical values.

Cases like *Re A* and *Bland* engage the attention of the whole community. Debates run concurrently, in courtrooms and out of courtrooms. In courts, the recognised reference points are in the established principles and precedents; out of court, the reference points are not so constrained and they might include not only a plurality of ethical viewpoints but also the more formal ethical guidance that we find in professional codes. While judges might be able to distance themselves from out-of-court ethical debates, if they want to carry the public with them on particularly contentious issues, then as Lord Hoffmann says, it is advisable to base judgments not only on the law but also on acceptable ethical values.

Whatever we make of the idea of justice in accordance with the law, it is more of a question than an answer. In pluralistic communities, cases such as those of *Re A* and *Bland* are likely to provoke ethical divisions. So, whether judges choose to keep ethics at arm's length or incorporate it into their thinking, it is unlikely to give a clear steer to decision-makers who seek a just outcome.

Aligning technological governance with justice

Where smart technologies are being deployed, it is commonly said that a major challenge is to align their operation with human values, such as the value of justice. Given what we have already said about justice, it is clear that there is no straightforward one-to-one alignment to be had because, on the human side, there are many different conceptions of justice. Unless the technology can reflect the plurality and creativity of human conceptions of justice, we have a problem.

What is more, whilst law's governance proclaims that it is just by virtue of its administration of the rules and the precedents, smart governance does not necessarily operate in the same way at all. For example, if the governance of disputes is left to smart technologies that operate by drawing on huge databases, complex algorithms, and machine learning techniques, we will need to think in terms of the justice of the way in which the data is collected, the justice of the processing of the data and the operation of the technology, and then the justice of the outputs.

Our concerns are likely to be various: for example, that the technology's inputs and processing will reflect biases that we already think are unjust; that it will be opaque to the extent that we cannot assess whether it operates justly (even if the machines do what they say they will do); that there will be injustice in the considerations taken to be relevant by the machines (for instance, taking into account data about unrelated third parties such as information about previous occupiers of an agent's present address); and, that the outputs will also be unjust in failing to treat what we humans would consider to be like cases alike.

Whether or not these concerns can be assuaged is open to question. However, the more that we rely on technologies to undertake governance functions, the less critical we are likely to be about the injustice as we see it of particular decisions. Overall, the culture will be tilted towards efficiency, utility, the collective good and, in the criminal justice system, crime control, and prevention. For those humans who are still wedded to liberal values and to individual justice, there is probably going to be a problematic alignment between man and machine.

27

ETHICS

Introduction

Ethics has an ancient pedigree and, even if we leave it to the philosophers to debate the best reading of Aristotle, we might spend some time wondering quite how 'ethics' relates to 'morals' and, indeed, to 'justice' (see, further, Chapter 40). However, as prospective lawyers, our interest nowadays is in the codes of ethics that spring up as the governance of each new technology becomes a debating point. Starting with biotechnologies and bioethics, we then have information and communication technologies and cyberethics. Before long, these are joined by neurotechnologies and neuroethics, nanotechnologies and nanoethics, and robotics and roboethics, and so on (Brownsword, 2008). For each new technology it seems that there is an ethical companion.

Although each technology has its own backcloth, and although the leading concerns can vary, the ethical thinking that is elaborated displays a familiar plurality and pattern. We can start by sketching this pattern before noting the 'politics' of ethical governance and then discussing the practical options for dealing with the plurality of ethics.

The pattern of ethical debate

At the price of some over-simplification, we can say that there are three ethical views that dominate debates and which can be conceived of as forming the points of an ethical triangle (recall what we said about these three viewpoints in Chapters 23 and 25). In response to the general question, 'What is the right thing to do?' these views respond that the right thing to do is,

DOI: 10.4324/9781003507802-31

respectively: (i) to act in a way that will promote some specified 'good'; (ii) to respect the rights of others; and (iii) to act in accordance with one's duties. Of course, the practical significance of these views only becomes clear when we fill in what constitutes the relevant 'good' (such as utility, the satisfaction of preferences, equality, the interests of women, or whatever), the substance of the 'rights' that are to be respected (including whether these rights are both negative and positive), and the substance of one's 'duties' (including whether these are duties to both others and to oneself).

The way in which these ethical viewpoints triangulate, and how they influence the content of law's governance of particular technologies will vary from one place to another. Occasionally, these three viewpoints converge to invite regulators to act on a consensus—as was the case, for example, with the agreed prohibitions on human reproductive cloning that followed the successful cloning of Dolly the sheep. Typically, though, there is not convergence and we will find tensions either within an ethics code or between ethical codes.

One of the key areas of tension will be in the drawing of any red lines. As we have seen in earlier chapters, for those whose ethics are duty-based, there might well be some technological applications which should be categorically prohibited. In no circumstances, it will be argued, should such applications be permitted. By contrast, utilitarians might want to keep their options open: in some circumstances, an otherwise prohibited application might promise hugely beneficial consequences. If so, those utilitarians who want to assess the utilities case-by-case, will reason that all options should remain open to governance. As for those whose ethics are rights-based, the starting point will probably be that technological applications should be permitted unless they intrude on the rights of third parties but that their use should not be required without the consent of the rights-holders.

The politics of ethics

The proliferation of ethics alongside the development of new technologies prompts several questions about, so to speak, the 'politics' of all this: in particular, who is initiating ethical debate, why are they doing so, what is their agenda; and, who is funding ethical bodies and why so? If it is the big tech corporations that are publishing ethical codes, some might accuse them of 'ethics washing' or of trying to control and shape the debate; but, similarly, if the funding comes from government, is this anything more than a public relations exercise? Is anyone above suspicion?

Ethics bodies, whether they are Councils, Commissions, or Committees, whether operating in the public or the private sector, whether established by governments or trusts or by industry, whether national, regional or international, do not come out of nowhere: there is always a background of policy, politics, and power. There is always a story (and there are always questions) about what prompted the establishment of the body, about whose idea it was, about the purposes and interests that its sponsors intended it to serve, about its funding arrangements, about its accountability, and so on. These features of the policy background invite further questions about the relationship between the body and those who fund it and to whom it accounts: the body may purport 'to do ethics' but to what extent is it (its membership, its agenda, and its recommendations) independent of its sponsors, to what extent do the latter exert control or influence over the former? To what extent might it be possible to insulate an ethics body from the policy background? Is it naïve even to ask such a question or to entertain such a thought (Bimber, 1996; Jasanoff, 2007)?

The practice of ethics

There is more than one way of doing ethics. Indeed, according to Harald Schmidt and Jason Schwartz (2016), there is a kind of North/South divide in the way that groups 'do their bioethics'—but, we can treat this analysis as applicable to ethics generally, not just to bioethics. While some groups adopt a 'rigid-grid' approach, declaring their ethical principles and then applying them consistently in a top-down way, others practise a 'flexible-focus' approach, an approach that 'does not impose ethical principles or norms in a top-down fashion, but identifies them anew for each topic or report' (Schmidt and Schwartz, 2016: 443). So, for example, if we were to apply this distinction to bioethics bodies in the UK, we might say that, while the approach of the now defunct Human Genetics Commission instantiates the former approach, the bottom-up consultative and deliberative approach of the Nuffield Council on Bioethics exemplifies the latter (Brownsword and Wale, 2018). Similarly, looking across the Atlantic, we might say that, in the US, this distinction captures the different approaches of the President's Council on Bioethics headed by Leon Kass (where the emphasis was on human dignity: Kass, 2002) and the Presidential Commission for the Study of Bioethical Issues that was chaired by Amy Gutmann (where the emphasis was on deliberative democratic process).

Adapting this insight, we can say that, broadly speaking, a group will seek to do its ethics by orientating itself to one or more guiding principles (or values) which it will consistently apply, or it will be guided topic by topic by the views that emerge from a consultative and deliberative process. Like any North/South distinction, this does not leave much room for nuance. Accordingly, we have to be ready to recognise that not all groups will do their ethics in a way that is guided consistently by top-down principles or by bottom-up processes; and that, even if groups are not inconsistent and ad hoc in their practice, they might operate in a way that combines these approaches.

If we now imagine an expert and truly independent ethics group, how might it operate? If the group operates in a top-down manner, it will be guided by principles; but, if it operates bottom-up, it will be the process that is crucial.

Principle

Let us suppose that our hypothetical expert group starts by surveying and mapping the literature. This is quite a task. The members of the group agree that there are many different and plausible approaches—various kinds of utilitarian, egalitarian, communitarian, and republican approaches, theories based on rights, theories based on duties, virtue ethics, and so on (Brownsword, 2003). Although some proponents of these approaches claim that their approach is 'right', the members of the group are not persuaded that any one approach is clearly right; and, indeed, they also agree that none of the standard approaches is clearly wrong. Rejecting the suggestion that some of these approaches might be welded together, the group reasons that their function is to apply the logic of each approach to the questions/topics as they arise for discussion and decision.

While each analysis undertaken by the group is rigorous and careful, some members of the group anticipate that their work might get mixed reviews. Where all approaches converge on a particular conclusion, there is an actionable outcome. However, where different approaches lead to different conclusions, the group fears that reviewers will find the outcome disappointing. Accordingly, in an effort to take their work to another (more normative) level, the members of the group agree that they will gloss their analysis with a statement of which approach they, as a group, judge to be the better view. Following this line of thinking, the group declares that it takes its lead from 'liberal' rights theory.

Having adopted this approach, however, the group now worries that this might compromise its position and that it will be seen as being partisan and lacking impartiality. Accordingly, it revises its declaration to say that it treats liberal principles as guiding, not only because it judges that this is the better view in bioethics but also because this is largely in line with the position taken in its community where there is a public commitment to respect human rights.

The work of the expert group is not well received. First, as the group feared, its early attempts simply to work through the logic of a plurality of approaches do not meet expectations; indeed, many are underwhelmed by the group's contributions. Secondly, while the group's change of direction (from 'descriptive-analytical' to normative) is welcomed, many are not impressed by its adoption and characterisation of a particular ('liberal') approach as being the 'better view'—'What exactly does that mean? Better relative to which criterion?' If the so-called 'better view' is simply a proxy for liberal values, then we are left with the question of why the group thinks it appropriate to take liberal values as criterial. Thirdly, to then switch from a supposedly better view simply to follow the commitments of the community seems like more than a concession; as many see it, it is to abandon the critical distance that an expert ethics group should have.

Process

By contrast, let us suppose that the expert group agrees that the best approach is to gather the community's views on a particular topic and to identify a consensus or, if not that, then to identify a range of plausible accommodations of interests. Following this approach, the group works topic by topic, its guiding principles and values being specified afresh for each new case. Sometimes, there is a clear consensus but, often, the group finds that it is pushed towards a middle ground, even a relatively anodyne, position that reflects the push and pull of the principal opposing views on a topic. For example, when the Nuffield Council on Bioethics addressed the topic of NIPT (non-invasive prenatal testing), the group staked out a compromise position that accommodated, on the one side, those who argued that the reproductive autonomy of women should be prioritised and, on the other, a number of views that expressed concern about the signals being given about respect for the disability communities (Brownsword and Wale, 2018).

After a while, the group becomes concerned about a number of features of this approach. One such concern is that there are often a number of middle ground positions that are plausible; but, then, there is no good reason for preferring one such position rather than another. In an attempt to respond to this, and to underline its 'ownership' of its favoured positions, the group agrees that, from the range of possible and plausible accommodations, it should specify its own preferred view. However, this is constrained by the process that it follows. The fact of the matter is that there is a worrying lack of consistency and coherence in the principles and values that it treats as relevant and in the positions that it takes up. To be sure, this reflects a degree of inconsistency and incoherence in the community's own thinking, but this is no comfort so long as the group sees its role as brokering an accommodation of interests that originate in the community's responses to its consultations.

In a further attempt to strengthen its approach, the group combines a processual approach with a principled privileging of what it takes to be the community's fundamental values. This has the attraction of eliminating some views as inconsistent with the community's own aspirations; there is now a degree of coherence in the process. However, other weaknesses that the group identified remain and, overall, the process seems to be one of 'messy' brokerage (Ashcroft, 2010).

Once again, many are dissatisfied with ethics by process and its outcomes. The processual approach seems to do no more than hold up a mirror to the community and its values. Doing ethics has to be more than that, and more than brokering compromises where the community's views do not all pull in the same direction. If we are to take ethics seriously, its judgments have to signify more than that a certain position is 'acceptable'. Moreover, if the group limits itself to engaging with the views expressed by a particular community, ethics seems to have no cosmopolitan aspirations.

Franklin's critique

The experience of the hypothetical expert group chimes in with Sarah Franklin's provocative assessment of the current state of bioethics (but it could as well be ethics applied to emerging technologies). Franklin (2019) claims that amongst bioethicists there is a 'sense of ethical bewilderment' with a 'feeling of being overwhelmed [being] exacerbated by a lack of regulatory infrastructure or adequate policy precedents' such that '[b]ioethics, once a beacon of principled pathways to policy, is increasingly lost, like Simba, in a sea of thundering wildebeest.' Indeed, '[i]n the wake of the "turn to dialogue" in science, bioethics often looks more like public engagement—and vice versa.' Or, putting this in the words of this chapter, Franklin detects the decline of bioethics by principle and the rise of a muddling bioethics by process—moreover, the resulting process is one that offers little resistance to the promoters of new technologies who are quickly able to persuade the public of the benefits to be gained.

Speaking to the decline of bioethics by principle, Franklin remarks that a 'single, Belmont-style umbrella no longer seems likely, or even feasible.' Instead, she concludes,

> the new holy grail is the ability to create trustworthy systems for governing controversial research such as chimeric embryos and face-recognition algorithms. The pursuit of a more ethical science has come to be associated with building trust by creating transparent processes, inclusive participation and openness to uncertainty, as opposed to distinguishing between 'is' and 'ought'.
>
> In short, expert knowledge and reliable data are essential but never enough to enable enduring, humane governance to emerge. So there is now more emphasis on continuous communication and outreach, and on long-term strategies to ensure collective participation and feedback at all stages of scientific inquiry. The result is less reliance on specialized ethical expertise and more attention to diversity of representation...

> The implication of this new model is that the most ethical science is the most sociable one, and thus that scientific excellence depends on greater inclusivity. We are better together—we must all be ethicists now.

Whether or not we agree with Franklin's assessment of the loss of expert direction in modern bioethics, the point is that a turn to bioethics by process is no more the way to respond to a lack of confidence in bioethics by principle than a reversion to the latter would be the way to respond to disenchantment with the former. We are missing something; and what we are missing is, actually, glaringly obvious.

If we ask ourselves what it takes to do bioethics in the first place—not the funding and the fancy facilities, but the minimal conditions for doing bioethics—we are on the right track. In response to our question, it goes without saying (but it is very important to say it) that there need to be humans (which implies that there need to be conditions for humans to exist) who understand that simply because we can do certain things it does not follow that we ought to do them (which implies that the conditions enable humans to form a view about what can be done and what ought to be done). So, the focus for the fresh start that we are looking for is not principle or process but the preconditions for the human enterprise of bioethical reflection and governance by bioethics (and ethics more generally). Bioethics has become a box that we now need to think outside—and, as we have indicated in Chapter 22, it is the conditions of possibility to which we now need to refer.

28

CONSCIENTIOUS OBJECTION AND CIVIL DISOBEDIENCE

Introduction

Throughout the foregoing discussion of values, it is apparent that where the context for law's governance is one of like-minded people, then it should not be too difficult to find a consensus; but, where the context is one of a plurality of views, then that is quite another story. In this chapter, we can consider the extent to which law's governance relies on a consensus, how it can ease some tensions of value plurality by allowing for conscientious objection, and how a more technological form of governance might avoid the problem of a plurality of views but with some implications for civil disobedience.

Law's governance and consensus

To the extent that law's governance aligns with the values of the community, we might think that, in seeking compliance, it is pushing at an open door. Here, it does not matter too much whether those who are governed are disposed to comply because they have a general respect for the law or because they believe that the law's particular provisions are ethically sound; either way, those who are governed will comply with the law.

Even in such favourable circumstances, circumstances that are so conducive to law's governance, there will be some members of the group who will be disposed to defect where the opportunity presents itself and where there is a self-serving gain to be made. Anticipating this possibility, legal requirements and prohibitions will be backed with sanctions (penalties) that are designed to nullify the self-serving gain and discourage non-compliance. Where members comply with the law only because they calculate that, all

DOI: 10.4324/9781003507802-32

things considered, non-compliance is not in their own interest, moralists might regard this as an imperfect reason for compliance but at least it is better than non-compliance.

Where the circumstances are less favourable for law's governance, where there is significant value plurality, some will find that legal provisions align with their values but others will not. With regard to the latter, law's governance might still attract some respect simply because it is the law and it is recognised that those who govern are trying to do the right thing; but, it is also likely that law's governance will have to rely more on prudential reasons that indicate that, in the long run, compliance will serve the interests of all members.

In what follows, we can consider how law's governance can ease the strain on those whose values are not reflected in the relevant legal provisions by allowing for a degree of non-compliance; and, thinking in a radical mode, we can imagine how governance by technological management can bypass both self-serving and value-based resistance but at some cost to the scope for civil disobedience.

Conscientious objection

Where a community is morally divided, where there is value plurality, there is a case for making some allowance for conscientious objection. Certainly, if the members of the community regard the matter in relation to which there is moral division as one about which members might reasonably disagree, there is a case for tolerating conscientious non-compliance; and, similarly, if the values of those who are in the minority are deeply held and go to their sense of identity there is a case for not compelling them to act in ways that offend their conscience and basic beliefs. Just how generous the proviso for conscientious objection should be is a matter to be contested both in recognising an exception for conscience and then in the interpretation and application of a conscience clause.

Formally to recognise that conscientious objection has its place—as is the case, for example, in the UK where section 4 of the Abortion Act 1967 provides that no person shall be under a duty 'to participate in any treatment … to which he has a conscientious objection'—is the first step: but, then, the question is how much scope and strength is to be accorded to a conscience clause such as section 4? The jurisprudence in the UK is markedly restrictive. In the leading case, *Greater Glasgow Health Board v Doogan* (2014), the concern of the petitioner midwives was that, following the closure of one of the three hospitals in Glasgow that provided maternity services, and the consequent reorganisation of such services, they might find themselves being expected to perform functions to which they had a conscientious objection. The question narrowed to whether 'delegating, supervising and/

or supporting staff to participate in and provide care to patients throughout the termination process' would qualify as activities from which the midwives might exempt themselves on the grounds of conscience. The midwives' application was unsuccessful at first instance but then succeeded on appeal. On final appeal, the Supreme Court ruled against the applicants.

In *Doogan*, Lady Hale declared that the restrictive reading was more likely to accord with Parliament's intention. The conscience clause, it was noted, related to acts made lawful by the legislation, from which it followed that it was unlikely that Parliament was contemplating an exemption from 'the host of ancillary, administrative and managerial tasks that might be associated with those [now lawful] acts' (para 38). However, at the best of times, reliance on 'legislative intention' is highly problematic and in the context of the 1967 Act, where a legal (and, for many persons, a moral) prohibition was being changed to a conditional permission, this might seem like a more than usually problematic reason for marginalising conscientious objection (which, unlike an objection that is based on prudential considerations, rests on an independent moral judgment).

Of course, if the context is such that the exercise of conscientious objection by midwives impedes the availability of health services or is treated as being incompatible with the rights of patients or employers, then a further layer of complexity is added. At the European Court of Human Rights, in the case of *Grimmark v Sweden* (2020.), the Court eased the complexity by observing that Sweden, by committing to provision of nationwide abortion services, 'has a positive obligation to organise its health system in a way as to ensure that the effective exercise of freedom of conscience of health professionals in the professional context does not prevent the provision of such services'; and, thus, the 'requirement that all midwives should be able to perform all duties inherent to the vacant posts was not disproportionate or unjustified' (para 26).

Technological management and civil disobedience

If governance relies on technological management, limiting the options that are practically available to those who are governed, there will be conformity regardless of whether, counterfactually, there would or would not be compliance with law's rule-based governance. Moreover, there will be conformity regardless of whether the values embedded in the technological management align with the values of those who are governed or whether prudential considerations would indicate compliance as the better option. When technological management applies, the only options are those left by design; the only possibilities are in the affordances given by the technology.

To the extent that technological management eliminates self-serving opportunism, we might have few, if any, objections. However, where technological management impinges on the ability of those who are governed freely to act in accordance with their own values, this is another matter. Here, the key point is that, in moral communities, the aspiration is to do the right thing; respecting persons is doing the right thing; and it matters to moral communities that such respect is shown freely and for the right reason—not because we know that we are being observed or because we have no practical option other than the one that the regulators have left for us. Quite simply, even if the technology channels regulatees towards right action, the technologically secured pattern of right action (as we emphasised earlier in relation to the use of golf carts at Westways) is not at all the same as freely opting to do the right thing. One agent might be protected from the potentially harmful acts of others, but moral virtue, as Ian Kerr (2010) protests, cannot be automated.

In the same vein, is there a risk that technological management might compromise the possibility of engaging in responsible moral citizenship? As Evgeny Morozov (2013) points out, Rosa Parks' historic act of civil disobedience (https://en.wikipedia.org/wiki/Rosa_Parks) was possible only because

> the bus and the sociotechnological system in which it operated were terribly inefficient. The bus driver asked Parks to move only because he couldn't anticipate how many people would need to be seated in the white-only section at the front; as the bus got full, the driver had to adjust the sections in real time, and Parks happened to be sitting in an area that suddenly became 'white-only'.
>
> *(204)*

However, if the bus and the bus-stops had been technologically enabled, this situation simply would not have arisen—Parks would either have been denied entry to the bus or she would have been sitting in the allocated section for black people. Morozov continues:

> Will this new transportation system be convenient? Sure. Will it give us Rosa Parks? Probably not, because she would never have gotten to the front of the bus to begin with. The odds are that a perfectly efficient seat-distribution system—abetted by ubiquitous technology, sensors, and facial recognition—would have robbed us of one of the proudest moments in American history. Laws that are enforced by appealing to our moral or prudential registers leave just enough space for friction; friction breeds tension, tension creates conflict, and conflict produces change. In contrast, when laws are enforced through the technological register, there's little space for friction and tension—and quite likely for change.
>
> *(205)*

In short, technological management disrupts the assumption made by liberal lawyers that direct civil disobedience will be, and should be, available as an expression of responsible moral citizenship.

Suppose that legislation is introduced that specifically authorises or mandates the use of a suite of smart technologies on and around buses in order to maintain a system of racial segregation on public transport. Those who believe that the legislative policy is immoral might have opportunities to protest before the legislation is enacted; they might be able, post-legislation, to demonstrate at sites where the technology is being installed; they might be able to engage in direct acts of civil disobedience by interfering with the technology; and they might have opportunities for indirect acts of civil disobedience (breaking some other law in order to protest about the policy of racial segregation on public transport). Regulators might then respond in various ways—for example, by creating new criminal offences that are targeted at those who try to design round technological management. Putting this more generally, technological management might not altogether eliminate the possibility of principled moral protest. The particular technology might not always be counter-technology proof and there might remain opportunities for civil disobedients to express their opposition to the background regulatory purposes indirectly by breaking anti-circumvention laws, or by engaging in strategies of 'data obfuscation', or by initiating well-publicised 'hacks', or 'denial-of-service' attacks or their analogues.

Nevertheless, if the general effect of technological management is to squeeze the opportunities for traditional direct acts of civil disobedience, ways need to be found to compensate for any resulting diminution in responsible moral citizenship. By the time that technological management is in place, for many this will be too late; for most citizens, symbolic and evocative expressions of conscientious objection and non-compliance will no longer be an option. This suggests that the compensating adjustment needs to be *ex ante*: that is to say, it suggests that responsible moral citizens need to be able to air their objections before technological management has been authorised for a particular purpose; and, what is more, the opportunity needs to be there to challenge both an immoral regulatory purpose and the use of (morality-corroding) technological management.

In Chapter 22, assuming non-ideal conditions, we suggested that all human communities should build a precautionary approach into their governance so that the global commons is protected and preserved. This implies a precautionary approach to the use of technological management; and, arguably, this is particularly so for those communities with moral aspirations. Given that we do not know just how much space a moral community needs to have in order to safeguard against the automation of virtue and to sustain critical citizenship, a generous margin of operational space for moral reflection, for moral reason, and for moral objection should be maintained.

PART 5

Law's imperfect governance and its many challenges

29

LAW'S GOVERNANCE

The range of challenges

Introduction

Law's governance is about the making and administration of the group's rules, about the settling of conflicts and disputes within the group, and about setting and maintaining the policies and direction of the group. However, none of this will happen unless the group has first allocated the relevant governance responsibilities to particular members of the group or unless the group acquiesces in the de facto governance that is led by certain members of the group. Another way of putting this is to say that the group's first step towards governance will be its response to the question of who is to be accepted as having which roles and responsibilities in the governance of the group. To whom, or to which body, is 'authority' to be allocated for making the rules, dealing with disputes, and making policy decisions for the sake of the collective interest of the group?

Parks, vehicles, and dogs

In Chapter 9, we mentioned the hypothetical rule that prohibits taking vehicles into a park, our point being that there might be some scenarios in which the meaning of the rule and its application to the facts is contested. Suppose, though, it is admitted that, on the facts, the rule has been broken, a vehicle has been taken into the park. However, the person who has taken the vehicle into the park challenges the authority of those who have made the rule. On what basis, it is asked, do those who have made the rule rest their rule-making authority? If the rule-makers can trace their authority directly to a decision made by the local community, and if that group includes the

DOI: 10.4324/9781003507802-34

challenger, then that answers the question in a way that precludes objection by the challenger. However, in the majority of instances of law's governance, it will not be possible to trace explicit and personal authorisation back to the current members of the group that is subject to governance.

Even if there is no challenge to the authority of the rule-makers, the rules that they make for the use of the park might be contested, attracting little respect and proving largely ineffective in practice. In their book, *Orderly Britain* (2022), Tim Newburn and Andrew Ward remind readers about the concerns that have periodically erupted where owners are permitted to take their dogs into public parks. In the mid-1970s, the risk that children might catch diseases from dog faeces was one such case. This concern was taken very seriously in Burnley where the Borough Council passed a by-law that excluded all dogs, except guide dogs, in three of the town's public parks. For many dog owners, this was totally unacceptable and they had no compunction about breaking the rule. As one such dog owner, Herbert Johns, facing four charges of contravening the by-law, told the court:

> [He] believed in law and order, but he didn't believe in the by-law and wouldn't abide by it. He had fought for democracy and freedom with the Eighth Army during the Second World War, but that freedom was now being denied him 'by park rangers adopting KGB tactics'. 'What harm is there in walking a dog in a park?' Johns asked the court. 'What authority do these petty, pompous, big-headed councillors have to prevent me taking my dog into the park? This is a ridiculous situation for anyone to be in. I cannot believe that I can possibly be committed to prison for walking my dog in the park.
>
> *(Newburn and Ward, 22–23)*

His protestations notwithstanding, Johns was fined for breach of the by-laws; and, a year later, still not having paid his fine, he was jailed for five days by the local magistrates. In the end, law's governance prevailed but Johns was not the only protester, and nor was he the only protester who spent time in prison for the sake of their opposition to the by-law. Indeed, the Burnley dog owners even brought their protest to Number 10 Downing Street.

Challenges, discontent, and more challenges

In the chapters that follow in this part of the book, we highlight the challenges that face law's governance and the various kinds of discontent to which it can give rise. We start with the prospectus for law's governance, with what it promises, with the obvious difficulties associated with its promise, and with some anticipation of how it will disappoint. Where there are reservations about law's governance—for example, we might already have reservations about the promise of law or its actual delivery—then claims made either for the authority of law or that law should be respected are likely to be problematic. Accordingly, the next challenge to consider relates to maintaining the authority of law and respect for its governance.

Not surprisingly, politicians present their administration of law's governance in a positive light, always regulating at just the right time and in the right way. However, this sets a high bar when, as is the case today, law's governance has to engage with a raft of new technologies that can present novel questions, divide communities, and exacerbate the challenges that already confront law's governance. Moreover, as a lawyer, one of the first things that we notice with emerging technologies is that they present major challenges with regard to regulatory connection and sustainability, that is, a challenge in knowing both when to make a new rule intervention (neither too early nor too late) and how to sustain the connection between the rule and the technology once the intervention has been made.

This leads to chapters on what are perhaps the two principal regulatory challenges, irrespective of whether emerging technologies are on the governance radar. These are the challenges of regulatory effectiveness and regulatory acceptability or legitimacy. The former is a challenge because law is a human enterprise and humans, often guided by short-term and self-interested considerations, are not natural compliers with rules made by others. The latter is a challenge where communities of humans have competing and conflicting preferences, different priorities, and a plurality of values. For example, the Burnley by-law was not acceptable to some local dog owners but, for those who were concerned about the health hazards, it would not have been acceptable (or legitimate) to leave the parks open to dogs.

Finally, turning away from rule-making and the channelling of conduct, we look at the challenges confronting law's governance as it lays down processes and rules for the resolution of disputes and managing conflicts. Whereas rule-making and channelling are nowadays not just dominated by legislators and politicians, but also guided by a Law 2.0 regulatory mindset, in the case of disputes we might expect to be able to revert to traditional Law 1.0 thinking. However, where governance now defaults to regulatory modes of reasoning, we will also find that some will argue in a way that is not only both regulatory and more technological but also more preventive and managerial.

30

LAW'S PROMISE

Order, democracy, and justice

Introduction

Characteristically, the headline promise in the prospectus for law's governance is that it will bring with it the Rule of Law; the legal enterprise is committed to governance by rules, to putting an end to both arbitrary rule and to might being right. This headline promise generates the expectation that law's governance will establish (or restore) and maintain 'order' (connoting security, predictability, calculability, consistency and so on). Law's governance promises a haven against disorder, whether it is the disorder of a brutal state of nature or of a lawless Wild West.

More ambitiously, law's governance might also promise democracy, respect for the fundamental values of the community (such as human rights and human dignity), and justice. In this more ambitious version, law's governance promises more than crime control, more than dispute settlement, and more than sound administration; it promises systems of criminal *justice*, civil *justice*, and administrative *justice* (compare Adams and Brownsword, 2006).

In this light, we can anticipate that doubts and discontent with the promise of law's governance might arise because:

(i) the prospectus for a well-ordered society is judged to be insufficient (we want more from law's governance);
(ii) the prospectus for law's governance is not sufficiently geared for flexibility and the ability to respond to changing conditions or novel circumstances;

DOI: 10.4324/9781003507802-35

(iii) the prospectus commitment to instate just order, and to achieve just outcomes, is not credible;
(iv) the prospectus commitment to democratic principles will be counter-productive (e.g., by impeding the group's articulation of a sense of direction and progress towards its goals); or
(v) the prospectus offers no credible strategy for managing the tensions that might arise between the different elements of the promise of law's governance.

Having considered each of these reasons for questioning law's promise, we can then take a more radical view, drawing into the discussion the impact of emerging technologies on our attitudes towards law's promise.

Five reasons to question law's promise

We can say a little more about each of the five reasons that might cause us to question law's promise. An obvious reason is that we are not happy with the scope of law's promise but, echoing two themes from earlier chapters, we will find our doubts intensifying where law has to adjust to changing conditions and where it is confronted by a plurality of views and values.

The prospectus for a well-ordered society is insufficient

At first blush, the prospectus offered by law's governance for a well-ordered society sounds attractive and reasonably straightforward. In a well-ordered society, there will be rules that enable citizens to know where they stand and to anticipate how others will normally act. To be sure, compliance will not be perfect; our expectations must be realistic. Moreover, there will be occasions when professional advice is required—for example, citizens will want to be sure that when making their wills, they follow the correct legal protocols—but, in general, citizens will know not only what is expected of them but also what they can reasonably expect of others in their rule-guided society.

The core commitment of this prospectus is to the ideal of legality (Fuller, 1969; Brownsword, 2022a: Ch 4). Essentially, those who govern commit to giving those who are governed a fair warning of what is prohibited or required, especially where the rules are backed by sanctions. Hence, the rules should be promulgated, they should be clear, they should not involve any contradiction, and they should be relatively constant (lest citizens are unaware that the rules have changed). In the same way, this prospectus promises that citizens will have a fair opportunity for compliance. In line with this promise, those who govern should eschew enacting rules with which compliance is impossible as well as rules that are retrospective in their operation.

Moreover, the governors also commit to governing by the public rule-book. It follows that if what passes for law's governance falls short relative to this ideal of legality, then law will not have delivered on the well-ordered society that it promised.

However, even if we were satisfied that law's governance has a realistic chance of delivering a well-ordered society, we might not be content with this prospectus and its commitment to legality. We might think, for example, that this prospectus does not go far enough in laying the foundations for an order that is fair, just, and reasonable; or, we might be unconvinced that the prospectus has a strategy for dealing with circumstances in which governance that is geared for predictability and consistency needs to become more flexible and agile.

The prospectus for law's governance is not sufficiently geared for flexibility and the ability to respond to changing conditions or novel circumstances

Unless a society is static, law's governance needs to have some capacity for adjustment of the existing order as circumstances change; where the context is dynamic, order needs to be flexible, agile and responsive; and the more dynamic the context, the more dynamic law needs to be. So, in dynamic conditions, a well-ordered society will be striving for both predictability and responsiveness. However, where some want predictability more than adaptation and, at the same time, others want adaptation more than predictability, law will not be able to satisfy everyone. Inevitably, some will be discontent and we know that this is so even if the prospectus does not declare it explicitly.

The prospectus for just order is not credible

By contrast with the promise of a well-ordered society, the prospectus for just order looks anything but straightforward. A culture of, and commitment to, governance by rules is not sufficient; the rules must also be just. If that is the promise, this invites doubts from those who question whether those who govern will be able to discharge the burden of justification. On what basis, or by reference to which criteria or standards, will those who govern determine or judge that a rule (or its application) is just?

As we have seen in earlier chapters, where there is a plurality of moral views, the justice of law's governance will be contested. In some areas of law's governance, for example medical law and ethics, we see this issue in an acute form (for example, in tragic cases where no decision will be universally accepted as just); and we also see a chronic problem in finding a satisfactory answer to the question that we have about the criteria of justice and the basis for justifying our judgments about what is and is not just. Whether the argument for the justice of law's governance relies on the integrity of a process or on some supposedly axiomatic principles, the governed might reject either basis. Similarly, in our information societies, where much of the law relating to privacy and confidentiality, the right to know, and so on, is based on 'reasonable expectations', we have problems in finding compelling reference points for determining what is and is not reasonable and, with that, difficulty in finding compelling anchoring points for law that claims to be just (Borghi and Brownsword, 2023).

To be sure, we might act on the basis that the reference point for fairness, justice, and reasonableness is no more and no less than the preponderance of views in the community. However, there are several problems with this. One problem is that it might be difficult to identify what that preponderance is. In some cases, it might be clear that most members of the community subscribe to a particular view and that, while there might be dissenting views, they are very much in the minority. However, in other cases, the plurality might be made up of two dominant views, each of which has widespread support; or, it might be made up of several views, each with a significant body of support. In these latter cases, it is unclear which view reflects the preponderance. Another problem is that the community's views of what is reasonable or acceptable might involve a compression of moral and prudential judgments, of impartial judgment and personal preference and inclination. For moralists, polls of positive and negative attitudes are no substitute for a focused discussion of what is fair and just. These problems aside, even if the community's morality is clear and distinct, it is at best the moral judgment of a particular group at a particular time. If we think that there should be a critical distance between judgments of what is fair, just, and reasonable and the moral view that happens to prevail in the community, we will want a more compelling (critically grounded) reference point.

What we are looking for are foundations that no human, whether one of those who governs or one of those who is governed, can rationally reject. If we accept that the only anchoring points that are beyond rational disputation by humans are those on which humans, rational discourse, and disputation themselves are predicated, then communities that commit to law as a just order cannot find the foundations that they are looking for within their own legal orders; the foundations in question are *pre-conditions* for such legal orders. So, building on the idea already floated in earlier chapters, the legitimacy of a particular legal order starts with its respect for those pre-conditions and then it rests on the community's acceptance of the particular constitutional arrangements that it has put in place for establishing and maintaining order and settling disputes in a just manner.

The prospectus for democratic order will be counter-productive

Law's governance matters because, as we have emphasised, groups of humans will not be viable unless they have agreed on a basic code of conduct which serves, so to speak, as the rules of the road. In so doing, they will take a position on which conduct is acceptable, which unacceptable. Conduct that is treated as unacceptable will constitute 'wrongdoing' and, the code will need to specify what are judged to be reasonable responses to wrongdoing—whether these responses are in the nature of penalties or compensation, restoration, or performance. As communities evolve, the code of conduct and its specified responses to wrongdoing will need to be revised. Alongside its code of conduct, a group's scheme of governance will also specify the goals and objectives of the community. Initially, these goals and objectives might be relatively static, but, again, as the community evolves, as its sense of collective purpose extends beyond subsistence and survival, its direction of travel and its targets will need some revision. In developed political societies, the 'policy' priorities adopted by the governing class will be under constant review. Unless all members of the community endorse the governance positions that are taken and the policy choices that are made, these are likely to be focal points for discontent.

Some years ago, for example, while I was visiting the University of Cape Town, I heard much discussion and no little concern about the possibility that Sol Kerzner (https://en.wikipedia.org/wiki/Sol_Kerzner), the developer of the Sun City resort in South Africa, might be planning to expand his hotel and casino operation to the Cape. For those South Africans who believed that gambling was plain wrong, such an expansion would have been unwelcome. However, the rights and wrongs of gambling were not the principal talking point. Rather, the point was that the proposed site for the development was in an area of outstanding natural beauty on the Atlantic coast just South of Cape Town. If the necessary approvals for the development were given, it was understood that Kerzner would put up the money that would enable the post-Apartheid government to build a stock of social housing that would provide accommodation for the poorest members of the community. Whatever choice the government made, environment or housing, it would provoke discontent.

But, of course, it is not just housing or environment: in modern societies, a broad sweep of policy choices is made in the name of law's governance—policies, for instance, that relate to consumer protection, taxation, transport, welfare, immigration, and so on. The list is a long one. Whichever way we view the matter, the problem is that, in pluralistic societies, a commitment to democracy not only accentuates division, it is likely to delay decisions and it leads to a loss of direction.

Elaborating this doubt, the question is not about democratic governance in small homogeneous groups; rather, the concern is that law's governance will become counter-productive as it tries to keep faith with democratic principles in large-scale heterogeneous groups—indeed, in groups such as those that we now find in many modern nation states. The point is that a commitment to democracy engenders an expectation that there will be an opportunity to hear the many different voices that are held by the members of the community. Sometimes there will be a major gulf between the protagonists; at other times, the differences might be fine-grained; but, to the protagonists, their views always matter and they want them to be given fair consideration. However, this will only work where members have the maturity to accept that some decisions will not go their way.

Even if democracy is not destabilising, processes of inclusive consultation and transparent deliberation take time. This can mean that important national projects—such as major infrastructural projects (for example, airports, high-speed rail connections, nuclear power plants, and so on)—can take many years to begin, let alone to be completed. Moreover, if those with governance responsibilities try to cut corners or expedite the process—for example, by narrowing the scope of the consultation—this will provoke discontent with the process (and its outcome). Similarly, in pluralistic communities where no political party can command a clear majority, this can either compromise a clear sense of direction or lead to constant changes of direction.

The prospectus offers no credible strategy for managing the tensions that might arise between the different elements of the promise of law's governance

Several tensions might arise between (and within) the different elements of law's mission—for example, between order and democratic process, or between the static and dynamic dimensions of order itself. However, for the purposes of illustration, we can simply concentrate here on the tension between order and justice.

Any prospectus that conjoins the promise of order with the promise of justice is likely to run into difficulty in practice. From this perspective, the picture of law as order will always come up short if it cannot adjust to the occasional hard case. However, where the law is settled, any adjustment for the sake of justice in the particular case is likely to cut against calculability and order. That said, where pretty much everyone agrees that it would be unjust to decide a case in the particular way that is indicated by the rules or the precedents, then the reputation of any kind of order of law is at stake if it has no mechanism to ensure that an unjust decision is avoided. For sure, there is a dilemma here—as Lon Fuller (1958) reminds his readers, before there can be a *just* order, there has to be *order*. Nevertheless, once a certain level of order has been achieved, law's governance needs to have a strategy for dealing with glaring injustice other than reliance on the happenstance instinct for justice that motivates some judges.

Law's governance also needs a strategy for managing conflicts between the community's fundamental values so that order is maintained and members know where they stand. Notoriously, for example, a free press reflects the importance of free expression but it can impact on individual privacy and reputation. How is this tension to be managed? With difficulty is the answer. We might rely heavily on the idea of 'proportionality' as a device to manage the tension but this is less a way of resolving the tension than a prop to support a decision that has been made. With or without proportionality, there is likely to be ongoing doubt about the basis on which law's governance prioritises one fundamental value rather than another.

The impact of emerging technologies

Thus far, we have not asked how emerging technologies impact on the assessments that we might make of the promises made by law's governance. However, the place of technology is central to our radical introduction to law. So, we must now ask how the promise of law's governance—the promise for order, democracy, and justice—is impacted by emerging technologies.

Order

We might already be discontent with the promise of order and nothing more. It might be that we want law's governance to be more ambitious, to be committed to democratic principles or just order. Or, it might be that order is our priority but we are not confident that law's governance has a strategy for managing change and smoothing the transition to a new order.

Once we factor in emerging technologies, our existing doubts and discontent might be accentuated in all sorts of ways. For instance, if we are discontent with the tendency of law's governance towards an authoritarian approach, emerging technologies might intensify our concern with the commitment of those who govern to little more than bare order. In particular, we might worry that regulatory red lines in relation to emerging technologies—for example, the use of robots to carry out policing functions, or the arming of robocops (Levin, 2022)—will not be drawn in the right place relative to the collective interest or to a particular moral viewpoint. Similarly, if our concern is that new technologies might lead to new forms of unfair discrimination (such as genetic discrimination by insurers and employers) or accentuate existing inequalities (Eubanks, 2018), then we will worry that law's governance offers no assurance about the justice of the order it upholds.

If our concern is that law's governance will not be successful in managing change, then the introduction of new technologies will amplify this concern. Like compound interest, these technologies and their disruptions build on one another. Technology is an accelerator. Here, law's governance is challenged to support innovation and capture the benefits of new technologies while, at the same time, managing risks and safeguarding systems and values. However, there is no guarantee that law will always make the right regulatory response (to prohibit or to permit, to incentivise or disincentivise) at the right time or in the right way. In our dynamic technologically-driven societies, how confident can we be that law's governance will have the agility to negotiate the liminal spaces that connect the old order to the new (Brownsword, 2023)?

Democratic order

If law's governance promises to instate democratic order, then we might reject this as committing to too much or committing to too little. In the former case, our discontent reflects a concern that opening up participation will undermine the possibility of order; and, in the latter case, the concern is that there might still be injustice, amplified by new technologies, that are not tackled by law's governance.

For those who think that the promise of democratic order is the right commitment to make, the concern will be that new technologies will open up new questions, surrounded by new uncertainties, that we are ill-prepared to answer—sometimes because the democracy is not sufficiently well informed or lacks understanding, sometimes because the conversation throws up too many different and incompatible views. There is a sense in other words that our technological futures are arriving—bitcoins are being mined, crypto is attracting investment, autonomous taxis are running in San Francisco, NFTs are being bought and sold, ChatGPT is a cat that is already out of the bag, and so on—before we are ready to guide and control them through democratic processes.

Moreover, after Cambridge Analytica and Russian bots, we might also worry that emerging technologies will threaten democratic processes. Can law's governance ensure that new technologies do not bring further problems for the already toxic information ecosystem, that they will not be used to interfere with free and fair elections, and that reliance on technical experts in conjunction with the automation of governance will not de-centre (non-technical) humans from the democratic process?

Just order

If the promise made by law's governance is for just order, we might reject this because we think that there is no practical way of dealing with moral plurality and no rational basis for one view of justice rather than another. If too many cooks can spoil the broth then too many views of justice can undermine confidence in law's governance. Adding to a legacy of such doubt, we will have concerns that emerging technologies will accentuate the injustice of the digital divide as well as will invite various kinds of unjust discrimination, and we will fear that profiling technologies will mirror and compound existing injustices (Eubanks, 2018).

A hollow promise?

Whatever promises are made for law's governance, we are likely to be sceptical. According to Hartmut Rosa (2015: 252), 'the superiority of modern, democratic models of politics with respect to their predecessors and competitors rested above all on their ability to react to emerging needs in the various spheres of society in a sensitive, fast, and flexible way'. However, the cumulative effect of the technological transformation of communication, transportation, and so on has created a context in which we might be drawn to the conclusion that 'the time of modern politics has run out' (267). If this is right, it is small wonder that democracy has its discontents.

Arguably, the same applies to law's governance. That is to say, law's governance no longer has the capacity to shape and re-shape the social order; it simply cannot 'get out ahead' of changing conditions to set the terms of new frameworks and codes; the best that it can do is to react and react again. What is more, the commitment to democratic participation is not credible unless deliberative democracy is given time; and time is the one thing that law's governance no longer has on its side.

On this analysis, we might concede that the prospectus can be full of good intentions and that promises can be made but we will know that the reality will be a disappointment; we will know that, in its performance, law's governance is now bound to be inadequate and to lead to further discontent. Taking this line, we should not under-state the impact of high-tech development: these technologies do more than aggravate prior discontent with law's governance, they disable this particular mode of governance. For law's governance, time is of the essence; and, arguably, time is now up.

31

AUTHORITY OF LAWMAKERS AND RESPECT FOR LAW

Introduction

As a novice law student, I expected that some time would be spent making the case for law. Of course, those persons whose particular interests are protected by the law would be expected to act as advocates for its governance; but, even those who are not so lucky might see some virtue in the law. Famously, for example, the left-wing historian E.P. Thompson (1975: 266) declared that the Rule of Law was an 'unqualified good'. What should we make of this? What is the best case for the authority of lawmakers and respect for law's governance?

When I refer to my initiation into the study of law, it should be recalled that this was the 1960s; it was a time when students questioned established authority and when, on the other side of the Atlantic, there was a good deal of discontent with the law—in particular, there was the civil rights movement as well as protests against the draft and US involvement in the Vietnam war. In this context of protest and civil disobedience, why was law thought to be better than the alternatives? Indeed, what are the alternatives? If we are thinking about dystopian alternatives, such as a violent state of nature, or an unpredictable anarchic state of disorder, then the case for law might seem obvious. Equally, if we are thinking about utopian alternatives, then the case for law is perhaps that we should be realistic: utopias are just that, idealised visions, not practical options. At law school, we did not debate such matters but, with legal systems operating all around the world, perhaps there was nothing to debate: if groups of humans are prudent and realistic, then perhaps it is clear that they will instate a scheme of governance and, in nation states, this will take them to law's particular mode of governance.

DOI: 10.4324/9781003507802-36

Fast forwarding, we still have legal systems operating all around the world but our questions about the virtues of law's governance have not gone away. What we can say is that, if those who are governed are generally positively disposed towards those who govern and towards the rules that are made, then this is a favourable context for law's governance; it should be viable. However, the less positively disposed those who are governed are to a particular regime and its rules, then the circumstances are more challenging, the resistance is likely to be greater, and there will be some turbulence. Here, those who govern will have to appeal quite regularly to their own 'authority' and, at the same time, demand that those who are governed should respect the law. In this chapter, we can consider both authority and respect.

Authority

The authority of those who purport to govern in the name of law can be challenged in more than one way. For example, the dog owners who challenged the authority of the rule-makers in Burnley, did not claim that they had no authority to make rules for the use of public parks; what they objected to was the particular by-law that had been made and which excluded dogs. By contrast, in some quarters, we might find a fundamental scepticism about any claim to authority that is made on behalf of law. For example, it might be contended that law's governance is nothing more than an instrument for protecting and legitimising historic privilege, colonial force, and the interests of the propertied and commercial classes; even the Rule of Law has a 'dark side' and might itself be 'illegal' (Mattei and Nader, 2008). In this vein, we can imagine that whatever unilateral assertions of legal authority Russia might claim over Ukraine, they will be contested and rejected by not only the Ukrainian government in Kyiv but also by many who live in the occupied regions.

One step down from such total rejection, while recognising the general authority of those who govern a particular place or space, it might be claimed that those who govern lack 'competence' in relation to a particular matter. Potentially, this kind of question can be raised in any regime of law but it is particularly prevalent where we have multi-level governance—for example, as in the US (where the competence of federal bodies is likely to be carefully checked) and in the EU (where the jurisprudence regularly involves questions about the basis for Union competence, as in the famous *Tobacco Advertising* case (2000)); and, similarly, even in the UK, we see this kind of authority issue in the reference by the Lord Advocate to the UK Supreme Court (2022), where the question concerned the competence of the Scottish Parliament to legislate for the holding of a referendum on Scottish independence.

Or, again, while recognising both the general authority and the particular competence of those who govern, it might be objected that the authorisation is being misapplied in some way—for example, in the way that some may complain that, over the years, the European Court of Human Rights has expanded and exceeded (illegitimately) the scope of its authority, or as in the case of the protesting dog owners in relation to their local council in Burnley.

In all these examples, a group's discontent with the authority of a governing body might result in a question that is put to a court. Typically, the court will look to the authorising legal instrument (to a constitution or to a Convention or a Treaty, and so on) and then it will hand down its ruling. Some questions will be more fundamental than others but, so long as it is accepted that the authorising legal instrument is itself determinative, we will not yet have hit a truly foundational challenge. However, if those who are discontent also reject the authority of the authorising legal instrument, as is the case with colonial or imperial occupation, we have a big problem.

Thinking inside the box

For many jurists, the answer to questions about the authority of an ostensibly legal body or its acts are given by the constitution of the group, by the way in which the authority to undertake legal functions has been allocated in the constitution. Thus, in HLA Hart's (1961) articulation of the concept of law, any question about the authority (title) of a body or person undertaking a legal function (or claiming to act in a legal capacity) hinges on there being an appropriate mandate in an authorising rule. In the case of legislative and judicial bodies, this authorisation might be explicitly declared in the founding constitutional rules; in other cases, the authorisation will be found in rules that have themselves been made by authorised rule-makers.

However, this account gives rise to a puzzle about what authorising basis lies beyond the formal constitutional framework or the operative or traditional constitutional arrangements. In other words, if the chain of legal title takes us back to the constitution, or (what Hart terms) the rule of recognition, or some such apex rule or norm within the particular legal system, is there some further (higher or deeper) authorisation, or do we need to accept that, in the final analysis, the system purports to be self-validating? If the latter, then this means that the plausibility of all claims to authority within the system are contingent on acceptance of the apex rule as the ultimate test of authority. Given this puzzle, the challenge is either to find a more adequate basis for legal authority or to concede that the authority of law and particular constitutional arrangements rests on acceptance and acquiescence.

Two radical questions

Thinking radically about the challenges to law's authority, we might ask two important questions. First, do new technologies increase or amplify the challenges to law's authority? Secondly, and conversely, do these technologies ease the challenges?

Increasing the challenge

Responding to the first question, while we might view the development of blockchain and cryptocurrencies as an *indirect* challenge to the authority of law's governance (compare De Filippi and Wright, 2018), it is with the development of cyberspaces that we find the most striking aggravation of the discontent that we might already have with regard to the authority of our governing bodies.

Already, we have met John Perry Barlow's (1994) Declaration of the Independence of Cyberspace and noted Joel Reidenberg's (2005) concerns about the way in which the 'Internet separatists' were prepared to flout the authority of law. In line with this analysis, Chris Reed and Andrew Murray (2018) argue that, whatever the plausibility of claims to authority in offline analogue legal systems, these do not translate across to the online environments of cyberspace. In the latter, where individuals are presented with a plurality of authority and legitimacy claims, the self-validating claims of national legal systems will not suffice. Taking acceptance by the individual as focal, Reed and Murray conclude that 'the legitimacy, efficacy and normative acceptance of law norms in the online environment are predicated upon their acceptance by the community and by the individual in that community' (at 228). In other words, claims to authority are not vindicated by constitutional declaration or by the practice of officials who are authorised by such declaration, but depend on recognition and acceptance by the community and its individual members. That said, we should not assume that self-governing techy communities will find it all plain sailing. Already, for example, we have seen blockchain groups fall out about the use of forks to make a fresh start following a hack (famously so in the case of the multi-million dollar hack at the DAO in 2016: see Low and Yeo, 2017).

Nevertheless, and to look ahead, if enthusiasts for the Metaverse (Ball, 2022) are right in predicting that many humans will spend most of their time 'immersed' in a parallel virtual world, and if those humans prefer either self-governance or the technological governance of the latter to law's governance of the 'real' world—indeed, especially so, if those who migrate to the Metaverse do so precisely because of their disenchantment with rule-based human governance in the real world—then we will have another space in which participants might present a challenge to the authority of law's real world governance.

Decreasing the challenge

Turning to the second question, might technology operate in the opposite direction by diminishing the challenge to law's authority? Recalling my earlier remarks about the design of modern airports (and the impact that this has on the channelling of passengers), the persistent radical thought is that technology might help us to 'do governance' better, not just at airports but generally. Might technology help to address not only some of our discontent but also the causes of our discontent? In particular, the idea is that governance might be improved in two principal ways.

First, there is the prospect of technologies reducing the influence of those self-serving and short-termist human considerations that weaken law's governance. For example, where new tools are deployed in the criminal justice system—for example, surveillance, recognition, and locating technologies—the signal to humans who see an opportunity for non-compliance is that they are more likely to be detected and convicted. Moreover, where governance is automated, the human factor (including reliance on humans to apply and to enforce the law) might be further reduced or even eliminated. As David Goddard remarks, '[c]omputers do not have overflowing in-trays or influential cousins, or require side payments to do their job' (Goddard, 2022: 130). On the face of it, the promise here is of governance that is both more effective and more efficient. Secondly, recalling the technological governance of the golf carts at Westways, there is the prospect, through technological management, of reducing reliance on rules and, thereby, narrowing the practical opportunities for non-compliance.

For the sake of argument, let us suppose that new tools for governance do improve the channelling of humans. Nevertheless, it does not follow that humans will more readily recognise whatever 'authority' is claimed for governance by smart machines. Humans might feel devalued by the transfer of governance functions to machines and some might question whether it makes sense to claim or concede 'authority' in relation to this kind of governance. In other words, radical thinking might take us to a point, not so much where concerns about the authority of law's governance are eased but where law's governance is replaced by a different mode of governance, a mode that changes the context in a way that makes the concept of authority redundant.

Putting this in another way, where humans cede authority to fellow humans, or to a body or group of humans, the former might well have reservations about how the latter will exercise their authority. However, freely to cede authority is to commit to respecting exercises of authority; our reservations (both initial and continuing) notwithstanding. By contrast, where humans cede control to smart machines, and where they do so in a context in which it is recognised that governance by machines is a better form of governance, then this threshold recognition overcomes whatever reservations there might have been. Once governance has been delegated to the machines, not only does it make no sense to have reservations about their authority, it makes no sense to ask whether the machines have authority—or, at any rate, it makes no sense unless we turn our idea of authority (with reservations) upside down and treat the paradigmatic case of authority as that in which we have no reservations about those who are responsible for governance.

These remarks imply that both claims to legal authority and the demand that law's governance should be respected take their meaning and practical significance from a context in which those who are governed might have reservations about those humans who have governance responsibilities or their performance. But, if governance by technologies takes the enterprise to super-human levels, the context changes in a way that impacts on our thinking about both the authority of law and our respect for law. This takes us to the next part of the chapter: the challenge facing law's governance in earning the respect of those who are governed.

Respect for law

A question that has troubled me from my first days as a law student is why we should respect 'the law', simply because it is 'the law' (Brownsword, 2022b). Why should we comply with and support the law even where we have reservations about it? In response to this question, we might expect the positives of law's governance—particularly, the commitment to legality and the Rule of Law—to be accentuated and/or law to be presented as being preferable to the alternatives. However, as Margaret Atwood (2023: 252) remarks:

> Some people are fond of invoking 'the rule of law,' but they should remember that there have been some very unjust laws. The Nuremburg Laws—directed against Jews—were laws. The Fugitive Slave Act was a law. The decree forbidding literacy for American slaves in the South was a law. The Roman grind-the-peasant tax laws were laws. I could go on for a very long time on that subject.

Point taken surely. Still, in the context of failed states, or in zones where there has been a breakdown of law and order, we might agree that law is better than the alternatives and that law's governance needs our support if it is to get off the ground in adverse conditions. However, this is not an unconditional endorsement of law or of the demand that law should always be respected simply because it is the law. In contexts that are more favourable for law's governance, those who are critical of its operation might argue that respect has to be earned rather than taken as read. In this kind of context, the argument is likely to hinge on how much respect law can demand simply by virtue of its commitment to legality and the Rule of Law.

Legality and the Rule of Law

As we have noted in earlier chapters, the idea of legality is taken to involve a commitment to governance by rules: those who govern will declare the rules, the rules will be enforced, and in the event of there being disputes they will be arbitrated by reference to the rules. In Lon Fuller's work (1969), this commitment to rule by rules reflects a practice of fair dealing with citizens; those who are governed are not tricked or trapped, they have a fair opportunity to comply, and they are fairly warned about the rules and the penalties for non-compliance. These are important considerations but they do not go as far as constraining the content of the rules.

When we turn to the Rule of Law, or the rule of rules, we again start with the procedural virtues of legality. But, how will respect be sustained in communities that are not only concerned about the content of the rules but also are morally and prudentially divided? Here, support for the Rule of Law is likely to evaporate as law's governance has to take a position on questions that are deeply contested (as, of course, they frequently are). On this view, the lowest common denominator is the procedural commitment to rules and this is where consensus and respect for the law has to be forged.

The upshot of this is that a case might be made for respect for the law, based on the procedural virtues of legality, but it cannot be a case for unconditional respect whatever reservations we might we have. For, our deepest reservations are likely to lie in precisely the area that the Rule of Law hesitates to colonise, that is to say, the area of substantive values. So, here is the dilemma: we can limit the Rule of Law to procedural features of law's governance and argue that *other things being equal* we should respect the law simply because it is the law—but this allows for respect to be withdrawn whenever we have significant reservations about the substance of law; or, we can try to neutralise at least some of these substantive reservations and strengthen respect by listing some substantive values as features of the Rule of Law—but, if we define the Rule of Law as not only the rule of rules but also the rule of some particular values, those who reject these values are unlikely to respect law's governance and very likely to renounce the Rule of Law (compare Bingham, 2011).

If we are to find a basis for respect for law's governance, simply because it is the law and our reservations notwithstanding, we will need to think outside the box. Moreover, it is by responding to this prompt for fresh thinking that we will illuminate the claim that law's governance, and legal education, is ultimately about being civilised.

Thinking outside the box

If law's governance is to merit our respect simply because it is the law and our particular reservations notwithstanding, those who are governed need to have trust and confidence that those who govern are doing so with integrity and in the interests of those who are governed. In this spirit, we can take it that governance should be (i) compatible with respect for the global commons (which, as we argued in Chapter 22, represent the foundational conditions for the possibility of governance), (ii) in line with the community's fundamental values, and (iii) socially acceptable within the community.

If the global commons is first base, humans start building their communities at second base. It is here that they declare their distinctive values, as well as their distinctive conception of cornerstone values (such as respect for human dignity) and define themselves as the particular people that they aspire to be. Where there are questions about the interpretation or application of these values, it will fall to the community's laws and legal institutions to respond. It is, of course, essential that whatever the fundamental values to which a particular community commits itself they should be consistent with (or cohere with) the commons' conditions. It is the commons that sets the stage for community life; and then, without compromising that stage, particular communities form and self-identify with their own distinctive values.

Beyond governance that respects the global commons as well as the fundamental values of the particular community, we expect that the positions taken or policies adopted must be socially acceptable. For law to command respect at this level, it must employ governance processes that have integrity. Hence, law's governance must have given the members of the community a fair opportunity to present their views and, where there are conflicting views, the accommodation reached must be (relative to the community's own standards) not wholly unreasonable.

Consider, for example, proposals for the adoption of new technologies (robots, AI, digital doctors, and so on) in healthcare as a case in point. The functions performed by the technology might be in the nature of governance (such as making triage decisions) or they might be diagnostic or surgical, and so on. Whatever the function, while some persons, regretting the loss of the human touch, will insist that the application of technologies should always be 'human-centric', others will welcome smart governance and 24/7 intelligent care. More generally, while some will push for a permissive regulatory environment that is facilitative of beneficial innovation, others will push back against healthcare practice that gives rise to concerns about the safety and reliability of particular technologies as well as their compatibility with respect for fundamental values. Yet, how are the interests in pushing forward with research into and the adoption of potentially beneficial health technologies to be reconciled with the heterogeneous interests of the concerned who seek to push back against them?

In such a scenario, the first priority will be to pick out those aspects of the proposals that touch and concern the global commons or the fundamental values of the community. To the extent that the proposals are incompatible with respect for these conditions, they are 'non-starters'. However, assuming that the proposals can satisfy these conditions, we get to the matter of their social acceptability. Let us assume that, following serious public consultation on the proposals and members of the community having had a fair hearing, regulators take a position on the proposals which they present as a reasonable (or not unreasonable) accommodation of the various interests. There are a number of ways in which we might think that such a model of social acceptability is less than ideal—for example, because it allows all interests (self-serving or community-serving prudential as well as other-regarding ethical) to be flattened in the balancing process; there is no ranking of interests; and, there are too many positions that can be presented as reasonable. Nevertheless, this might be the best that we can expect at this level.

Of course, at each point, law's governance might take up positions that are not the ones that we would favour. To some extent, it might be possible to mitigate the hardship for those who have reservations, not just as a matter of preference or personal advantage, but as a matter of moral commitment—for example, as we have emphasised before, the law should recognise some space for conscientious objection and it should be open to review and reconsideration. However, where law is faced with a plurality of conflicting and competing views, it cannot satisfy everyone; and, as we emphasised back in Chapter 3, the mark of a civilised society is that members understand that their view cannot always be the one that prevails. Law's governance is civilising but it needs help from communities whose members also conduct themselves in a civilised way.

In sum, what we humans should categorically respect is not so-called legal systems or particular laws but governance that makes a serious attempt to maintain and protect the global commons. If we have reservations about particular laws, we should recognise that it might not be possible to please everyone; and, if we are to act on and press our reservations, we should ensure that we do not jeopardise the global commons and always give credit to governance that is generally directed at sustaining the commons' conditions.

32

GETTING REGULATION RIGHT

The politicians' claim

Introduction

At the time of the pandemic, senior members of the government regularly assured the British public that they were confident about the regulatory interventions that they were making—that these were the right interventions being made at the right time. Even though tens of thousands of people had died, even though there were obviously difficult choices to be made about protecting public health as well as the economy and the public finances, and even though there were plenty of critical voices—not least, highlighting the impact of the lockdown restrictions on freedom of movement and association and the implications for privacy of the surveillance and reporting measures—the government insisted that it had got the regulation right. While the government might have been right in reminding the public that the pandemic presented an unprecedented challenge, the confident claims made by the government for its regulatory interventions were actually political business as usual.

Introducing new laws or regulations, politicians like to insist that their regulatory interventions are fit for purpose, that they will be effective in serving government policy. Expanding this claim, politicians will claim that they are making the right kind of intervention (neither over-regulating nor under-regulating), that they are using the right tools (which, traditionally, would be rules or principles, and which would represent the optimal mix of clear guidance and flexibility), and that they are making their intervention at the right time (neither regulating too early nor too late). However, when technologies emerge and catalyse rapid change, each part of the politicians'

DOI: 10.4324/9781003507802-37

claim is bolder because, if not unprecedented, the governance challenges are all the more difficult in such a context.

In this chapter, we can begin to address the politicians' regulatory claim by saying a few words about the pace at which new technologies develop and move on before considering the implications for regulatory connection and sustainability. We will deal with other elements of the claim in the following two chapters.

A workshop in Israel

About 25 years ago, a colleague and I were invited to speak at a consumer law workshop in Jerusalem. At the workshop, the participants were trying to assess the legal implications of the early development of e-commerce and e-money. Of course, at that time, AI and machine learning did not figure in those conversations. Rather, I recall conversations about the applicability of the principles of contract law to online transactions—for example, there were questions about how we contract lawyers should characterise the kind of online advertisements that we could then see and when precisely an online acceptance would be treated as taking effect (Brownsword and Howells, 1999); and, I also recall conversations about the acceptability of e-money, this being prompted by an early trial of the Mondex card in Swindon which suggested that, even if consumers might be happy enough with payment cards, there was likely to be some push-back from traders if they were required to pay for the terminals (https://en.wikipedia.org/wiki/Mondex). However, the conversation that has stayed with me is one that I had at the airport, with a security officer, as I was leaving Israel.

This conversation at the airport did not start well. The security officer wanted to know why I had been in Jerusalem and what I had been doing there. Not anticipating this parting interrogation, I had packed my letter of invitation from the Ministry of Justice together with the workshop papers in my suitcase which, by now, I had checked in. However, as soon as I said that we had been discussing online shopping at the workshop, the mood changed. The officer expressed surprise: evidently, she was not aware that consumers could buy things online. What followed was less about me and more about the kind of goods that were already being offered for sale online (mainly books and CDs) and about how e-commerce might evolve and grow.

Had I known then what I know now about the growth of the online marketplace, about digital goods and services, about the harvesting of data, about the Internet of Things, about AI and consumer profiling, about platforms for consumer goods and services, and about online payment rails, this conversation would have been somewhat different. To be sure, even with the displacement of both offline retailing and the traditional cash economy, the conversation might have ended in a positive way with the security officer, qua consumer, looking forward to online consumer marketplaces together with the AI-enabled provision of digital goods and services. On the other hand, there might have been some reservations about where we were heading including questions about the governance challenges that we might face—for example, questions about the governance of data, about liability for various kinds of harm that is caused by AI, about the legal obligations to be placed on suppliers of digital goods and services, about the responsibilities of platform operators, and about the risks to which consumers might be exposed in these online transactional environments. Moreover, looking ahead, there might have been speculation and questions about how AI and consumer markets might evolve. For example, there might have been questions about the extent to which digital assistants would act for individual consumers; about whether consumption (from the ordering of goods and services, through to their supply, and any compensatory adjustments that need to be made) would be fully automated; about whether commerce and consumption would largely become a conversation between machines; and about whether consumers who crave for old-style retail experiences might find them in high-end immersive malls or in the everyday Metaverse. How, we might have wondered, would the law protect the interests of consumers in such a world?

Whatever the future may hold for consumers, for AI, and for the suite of technologies that will provide the infrastructure for the provision of goods and services, the question for the next generation of lawyers is whether we are ready for it. Twenty-five years ago, we did not really know where e-commerce would take us or what the legal issues would be. Today, we certainly know more than we did back then but one senses that, as the technologies associated with online transactions and interactions become more sophisticated, the regulatory learning curve gets steeper.

No doubt, politicians will continue to claim that their regulatory interventions are made at the right time. However, with the acceleration in technological development and the variety of applications, how confident can we be that politicians are on the appropriate learning curve? How confident can we be that law's governance can be operationalised in a way that ensures making a timely and sustainable connection?

Regulatory connection and sustainability

For some time, it has been understood that the pace at which modern technologies are developed and applied presents a distinctive challenge to lawmakers who seek to enact a regulatory framework in a traditional legislative form. The challenge is: How do regulators get connected to these technologies, and how do they stay connected? As John Perry Barlow (1994) famously remarked:

> Law adapts by continuous increments and at a pace second only to geology in its stateliness. Technology advances in…lunging jerks, like the punctuation of biological evolution grotesquely accelerated. Real world conditions will continue to change at a blinding pace, and the law will get further behind, more profoundly confused. This mismatch is permanent.

Whether one looks at the regulation of information technology or the regulation of biotechnology—or, for that matter, at the regulation of nanotechnology or the technologies associated with the new brain sciences, let alone blockchain, AI and machine learning—there seems to be ample support for Barlow's thesis. Indeed, it is arguable that the pace of technological development, already too fast for the law, is accelerating. Whilst this is not an easy matter to measure, there are at least three respects in which modern information technology, in addition to being significant in its own right, plays a key enabling role relative to other technologies—facilitating basic research in biotechnology (spectacularly so in the case of sequencing the human genome), providing the computing power for the development of machine learning, and enabling the commercial exploitation of the products of other technologies.

Given that technological innovation speeds up the pace of change, it follows that the faster the innovation, the faster law's governance needs to go (Rosa, 2015). This tests the flexibility of law's governance and its ability to maintain effective order during the transition to a new order. How, then, is law's governance going to respond in the right way and at the right time? In easy cases, it will be very clear what the right response is—it will be clear, for example, that a particular application of a new technology needs to be prohibited—and from this it follows that an urgent intervention is required (the right time for intervention is not in doubt). For most nation states, the prospect of human reproductive cloning was wholly unacceptable and legal prohibitions were introduced at once. However, there will be other technologies, such as cryptocurrencies or the platform economy, where some communities see the clear need for urgent intervention but others want to wait and see, delaying their response until they have a clear profile of the risks and benefits. Famously, as David Collingridge (1982) pointed out, regulators face a dilemma: whichever approach is taken, it might prove to be a mistake. Intervention that is premature might not only miss the target but also it might stifle beneficial innovation; conversely, intervention that is delayed might eventually identify the right target but, in the meantime, delay will create some uncertainty (people will not know where they stand, this hindering the effectiveness of order) and, in some cases, it might be impractical to make the desired intervention because the technology is already too widely embedded in the practices of the community.

Technology is capable of leaving the law behind at any phase of the regulatory cycle: that is to say, before regulators have anything resembling an agreed position, before the terms of the regulation are finalised, and once the regulatory deal is in place. For example, a new technology might emerge very quickly, catching regulators (at any rate, national legislators) cold; or it might be that a controversial new technology develops and circulates long before regulators are able to agree upon the terms of their regulatory intervention. While regulators are getting up to speed, or pondering their options and settling their differences, the technology moves ahead, operating in what for the time being at least amounts to, if not a regulatory void, at least a space in need of regulatory attention. As Michèle Finck (2018: 64) (thinking about the Internet and, potentially, distributed blockchain technologies) rightly remarks: 'When systems with regulation-defiant features are adopted on a large scale, social norms will shift to reject regulatory intervention. In such a setting regulation not only becomes hard from a technical perspective; it also becomes politically unattainable'.

Even (or especially) when regulatory frameworks have been put in place, they enjoy no immunity against technological change. For example, the UK Human Fertilisation and Embryology Act 1990 was overtaken by developments in embryology (in particular, the ability to carry out genetic engineering in eggs which are then stimulated without fertilisation rather than in embryos) as well as by the unanticipated use of new embryo-screening procedures to identify embryos that would be tissue-compatible with a born child who was in need of a bone marrow transplant (the so-called 'saviour sibling' cases); and, notoriously, data protection laws are soon outpaced by both technological development and the purposes for which personal data are collected and processed.

Currently, EU lawmakers are undertaking a comprehensive updating of the regulatory deals that were put in place for the governance of the early years of the online world. As we emphasised earlier in this chapter, this is not ancient history; these original deals were negotiated only a couple of decades ago. However, it is salutary to note just how quickly the laws that were once thought fit for purpose in protecting the interests of consumers and data subjects are now so disconnected from our online environments.

33

REGULATORY EFFECTIVENESS

Introduction

As a law student in the 1960s, the question of whether laws were 'effective' was not part of the curriculum; and, if there were systematic attempts to follow-up on regulatory interventions to check that they were having the intended impact, I was not aware of them. Yet, it was pretty obvious that criminal law, contract law, and tort law did not work—or, at any rate, did not work *perfectly*—in the sense that, these laws notwithstanding, crimes were committed, contracts were broken, and accidents happened. To the extent that these laws were about correcting wrongs (by punishing wrongdoers and compensating victims), perhaps a qualified case for their effectiveness might have been made out. But, by the 1970s, socio-legal scholars were taking a much harder look at the impact of laws that clearly had regulatory purposes to assess whether they were effective. In some cases, notably the prevention of crime and criminality, the verdict was pretty negative; little if anything seemed to work. In other cases, laws were worse than 'damp squibs'; not only did they fail to achieve their intended effects, they had unintended negative effects.

Since that time, a good deal of research effort has been expended in tracking the impact of particular legal interventions. Some interventions work reasonably well; but, as we have said, many do not—many are relatively ineffective or have unintended negative effects (see Gash, 2016). Moreover, in our connected world, we also know that the cross-boundary effects of the online provision of goods and services have compounded the challenges faced by regulators. If we synthesise this body of knowledge, what do we understand about the conditions for regulatory effectiveness?

DOI: 10.4324/9781003507802-38

The conditions for regulatory effectiveness

Broadly speaking, what we now understand is that context and circumstances matter, that people matter, and that the effectiveness of regulation can be impacted by third-party interference.

The first thing that we know is that context and circumstances matter. Some contexts are more conducive than others to making effective regulatory interventions. In some contexts, regulators will be pushing at an open door. By contrast, where the context encourages corruption (whether in the way that those who govern set the standards, or in their monitoring of compliance, or in their responses to non-compliance), or where the circumstances invite 'capture' by regulatees, or where regulators are operating with inadequate resources, the effectiveness of regulatory interventions will be compromised. We also know that attempts to improve the efficiency and effectiveness of regulators by highlighting performance indicators and setting targets are likely to have mixed results including some serious unintended effects (Bussani, Cassese, and Infantino, 2023).

Secondly, we also know that it might be regulatees who are the problem. Generally, it seems that regulators do better when they act with the backing of regulatees (with a consensus rather than without it). Putting this another way, compliance or non-compliance hinges not only on self-interested instrumental calculation but also (and significantly) on the normative judgments that regulatees make about the morality of the regulatory standard, about the legitimacy of the authority claimed by regulators, and about the fairness of legal processes (Tyler, 2006). However, regulatee resistance can be traced to more than one kind of perspective, including the perspective of groups who prefer to operate in a self-governing way. Business people (from producers and retailers through to banking and financial service providers) may respond to regulation as rational economic actors, viewing legal sanctions as a tax on certain kinds of conduct, and, famously, business contractors tend to be guided by their own market norms rather than the formal rules of contract law (Macaulay, 1963); professional people (such as lawyers, accountants, and doctors) like to, and are expected to, follow their own codes of conduct; the police are stubbornly guided by their own 'cop culture'; and, occasionally, resistance to the law is required as a matter of conscience—witness, for example, the peace tax protesters, physicians who ignore what they see as unconscionable legal restrictions, members of religious groups who defy a legally supported dress code, and the like.

In all these cases, the critical point is that regulation does not act on an inert body of regulatees: law's governance is directed at humans who have their own minds and their own agendas. Accordingly, those who are governed will respond to regulation in their own way—sometimes by complying with it, sometimes by ignoring it, sometimes by resisting or repositioning themselves, sometimes by relocating, and so on. Sometimes those who oppose the regulation will seek to overturn it by lawful means, sometimes by unlawful means; sometimes the response will be strategic and organised, at other times it will be chaotic and spontaneous. But, regulatees have minds and interests of their own; they will respond in their own way; and the nature of the response will be an important determinant of the effectiveness of the regulation.

Thirdly, the problem might be various kinds of external distortion or interference with the regulatory signals. Some kinds of third-party interference are well-known—for example, regulatory arbitrage (which is a feature of company law and tax law) is nothing new. However, even where regulatory arbitrage is not being actively pursued, the effectiveness of local regulatory interventions can be reduced as regulatees take up more attractive options that are available elsewhere.

Although externalities of this kind continue to play their part in determining the fate of a regulatory intervention, it is the emergence of the Internet that has most dramatically highlighted the possibility of interference from third parties. As long ago as the closing years of the last century, David Johnson and David Post (1996) predicted that national regulators would have little success in controlling extra-territorial on-line activities, even though those activities have a local impact. While national regulators are not entirely powerless, the development of the Internet has dramatically changed the regulatory environment, creating new vulnerabilities to cybercrime and cyberthreats, as well as new on-line suppliers, and community cultures. For local regulators, the question is how they can control access to drugs, or alcohol, or gambling or direct-to-consumer genetic testing services when Internet pharmacies, or online drinks suppliers, or casinos or the like, all of which are hosted on servers that are located beyond the national borders, direct their goods and services at local regulatees.

Reacting to these challenges to Law 2.0 regulatory effectiveness, the thought occurs that social control might be more effective if new technologies were to be utilised as regulatory instruments. In particular, if human regulators were to be taken out of the equation, this might prevent corruption and capture; and, if those humans who are governed have no practical option (because of technical measures) other than 'compliance', then this might eliminate regulatee resistance. With these radical thoughts, we are on the cusp of Law 3.0.

The seeds of ineffectiveness; the human factor

Following up on the remarks just made, it bears emphasis that law's governance is a *human* enterprise. Just as political commentators are fond of explaining things by saying 'It's the economy, stupid!', commentators on law's relatively ineffective governance should explain this by saying 'It's the human factor, stupid!'

Of course, some humans might try to 'perfect' themselves but, for the most part, humans are what they are: they incline towards self-governance; they default to self-interest and are prone to acting on short-term calculation; they have a range of dynamic capacities—imaginative and innovative, enquiring and questioning, constructive and critical; they are heterogeneous in their preferences and principles; they are driven by their basic needs; and, they are 'at risk' because of their physical vulnerabilities and biological characteristics. From this list, we can highlight the significance of the human tendency to default to self-interest and short-termism, and the human capacity for innovation.

Self-interest and short-termism

According to the philosopher AC Grayling (2022: 8), the human condition is characterised by a 'double-edged Law … of self-interest'. The leading edge of this Law states that 'Anything that CAN be done WILL be done if it brings advantage or profit to those who can do it'. Its corollary states that 'What CAN be done will NOT be done if it brings costs, economic or otherwise, to those who can stop it'. So, where x can be done, for law's governance to control the undesirable exercise of self-interest, it has to take on those who will benefit from legal permission or support for the doing of x and who will resist legal prohibition or restriction on the doing of x; and, where x can and should be done, law has to face up to those who will incur costs if the doing of x is permitted and who will resist legal requirements or permissions in relation to the doing of x.

That said, humans do not act only in self-interested ways. As the social and cultural psychologist Jonathan Haidt observes, humans, as we know them today, exhibit a 'strange mix of selfishness and selflessness' (Haidt, 2012: 222). Human nature might be 'mostly selfish' (Haidt, ibid.) but humans are capable of acts of altruism and, in many cases, 'they are willing to cooperate and work for the good of the group, even when they could do better by slacking, cheating, or leaving the group' (Haidt, ibid.). Humans, we can concede, are not one-dimensional, and their behaviour is not entirely predictable.

Starting with those who have governance responsibilities, it is clear that the effectiveness of the intended legal order can be compromised by a self-serving lack of integrity, by corruption and capture, and the like. Moreover, some governance regimes encourage those who govern to act on a short-term basis. But, this is not the whole story. For example, the effectiveness of law's governance can be limited by a lack of resources (particularly where regulatory agencies are understaffed or are constrained by inadequate budgets or where, as increasingly is the case, effective governance of new technologies presupposes a certain level of specialist expertise).

On the part of those who are governed, self-interest and short-term satisfaction certainly weaken the order by encouraging opportunist crime and they also militate against longer-term planning and policy (which one would expect to be benefits of a well-ordered society). However, the responses of those who are governed to the legal order are more complex (Newburn and Ward, 2022). As we have already noted, compliance or non-compliance hinges not only on self-interested instrumental calculation but also (and significantly) on the normative judgments that regulatees make about the morality of the regulatory standard, about the legitimacy of the authority claimed by regulators, and about the fairness of regulatory processes.

The human capacity for innovation

In industrialised societies, it is hard to separate 'innovation' from '*technological* innovation'. Nevertheless, even in a low-tech context, we can see in any kind of human innovation (such as the adoption of a division of labour or specialisation, or the development of a credit economy and novel financial instruments) the creation of a pressure for change and the seeds of discontent with law's governance.

First, law's governance will be challenged by the tension between the conservative inclinations and interests of some members of the community confronted by the progressive inclinations and interests of others who propose new ways of doing things (new business models, for example) and new things to be done.

Secondly, innovative practices are disruptive and law's governance needs to manage change. As we have said several times, it will not do for law's governance to set the basic order of the community and then sit back. Innovation introduces dynamic elements which demand an agile response by law. The more innovation that there is, the more difficult it is for law to govern in a way that smooths the process of change, satisfying the interest in continuity as well as the interest in progress and efficiency.

Thirdly, there is no guarantee that those who benefit from innovation are also those who bear the risks or downside burdens (Wolff, 2010). This can provoke a good deal of discontent about the distributive injustice of the situation and law's governance will do well to manage the inevitable discontent that will follow once a regulatory position has been taken.

In sum, we should never forget that law is a human enterprise; it is governance of humans by humans; and, whether we focus on those humans who govern or on those who are governed, we can see all too well the ways in which the human factor will challenge the effectiveness of laws.

34

REGULATORY ACCEPTABILITY AND LEGITIMACY

Introduction

When Burnley Borough Council considered closing some of its public parks to dogs, it was faced by a range of views, some arguing for more restriction and others arguing for less. The challenge was to find an accommodation of these conflicting and competing views that was at least reasonable and workable. Local politics like national politics involves a high degree of pragmatism. However, even if we were to concede that, in the circumstances, the council made the best accommodation that we could reasonably expect it to make, we might still ask whether the by-law was 'really legitimate'. In other words, even if we conceded that, in the circumstances, the by-law was 'acceptable', we might still demand more. But, what is the test of regulatory acceptability and what would it take for a particular act of law's governance, such as the Burnley by-law, to be *really* legitimate?

Regulatory acceptability

There are several ways in which we might characterise a regulatory intervention that we judge to be 'acceptable'. For example, we might take a particularly undemanding line, holding that it suffices if those who are governed are ready to accept, or acquiesce in relation to, some particular act of governance. In other words, it is enough for regulatory acceptability if those who are governed simply go along with their governance. This allows for all manner of 'legitimating' narratives and pathologies on the part of the governing class and regulatory acceptability in this sense should not be confused with legitimacy.

DOI: 10.4324/9781003507802-39

Taking a more demanding approach, we might judge the matter entirely by reference to the process that has led to the rule or ruling. Provided the process has been conducted in a way that meets whatever criteria we specify (such as transparency, inclusivity, equal voice, integrity, and so on), then we will judge it to be acceptable. Whether or not we, or anyone else agrees with the outcome, is irrelevant. Or, we might qualify a purely processual test by demanding that the outcome falls somewhere within the community's bandwidth of reasonableness (on which, see Chapter 16).

A somewhat different approach holds that 'acceptability' is to be differentiated from legitimacy. The context for judgments of regulatory acceptability is one in which members of a community express their preferences and priorities in relation to their own interest, or their assessment of what is in the community's collective interest. In other words, the considerations here are entirely prudential (see, e.g., our discussion of regulatory signals in Chapter 14). This is to be distinguished from judgments of 'legitimacy' where the considerations are exclusively ethical or moral. It follows that, while a pragmatic accommodation of interests might meet the standard of regulatory acceptability it should only qualify as legitimate if it meets whatever the ethical or moral criteria are taken to be.

Regulatory legitimacy

Where regulators are faced with a plurality of competing and conflicting views about the position they should take, or the policy to be adopted, or the like, it seems less than satisfactory to treat any position or policy taken as being legitimate simply because that is the particular position or policy that law's governance has adopted. Even if, for the sake of argument, we grant that law's imprimatur is necessary for legitimate governance, it surely cannot be sufficient. Legitimate governance is surely more demanding.

What might it take for a regulatory intervention to be really legitimate? If we hold that this requires that the rule must pass ethical or moral muster, we might argue that this means we should test it relative to the fundamental values of the community. For example, where a community is committed to animal welfare as one of its identifying values, we might ask whether the particular regulatory accommodation is compatible with this commitment. On this approach, what is really legitimate might well vary from one community (and its fundamental values) to another.

There is another possibility but this requires a radical rethinking outside the box. What we are looking for is an Archimedean vantage point from which, regardless of the particular community, we can pronounce on the legitimacy of law's governance. By now, we know where this radical rethinking will take us; that is, we know that we will find that vantage point, and the ultimate test of regulatory legitimacy, in the preservation of the global commons and, concomitantly, in the bigger picture of human needs and regulatory responsibilities (see Chapter 22 and Brownsword, 2023).

In this bigger picture, there are two key dividing lines. First, there is the line between the global and the particular community, a line that divides what is rightly cosmopolitan from what is merely local; and, secondly, within each particular community, there is the line between the fundamental values of the community and its non-fundamental values and interests. What this line anticipates is that the community will declare its constitutive values which will then be privileged over whatever non-constitutive values and interests it recognises. Accordingly, in this bigger picture, regulatory legitimacy is to be judged relative to, above all, cosmopolitan standards and then, within the particular community, relative to its fundamental values and then to its non-constitutive standards.

In principle, we might appeal to certain values, such as human dignity, at any one of these three reference points (Brownsword, 2017b). For example, we might claim that respect for human dignity is a cosmopolitan principle that takes priority over any national or local considerations; or, we might locate human dignity in the constitutive values of a particular community; or, we might argue that, in a particular community, there is a legitimate interest in human dignity (or in dignified treatment, or in not suffering an indignity) that needs to be taken into consideration when regulatory decisions are made.

At all events, on this radical view, for law's governance to be judged to be legitimate, we have to demand more than the mere fact of its enactment, more than the acceptability of the rules, and even more than compatibility with the fundamental and constitutive values of the particular community. Governance is only really legitimate when it respects and supports the cosmopolitan standards of the global commons.

35

DISPUTES

Resolution, prevention, and technical solutions

Introduction

According to the standard view, national legal systems are to be conceived of as systems of primary rules directed at citizens supported by secondary rules that authorise certain bodies and persons to make and administer the primary rules. The logic of this view is that the reference point for legal disputes will be the rules of law, that processes will be orientated to the application of the rules to particular fact situations, and that the core of the dispute will concern the relevant rule, the application of the rule, or the facts. In all cases, the pathway for the dispute will lead to courts (or to court-like tribunals or arbitrators). It follows that legal disputes take shape, are settled, or are resolved either in the courts or in the shadow of the courts. However, just as new technologies operate to de-centre the standard view of law, of rules as the primary instruments of law, and of humans as the primary appliers of legal rules, so too they put pressure on the traditional court-centred view of disputes.

Once a Law 2.0 mentality takes hold, we will ask not only whether rules and regulations are fit for purpose but also whether the courts (together with those professionals who provide advice and assistance to disputants) are fit for purpose. Notoriously, if we aspire to universal affordable justice, then the current version of law's governance is not fit for purpose. This was all too evident in Dickens' time; and it is still evident today that there is an iceberg of unmet legal need. For example, in the World Justice Project's report for 2019, the UK does relatively well, standing at 12 out of 126 globally, but the lowest mark that it has for any one of the 44 indicators—and, what is more, the only mark below 0.60—is the mark of 0.53 for the 'accessibility

DOI: 10.4324/9781003507802-40

and affordability' of civil justice (World Justice Project, 2019: 151). Given these rankings, the position in the UK could be worse, but it also could be very much better.

That said, there has been a good deal of rethinking about dispute settlement, with court-based adjudication being complemented by less formal arbitration, and by less adversarial conciliation and mediation. While these particular forms of alternative dispute resolution were not responses either to new technological challenges or to new technological opportunities, they have paved the way for more radical thinking. Thus, as a Law 3.0 mentality takes shape, online technologies supporting online activities invite a further rethink about how disputes might be resolved—a rethink, for example, of the kind represented by the path-breaking online Resolution Centre, operated by eBay in conjunction with PayPal, and handling more than 60 million disputes each year.

In this chapter, we can introduce three lines of radical thinking: one is to employ new tools to support online dispute resolution (ODR); a second is an exercise in thinking outside the box by putting the emphasis on delivering compensation rather than establishing fault; and, a third is to develop technical solutions such as automation that can both prevent wrongs occurring as well as ensure that, in the event of wrongdoing, compensation is delivered.

Radical thought #1: Online dispute resolution

In May 2013, the European Parliament and the Council of the EU adopted Directive 2013/11/EU on ADR for consumer disputes and Regulation No 524/2013 on ODR for consumer disputes. According to Article 1 of the former, the purpose of the Directive is 'to contribute to the proper functioning of the internal market by ensuring that consumers can, on a voluntary basis, submit complaints against traders to entities offering independent, impartial, transparent, effective, fast and fair alternative dispute resolution procedures'. Article 1 of the accompanying Regulation expresses its purpose in very similar terms, but it emphasises 'the digital dimension' of the internal market. The conjunction of the Directive and the Regulation signals an awareness of the problems that consumers might have, particularly in cross-border commerce, in accessing convenient, affordable, and fair dispute-resolution procedures, as well as an appreciation that these problems might impact on the confidence of consumers.

Surveying the rapidly changing landscape of online dispute resolution (ODR) and analysing the insinuation of technologies into dispute resolution, both in courts and out of courts, Ethan Katsh and Orna Rabinovich-Einy (2017) detect three key shifts as follows. First, there is a shift from physical to virtual, or semi-virtual, settings: with this shift, individuals 'can access courts, evaluate their legal stance, communicate with the other party, and have a third-party decide their dispute, all without having to physically attend the court or be restricted to court operating hours … ' The second shift is 'from human intervention and decision making to automated processes'; and the third shift is 'from dispute resolution models that value confidentiality to models focused on collecting, using, and reusing data in order to prevent disputes….' (162–163). Had Katsh and Rabinovich-Einy been writing after, rather than before, the pandemic, then surely these shifts would have been even more pronounced.

These shifts notwithstanding, attachments to Law 1.0 processes persist. Indeed, as Katsh and Rabinovick-Einy ask:

> Will parties who participate in these processes feel that they have received their 'day in court' and have been 'heard'? Will users perceive these processes as fair? Will judges sustain their neutrality and authority, and will courts, relying on algorithms, maintain their legitimacy?
>
> Adopting technology in the courtroom opens up new opportunities not only for making our existing processes less expensive and cumbersome and more accessible at all hours. It could also change the very nature of court processes, with software playing an increasingly significant role in streamlining, resolving, and preventing claims. Indeed, there is promise for transforming our very understanding of the meaning of *justice*.
>
> *(164–165)*

While our ideas about what is convenient and what is efficient might remain fairly constant, there is no guarantee that citizens will judge that the gains in convenience and efficiency offset their questions about 'trust' in automated processes; and, the idea that our understanding of 'justice' might be transformed by these technology-driven forms of dispute handling might seem less a promise than an unwelcome threat. If automated processes and technological dispute-handling are thought to be more about getting disputes *settled* rather than getting them settled *justly*, there might be resistance to rethinking the meaning of justice and, concomitantly, to the de-centring of courts, rules, and humans.

Following up on these caveats, we might reason that, while incremental adoption of technologies that make dispute resolution smoother, more convenient, and more efficient is one thing, end-to-end automation of the process is something else. Nevertheless, in some parts of the world, various forms of automated civil justice are being piloted. For example, according to Santosh Paul, China is leading the way in developing AI Internet Courts (see www.barandbench.com/columns/is-artificial-intelligence-replacing-judging). Thus:

> Hangzhou, a city in north China, powers the country's cutting edge technological revolution. It is here that the first justice delivery system run

> by AI was introduced in 2017. Beijing and Guangzhou quickly followed suit. The three AI Internet Courts in China are judging disputes relating to online transactions of sale of goods and services, copyright and trademark, ownership and infringement of domains, trade disputes, and e-commerce product liability claims.

On average, a trial lasts 28 minutes and the entire process, start to finish, takes 38 days. Meanwhile, in Europe, it is Estonia that has the reputation for being in the vanguard of e-government; and, predictably, the development of robot judges (for small claims disputes) is one of the items on the Ministry of Justice's agenda. What should we make of this? Are 'robot judges' next?

In response, we should recall that judges perform more than one function, from finding facts to applying rules, to assessing the credibility of witnesses and the purpose of rules. While machines might be able to outperform humans in predicting how an agreed rule might be applied to an agreed set of facts, this is not adjudicating a dispute. Presented with a dispute, judges not only have to decide the case rather than predict an outcome, they also have to find the facts, draw inferences from the facts (about the intentions of the party), interpret and apply contested concepts in the agreed rules and principles, and determine which rule is the applicable rule. Accordingly, if smart machines are to outperform humans in all these respects, there is some way to go. Smart tools will surely play a role in the judicial process, but reliance on 'robot judges' is another matter.

Radical thought #2: Rethinking fault, liability, and compensatory responsibility

Traditional thinking is that those who are at fault in relation to some harm or loss that is caused should bear the compensatory responsibility (the line of thinking is from blame to claim to compensation). Victims should look to wrongdoers (to the blameworthy) to correct the wrong. It follows that victims who seek compensation will need to identify the party who was at fault.

For example, in the case of *Carmarthenshire County Council v Lewis* (1955) a nursery schoolteacher supervising a three-year old child was distracted when a second child fell and was hurt. While the teacher was attending to the second child, the first child wandered off out of the school building and through an open gate onto an adjoining road. In order to avoid hitting the child, a lorry driver swerved, collided with a telegraph pole and was killed. The claimant was the lorry driver's widow. In these circumstances, the House of Lords (disagreeing with the lower courts) found that the teacher was not personally at fault—she had acted responsibly. However, it was held that the Council had failed to explain how the child had been able to get out of the school; and, without such an explanation, it was to be inferred that the County Council had failed to take reasonable precautions to prevent an unattended child leaving the school and causing an accident of this kind.

This was very much an exercise in Law 1.0 thinking. The principles of tort law were applied to determine whether, on the facts, the schoolteacher had failed to take reasonable care or whether the County Council was to blame in the steps that it had taken to keep the children safe when they were attending the school. If the defendants were not at fault, if they could not be blamed for the accident, they would not be required to pay compensation to the claimant; and, this would mean that, unless other eligible defendants could be identified, the claimant would not be compensated for her loss.

Once we start to think outside the box and adopt a Law 2.0 perspective, this seems a somewhat unsatisfactory approach. Instead of searching ex post for a party who might be characterised as being at fault in the particular circumstances, far better surely to establish ex ante who could best compensate for accidents of this kind and then place the liability on their shoulders. This would imply no blame, but it would mean (i) that being at fault was not a condition for having the responsibility to compensate and (ii) that not being at fault was not necessarily an exemption from the responsibility to pay compensation. Attribution of fault and allocation of compensatory responsibility become two independent matters.

Following this line of thinking, in many legal systems, we see attempts to take the complexity and unfairness out of accident claims by adopting 'no-fault compensation schemes' (such as that administered by the Accident Compensation Corporation in New Zealand; see, https://en.wikipedia.org/wiki/Accident_Compensation_Corporation) or switching from fault-based liability to strict liability. For a long time, schemes of the former kind have been advocated as a rational response to the risk of road traffic accidents; and they are being touted again as the smart response to the risks presented by autonomous vehicles. Rather than tying compensatory liability to fault, the challenge is seen as being to articulate the most acceptable (and financially workable) compensatory arrangements that accommodate the interests in transport innovation and the safety of passengers and pedestrians. For example, one proposal, advanced by Tracy Pearl (2018), is that there should be an autonomous vehicle crash victim compensation fund to be financed by a sales tax on such vehicles. Of course, as with any such no-fault compensation scheme, much of the devil is in the detail—in particular, there are important questions to be settled about the level of compensation, whether the option of pursuing a tort claim remains open to victims, and what kind of injuries or losses are covered by the scheme.

Similar thinking underlies product liability regimes. So, for example, in one of the leading US product liability cases, *Beshada v Johns-Manville Products Corp.* (1982) the defendant asbestos manufacturers argued that they could not reasonably know that their finished products supplied for use in the shipyards were still hazardous and could cause dust-diseases. However, as the Supreme Court of New Jersey emphasised, in a product liability regime, arguments of this kind are not relevant; as the court expressed it, 'Strict liability focuses on the product, not the fault of the manufacturer' (204). A finding that the defendants have been assigned the compensatory responsibility in the circumstances does not imply a negative judgment about the way in which they have conducted their business. Moreover, at least in theory, provided that the compensatory burden is spread across the community by insurance and pricing mechanisms, the risk is borne collectively.

Once we are thinking out of the box, we can just as easily rethink the principle of 'if blame then claim' as that of 'if no blame then no claim'. Strict liability disrupts the latter; legal immunities disrupt the former. So, for example, if we wish to minimise disputes about whether Internet Service Providers (ISPs) have taken reasonable care to avoid carrying objectionable or illegal content, we could either adopt a strict liability standard (which would be opposed by ISPs) or, equally well, confer an immunity on ISPs (which would be opposed by potential claimants). In the EU, and a number of other jurisdictions, the legal position initially adopted was that of a qualified immunity for ISPs (no liability provided that content was taken down reasonably promptly after notice had been given). While this rethought the relationship between blame, claim, and compensation, and served to reduce disputes, it now strikes many commentators as over-protective of what were once small enterprises.

Radical thought #3: Technical solutions—Automate, prevent, manage

According to Richard Susskind (2017), one of the themes of his conversations with in-house lawyers is that dispute avoidance is to be preferred to even the neatest of resolutions; that it is better, in Susskind's words, to put 'a fence at the top of a cliff rather than an ambulance at the bottom' (95); that there should be 'a shift from legal problem solving to legal risk management [this anticipating] a world in which legal problems are often dissolved before needing to be resolved' (127). If we truly embrace Law 3.0 thinking, then we should deploy the full range of our regulatory resources, including technical measures and technologies, to prevent disputes arising in the first place.

The thought is simple and attractive: why not design our transactions and interactions in ways that reduce or eliminate the triggers for disputes? In our radical imaginary of automated futures, why not fully automated transactions, automated payment for automated provision of goods and services? If there are any technological glitches or errors, accounts will be automatically adjusted. Similarly, why not prevent accidents that cause injury to humans or damage to their property by taking humans out of the situation whether as operators who cause the injury or damage or who are the parties injured? No doubt, implementing this simple thought is much less simple. Nevertheless, if we can automate the back end of disputes why not also the front end?

Prevention I: Transactions

Where contracts are constituted by an exchange of promises, typically a promise of payment in return for a promise of the supply of goods or services, both parties are at risk if they perform first. From the supplier's point of view, the risk is greatest if payment is made only on delivery or completion. This risk can be reduced if payments are made in stages; but, to eliminate the risk of non-payment, the contract price needs to be paid in full upfront. However, if the price is paid upfront, this transfers all the risk to the customer. In international trade, where the exposure to risk is particularly acute, the use of trusted third parties (banks) and letters of credit reduces the risk to an acceptable level. However, if transactions, or parts of transactions, were automated, removing potentially defecting humans from the loop, might this prevent non-payment or non-performance and put transactions on a more secure footing?

In this spirit, imagine a world of automated transactions, a world where, as Michal Gal and Niva Elkin-Koren (2017) foresee it,

> [y]our automated car makes independent decisions on where to purchase fuel, when to drive itself to a service station, from which garage to order a spare part, or whether to rent itself out to other passengers, all without even once consulting with you.
>
> *(309–310)*

In that world, humans have been taken out of the transactional loop, leaving it to the technology to make decisions that humans would otherwise be responsible for making. The relevant humans include not only the primary contractors but also trusted third parties (such as banks that administer letters of credit or other documents in international trade). For example, in the context of carriage of goods by sea, electronic bills of lading promise to be a smart response to the problem of ships reaching the port of discharge before paper bills; and, as Paul Todd (2019) has argued, the use of blockchain and smart contracts might be part of an even smarter response, overcoming a lack of trust in central registries. Similarly, just like imperfect attempts to protect IPRs through contractual provisions, perhaps the required protections can be incorporated in relevant products and processes. In this world, transactional disputes between humans would be reduced or even eliminated, and if there are glitches to be resolved, this would be a conversation for the machines.

If this seems to project too far into the future, we can imagine instead a world in which performance of parts of the transaction at least can be entrusted to the technology. Most straightforwardly, as with smart contracts, the performance of those parts of the transaction that involve payments being made could be irreversibly entrusted to the technology. Let us suppose that a smart contract takes the form of a coded instruction for a 'payment' to be made by A to B conditional on the occurrence of some event (if x, then y). Where the 'event' is performance by B, then (provided that the technology is reliable) B will be paid and (provided that the 'performance' is as agreed) neither A nor B will have any grievance. There should be no dispute. Further, as a second-best, in the event that A is in breach of its obligations (for example, where an airline overbooks or is late in arriving) then compensation will be automatically and immediately paid to B. Of course, there are provisos here; there is plenty to go wrong; and there are other ways for parties to ensure that they get paid. Nevertheless, this is a pointer to how technology might be used as a means of preventing disputes arising.

Prevention II: Accidents

Humans, it might be said, are accidents waiting to happen. So, to prevent disputes arising, we should take humans out of accident scenarios. If we replace human operators with mechanical operators that are more reliable, this should reduce 'accidents'—this applies whether we are thinking about robots operating machines, or taking over the role of pharmacists in hospitals, or the automation of transport systems, and so on. Similarly, if we can take humans out of places where they are likely to be injured (in dangerous work environments, for example), we again should reduce accidents that cause harm to humans.

Imagine, then, that in the Carmarthenshire case, we have a robot looking after the schoolchildren. On these facts, what would we say about the liability of the robot or of the County Council who rely on the robot to look after the young children at the nursery school? This, of course, will depend on whether we are viewing the situation through the lens of Law 1.0, Law 2.0, or Law 3.0.

Briefly, if we view the situation through the doctrinal coherentist lens of Law 1.0, we will ask whether robot supervisors are analogous to human supervisors; and, whether we can treat robots as being 'personally' responsible or 'at fault'. By contrast, if we take a Law 2.0 regulatory approach, our thinking will be along the lines that, before schools are permitted to introduce robocarers, there needs to be a collectively agreed scheme of compensation should something 'go wrong'. On this view, the responsibilities and liabilities of the parties would be determined ex ante by the agreed terms of the risk management package. By further contrast, if we adopt a Law

3.0 technologically-sensitive and preventive approach, we will be thinking about technical solutions—possibly something as simple as a locked gate or a more sophisticated technological fix such as an invisible 'fence' at the edge of the schoolyard so that children simply could not stray beyond the limits. Thinking about the matter in this way, the question would be entirely about designing the machines and the space in a way that collisions between schoolchildren and passing vehicles could not happen. That way, humans would not be harmed, there would not be grievances, and disputes would not arise.

Consider now a further variation on the original facts of the Carmarthenshire case. Imagine that the lorry was not driven by a human but was fully autonomous and that it had been programmed to swerve if there was a risk of colliding with a human. If the vehicle was empty, the question would be about covering the costs of whatever damage was caused to the vehicle—a question that we can assume to be an everyday insurance matter. Let us suppose, though, the claim for compensation is by the widow of a passenger who was in, but not driving, the vehicle. What would we say about such a situation?

The first thing to say is that this reminds us that there are limits to preventing death and injury: try though we might, we cannot take all humans out of all potentially harmful situations. Fortunately, situations of this kind should arise only exceptionally and any questions about liability or compensation should have been settled way in advance of autonomous vehicles getting on the road. For many, the principal point of discussion would be whether the vehicle should have been programmed to save the life of the child at the possible expense of any passengers in the vehicle. In fact, one of the main questions generated by the development of autonomous vehicles has been the ethics of dilemmas of just this kind. Let us suppose though that the community has debated the ethics, agreed on a standard design, and that the vehicle in question has the standard coding for situations of this kind. What can we now say about the question of legal liability? Provided that there has been a proper democratic debate about the standard design, then regulators should at least be able to forestall disputes relating to particular incidents if not renewed discussion of the social licence for autonomous vehicles and, concomitantly, the fitness of the regulatory position.

Concluding remarks

In the context of disputes, LawTech starts in a relatively modest and uncontroversial role. Criticisms of court-centred civil justice are legion: processes are slow and cumbersome; lawyers are expensive; and, as a result, access to justice is delayed or denied and unmet legal need continues to be unmet. To the extent that technologies can be deployed in ways that mitigate these complaints, that is all to the good. It is in this way that ODR responds to a situation that most commentators agree is unsatisfactory.

However, once we turn to technology to rethink disputes in a way that goes beyond this core project, we find a paradox. On the one hand, we look to technology to make it easier for disputants to seek resolution or settlement of their disputes; and we look to automation to expedite the process. Otherwise, disputants are being denied access to either a service or to justice. On the other hand, we also look to technology to make it more difficult for disputes to arise in the first place. On the one hand, we are trying to open up and facilitate the disputing process; on the other, we are trying to shut the door on disputes.

This paradox results from two prongs of radical thinking. One prong is that we should try to reduce or even eliminate disputes by using technology to design out the causes of disputes. If grievances do not arise, disputes should be a thing of the past. At the same time, though, there is another prong of thinking that invites exploring the possibility of developing technologies that are able to resolve disputes in a way that outperforms any human. Our interest in AI-enabled judging machines is not so much efficiency or convenience but, if you believe it, fairness and expertise.

Finally, not only is there paradox, there is also a degree of homology. For both prongs of our radical thinking (preventing disputes arising and automating dispute resolution), the lowest hanging fruit are similar, notably, dealing with debts. For one prong, through technological management, we can ensure that payments due are paid (paid on time and paid in full); and, for the other prong, it is simple enough for smart machines to order payment of debts that are clearly due (these are easy cases). For both prongs, the challenge is to take the technology to more difficult cases; and, for everyone, the underlying questions are: how far do we want our communities to be dispute-free zones; and, to what extent are we content for humans to be taken out of the loops of dispute-resolution?

PART 6

Lawyers and legal services

36

LAWYERS

Introduction

What shall we say about lawyers? Famously, in Shakespeare's *Henry VI, Part II*, the rebellious character, Dick the Butcher, proclaims that the first thing to do is to 'kill all the lawyers'. Evidently, Dick has a pretty low opinion of lawyers but, as a rebel, this is likely to be because he sees the lawyers as defenders of the existing order. If so, and if the order that the lawyers are defending is just, then killing them off would be a backward step; but, if the existing order that the lawyers defend is unjust, then perhaps Dick has a point.

However, the matter is not so straightforward because it is one of the key claims of this radical introduction that we can have many competing views about the justice of particular orders; justice is a contested concept; and, in all contexts, the critical imperative is to respect the preconditions for the possibility of governance and for order. Accordingly, if the justice of the existing order is reasonably contested, then the disputants need to press their case in a way that will not jeopardise the possibility of civilised life. Given that lawyers have a critical role to play in building and maintaining civilised communities, and if they are taking that role and responsibility seriously, then killing them off would not be the smart thing to do.

So much for Shakespearean characters. Our assessment of lawyers needs to be made in modern times, not in the context of Elizabethan England. What should we say about lawyers today?

DOI: 10.4324/9781003507802-42

Lawyers today

To start with the public perception of the legal profession, books could, and have been, filled with jokes about lawyers—who, at best, are thought to be self-serving, elitist, and expensive (Auerbach, 1976); and who, at worst, evoke images of ambulance-chasing, dilatoriness, and less than competent service. Compounding such discontent, at any rate in the UK, there is evidently serious dissatisfaction with the service provided by the Legal Ombudsman to whom complaints about lawyers may be made (Ellson, 2022). As for those who make the laws, we read that working-class Americans see 'government … as being made up of two sorts of people: "politicians," who are blustering crooks and liars but can at least occasionally be voted out of office, and "bureaucrats," who are condescending elitists almost impossible to uproot' (Graeber, 2015: 10).

Moreover, it is not only the lay members of the community who can express discontent with law's officials and its practitioners; the legal profession too can be critical of those who are responsible for law's governance. For example, as Robin Ellison has remarked, while we all support the Rule of Law, the Rule of too much Law is another matter. Although those who govern will often understand that, by over-regulating, they will invite discontent, few manage 'to curb their own regulatory enthusiasm' (Ellison, 2018: xii). As a result, 'we have too many rules, inadequately briefed rule makers, over-zealous regulators and under-trained and too few judges. It is also clear that the over-government evident in many countries causes irritation, substantial cost, and unintended and adverse consequences for us all' (Ellison, 2018: 433).

Within the legal profession, we also hear judges who, like Ellison, are critical of the quality and opacity of legislation (Goddard, 2022), not least where they are required to give juries clear directions on complex criminal law defences—as one highly experienced Old Bailey judge has remarked, the fact that Parliament can legislate 'in such terms says a lot about its belief in the UK's elementary education system' (Joseph, 2022: 262).

Reverting to the general public, many might think that the test of a just legal order, serviced by lawyers, is actually having access to the courts and, as we saw in the last chapter, the situation here is less than satisfactory. It is all very well saying that the Courts of Law, like the Ritz, are open to all; but, the reality is that, for many, neither the Courts nor the Ritz is an option. Similarly, for many in the US, justice is out of reach. Quite simply, obtaining legal advice and assistance or taking legal action will not be a practical option. As Benjamin H. Barton and Stephanos Bibas (2017: 4) observe of the situation in the USA:

> Mothers seeking child support, tenants fighting eviction, and laid-off workers claiming unemployment or disability benefits usually cannot

afford lawyers. They routinely endure long delays and great difficulty navigating courts by themselves before they can receive justice.

Meanwhile, back in the UK, some think it a scandal that celebrities, from footballers' wives to Hollywood A-listers, can rack up huge legal bills in an attempt to protect their reputations (Waterson, 2022)—but, then, these are people who might frequent the Ritz and for whom nothing less than Rolls Royce justice will do.

Improving the image

To be sure, there are ways of improving access to lawyers and responding to unmet legal need—for example, by making public funding (legal aid) available to support the cost of providing legal advice, assistance, and representation; by making the market for legal services more competitive; and by introducing more flexibility into charging regimes (as is the case, for instance, with permitting lawyers to provide their services on a no-win no-fee basis). In the UK, publicly funded legal services for civil work were introduced in the post-War years when many families who were experiencing matrimonial problems were in need of legal advice and assistance; and, several decades later, a hard look at restrictive practices in the legal profession resulted in a much more competitive market for conveyancing services.

Over and above such initiatives, the legal profession itself can do pro bono work; and, for many years, the Law Centres and the Citizens Advice Bureaux (now Citizens Advice) have played a valuable supportive role. However, even with these measures, a significant amount of unmet legal need will remain—and even more so, of course, in the absence of such measures.

When access to justice depends on public funding and volunteers, it is likely to be under-resourced and vulnerable. Discontent with both law's governance in general and lawyers in particular will persist. Of course, against this background of under-provision, we celebrate the success of emblematic figures such as Erin Brockovich not only for the justice that she achieved in her lawsuit against the Pacific Gas and Electric Company (https://en.wikipedia.org/wiki/Erin_Brockovich) but even more so for her resilience and determination in getting *access* to justice. However, it really should not be so; accessing justice should not require such Herculean efforts. There surely must be a better way.

At this point, the more radical strategies that we have outlined in previous chapters—such as rethinking liability regimes, preventing disputes arising, and automating legal services—are likely to come on to the agenda. The thought will be that smarter, and more technological, solutions should be sought—and, one of the corollaries of a more technological approach might be that we need fewer lawyers because legal functions (or, at any rate, traditional legal functions) have been taken over by machines (see, further, Chapter 37).

Lawyers really do matter

Their typically bad press notwithstanding, lawyers could be seen in a far more positive light. To return to one of the central threads of this introduction, governance matters and lawyers have a key role to play in making governance both possible and good. Recall, again, Nicholas McBride's remarks:

> So we in the West owe everything to the legal systems under which we live. Without them, our lives would be unimaginably different, and unbelievably difficult. And as you can't have a legal system without lawyers to run it, it follows that we should regard the lawyers who help to keep our legal system running as public heroes, in the same way that we regard doctors and nurses and teachers as heroic for the work they do.
>
> *(McBride, 2022: 28–29)*

To many, the idea that, during Covid-19, we should have been going out once a week to applaud the lawyers might seem absurd. The idea that lawyers are key workers playing a vital role in helping the members of human communities to live together in a civilised way will seem ridiculous: first, we need to be persuaded that we should see lawyers in at least a positive light and, even then, there is a long way to go before we should view them as public heroes. Nevertheless, the traditional disdain for lawyers needs to be corrected; if lawyers play the role in the community that they should be playing, the light in which they will be seen will be, and rightly will be, far more positive. The present generation of lawyers has earned a certain reputation; the long hours and hard work will remain; but lawyering and lawyers need to be, and need to be seen to be, about good governance.

37

THE AUTOMATION OF LEGAL SERVICES AND SOCIAL ACCEPTABILITY

Introduction

To what extent will the provision of legal services be taken over by machines? To what extent will LawTech undertake the functions traditionally undertaken by lawyers? To what extent will RegTech automate regulatory functions?

According to Mark Fenwick, Wulf A. Kaal, and Erik P.M. Vermeulen (2020), there is already a flourishing market for the supply of LawTech with four categories of start-up companies being distinguished. Thus:

> The first category includes startup companies that offer a range of online legal services, removing the in-person legal consultation process and guidance process for clients. The second ... involves online 'matching' platforms that connect lawyers with clients. Such platform startups help consumers find a fitting lawyer without the costly involvement of a law firm. The third ... use[s] AI tools to take over their lawyers' time-consuming and expensive legal research activities such as reviewing, understanding, evaluating, and reapplying contracts. Finally, startups with expertise in blockchain technology attempt to replace lawyers as intermediaries in certain types of transactions.
>
> *(358–359)*

Tools of this kind will extend the options for the provision of legal services. However, what will those who are consumers of legal services make of the technological options that are already, and will increasingly become, available?

DOI: 10.4324/9781003507802-43

Social acceptability

Research conducted for the Legal Services Board and the Solicitors Regulation Authority (LSB and SRA, 2022) offers some insights into public attitudes towards the use of technology for the delivery of legal services. The research also offers some interesting insights into attitudes of practitioners in relation to the use of technology for this purpose as well as their views as to whether their clients would treat such use as acceptable. For present purposes, however, we will focus on what the research tells us about public attitudes.

Summarising the results of the research, the report concludes (LSB and SRA, 2022: 55–56):

> There is majority support amongst the public for the use of technology in legal services, both for themselves personally, and for society more generally. Most people think technology can bring benefits to legal services, helping the sector keep up with advances in wider society, and potentially offering faster, more convenient/accessible and more affordable services. People are—perhaps unsurprisingly—more comfortable with technology that is well established and familiar (such as video consultations). They are more wary of newer concepts (like smart contracts and decision making tools), and particularly tools that use artificial intelligence (including chatbots).
>
> However, a tenth of people are firmly against the use of technology in legal services. This links to their own reticence to use technology more generally, and for this minority the risks of technology (particularly the lack of human interaction and data security risks) reinforce their opposition to it ...
>
> Both audiences [legal professionals and the public] readily acknowledge that the use of technology in legal services brings risks. The complexity of the law; the human factors at play; and the sensitivity of issues all mean that abuse, mistakes and failures have greater consequences than in other sectors ...
>
> There are limits on the use of technology in legal services. The public and legal professionals both think its use is not suitable in all circumstances, and there is less support for its use in more complex, sensitive or higher stakes cases. They do not want final decisions to be made automatically by technology. They also strongly believe that clients should be able to choose not to use technological tools (without facing penalty or disadvantage), particularly as they believe technology is less acceptable for some people (including those who do not have access to—or confidence in using—technology; those with low literacy in English).
>
> The public and professionals say that building confidence in legal technology involves a combination of clear regulation and local governance;

> raising the profile of tools and their benefits; providing practical support to use technology; a system of quality checks; and ensuring an easy and visible route to redress if things go wrong. As a result, regulators, developers and legal businesses all have a role to play in building confidence in legal technology and realising its benefits.

Translating this into a brief for law's governance, we would say that public attitudes—which, in this particular case, are likely to be dominated by prudential preferences—are broadly supportive and positive. However, there is a minority view that is negative and, even those who are positive, expect there to be red lines and limits. In this respect, considerable value is attached to having *human* professional involvement—for example, humans are more empathetic, more intuitive, and more responsive to individual cases and contexts (p. 27); and, similarly, there is a mistrust of automated decision-making where the issues are more complex or nuanced (p. 33). Moreover, where the use of a technology is permitted (not subject to a red line restriction), it should be for clients to choose whether it is actually used in their case. On this basis, we can anticipate discontent with law's governance where the particular red lines or restrictions are not socially acceptable or where the use or non-use of permitted technologies is not at the option of clients (whether by opt-in or opt-out).

So much for the social acceptability of some technologies (the research focused on video consultations, e-signatures, smart contracts, predictive and decision-making tools, and chatbots) in relation to the delivery of legal services (many of which would be provided in non-contentious contexts). What, though, might be the position where technologies are available for the performance of primary governance functions and they are either not used or they are used?

Where technologies are not used

In the UK, it is clear that the SRA is keen to encourage the use of technologies that offer significant benefits to consumers and that address unmet legal need. After the pandemic, the use of some technologies (video-conferencing in particular) is commonplace but the take-up of many other technologies (such as blockchain) is quite low. While demand will vary from one sector of practice to another and while the costs of investing in technology will vary from one tool to another, we can take it that the regulatory environment will be tilted towards a more technological approach to the delivery of legal services (see, for example, the LSB presentation at www.youtube.com/watch?v=FZRUrBrACu4).

Given this regulatory background, if legal officials or practitioners choose not to make use of technological resources that are available to them, this is likely to provoke discontent on the grounds that effective and efficient means for dealing with some matter are being eschewed. As the research for the LSB and SRA suggests, if the cost of providing legal services could be reduced by automating the provision or if the quality of the service could be improved if technologies were employed by practitioners in an assistive way, then if these options were not taken up, clients and others would express their discontent and wonder why there was such reluctance. If legal practitioners were operating with technology-restrictive practices in order to preserve their jobs or their profit margins, they would be on the back-foot in defending their approach; and, if clients were themselves large commercial enterprises where technology was employed for the sake of efficiency, the lawyers' defences might not be sustainable.

But, what about a reluctance by regulators to make use of available technologies? What about regulators who, as it were, do not buy into RegTech? Recall the case of the drones at Gatwick airport. Suppose that a technological fix were available but regulators declined to require its application. Instead, they relied exclusively on rules. Once again, the burden of justification would be on the regulators. In this case, they perhaps might not say that they felt the need to retain humans in the (rule-based) enforcement loop—although this might be precisely what they should say because, in some places, this might be a priority for social acceptability. However, they might say that the technological fix, and enforcing the fix, would be too expensive relative to what they judged to be the low risk of a Gatwick situation re-occurring. If this were the best defence of the approach, discontent with the regulators (and legal officials) would depend on whether this was judged to be socially acceptable—which, in turn, would depend on whether the regulators' risk assessment and cost/benefit analysis were generally shared, whether over time the assessment was borne out, and whether the approach taken by regulators was judged to be both economical and effective.

Where technologies are used

Where legal officials, practitioners, or others with governance responsibilities choose to make use of legal technologies (whether in an assistive or a substitutive capacity), this should please those who are in favour of these tools being used. However, where it is risk-assessing tools or compliance-related tools that are being employed, there might be dissatisfaction if the perception is that the law is either under-enforced or over-enforced; or if there is a lack of confidence in the oversight exercised by humans; or if the avenues for appeal are not appropriate.

Under-enforcement and over-enforcement

Whatever the extent of human reliance on the technologies, governance needs to avoid both under-enforcement (false negatives) and over-enforcement (false positives). If governance is to be accurate, it will not do to correct under-enforcement if reducing false negatives means that we increase false positives; and, conversely, it will not do to correct over-enforcement by reducing false positives if this means that false negatives are increased. Where, as Andrea Roth (2016) suggests, popular support for more accurate decisions in the criminal justice system leads to a prioritisation of a reduction in false negatives without a corresponding concern about false positives, this is a recipe for injustice; and, if Roth is right, this is an injustice that is unlikely to be corrected.

Similarly, where the law to be enforced is in the form of a general rule to which there are some fairly flexible exceptions—such as the general rule against infringement of copyright and the exception for fair use of copyrighted material—the technologies that are employed to take down material that infringes copyright might work in a way that either ignores the fair use exception or applies it only in the clearest of cases. Once again, governance corrects for under-enforcement by means that lead to an increase in false positives. And, once again, where powerful interests favour an over-restrictive approach to the exceptions, these are injustices that will not be corrected.

Human oversight

As a corrective or insurance, a provision for 'human oversight' might be adopted. But, by whom, when, and how might such oversight be exercised? The jurisprudence waiting to be developed around such a provision is far from unproblematic. Moreover, how realistic, reasonable or rational is it for humans, exercising oversight, to override an automated decision (see, e.g., Cathy O'Neil, 2016: and Hin-Yan Liu, 2018)? Where technologies are more reliable than humans, might we be tempted to think that the better rule in the long run is that humans should *never* override automated decisions rather than that they should have a discretion (however specified) to override the machines?

Given such a context, how likely is it that human review of the technological (AI-enabled) risk assessment will reject its recommendation? How likely is it that, in the terms of Article 14(4)(d) of the EU's Regulation on AI, a human official will decide to 'disregard, override or reverse the output of [a particular] high-risk AI system' and thereby to err on the side of possible under-enforcement? To do this would be to direct all subsequent discontent at the human official. If human officials apprehend that their oversight actions or inactions are likely to provoke discontent, their default will be to follow the indication given by the technologies; and, this will provoke discontent on the part of those who are concerned that keeping humans in the governance loop should not be merely a token gesture.

In the same vein, we can also detect a risk that, in cases where there is public discontent with a technology that undertakes governance functions, the machines might insulate humans from being held accountable or responsible and thereby aggravate the initial discontent. This is another reason why we might argue the case for keeping skilled humans in the loop for the performance of governance functions and, at the same time, keeping accountable humans in the loop of responsibility.

Appeals

One of the most promising candidates for automating criminal justice is in the field of road traffic law. Technologies can be employed to detect offences, to identify offenders, and to enforce the penalties. If a mistake is made in the detection of the offence or the identification of the offender, the person to whom the penalty is applied might wish to appeal. However, if the appeal system is also automated and does not recognise the ground for appeal that is pleaded, this will intensify discontent. Similarly, if the appeal is to a human whose remit is constrained in the same way, this will provoke discontent with the human originators of the 'system', with the technology itself, and with the official who fails to correct an error.

Scratching the surface

Academic lawyers, having written at great length about a particular topic, will sometimes feel that they have done little more than scratch the surface. Looking back at the short remarks in this chapter about the social acceptability of the future use of technologies in law enforcement and in the delivery of legal services, there is no doubt that we have barely scratched the surface. While this might be appropriate in an introductory book, in this instance, it is not a case of knowing what lies below the surface but sparing readers the detail. In this instance, we do not know what lies below the surface because we are anticipating a future in which the acceptability of automated legal services will almost certainly vary from one community to another and will vary as new technologies are proposed. We will say a bit more about this at the beginning of the next chapter but, before we can get below the surface, we will have to wait and see how far and how fast different communities accept governance by technology.

38

SMART LAWYERS AND SMART LEGAL INSTITUTIONS

Introduction

We know that machines can outperform humans in various functions, from game-playing to image recognition to document scanning, and much else (Russell, 2020). What if we decide that smart machines make better governance decisions than humans (Brownsword, 2023a)? What does an institutional design that is fit for governance in such circumstances look like?

Unless a community decides, ab initio, either that it will not employ smart tools or that it will hand over all governance functions to the machines, there will need to be an ongoing discussion about just how far and fast the community wants to go with governance by smart machines. Questions about who is entitled to use smart governance tools, about what red lines there are to be, and about when and how there has to be public engagement will be standing items on the agenda for discussion. It will be work in progress and the institutional design will need to be geared to facilitate as well as to be responsive to this ongoing discussion.

While we can expect that different communities will run at their own pace in adopting smart tools for governance, and that there will be more than one institutional design that is fit for purpose, there will need to be the building of governance intelligence. In particular, as we have already intimated, it will be important to understand how humans operate alongside smart governance tools—for example, when it is appropriate for human legislators and judges to be guided by smart tools or even replaced by them; and, of course, the social acceptability of the use of smart tools will set limits to what is practicable at any particular time. This is a brave new world and we need to enter it with our eyes wide open—we need to be smart. If it goes

DOI: 10.4324/9781003507802-44

badly, if the promise of new technologies is not delivered, and if humans are still around to experience and to express their concerns, then there will be discontent with ostensibly smart high-tech governance.

To be prepared for our future worlds, our governance might need to be AI-enabled and, in a general sense, 'smart' (deploying the optimal combination of governance tools to achieve its purposes). However, this will not happen unless the institutional support for governance is itself fit for the purposes of smart governance. Given that much of our governance relies on legacy institutions from a low-tech setting, we should not assume that they will be fit for purpose in a very different world of high-tech governance.

In this chapter, we can say a few words about institutional fitness for purpose and the use of smart tools, in both cases treating the Metaverse as an illustrative case.

Fitness for purpose

In a high-tech setting, no institutional design will be adequate unless two conditions are satisfied. One condition, the 'governance' condition, is that there is a clear understanding in the community about who (or which body) has the relevant responsibility in relation to the regulation of emerging technologies and about the operating procedure. The other condition, the 'intelligence' condition, is that the community has arrangements in place to gather up, synthesise, and disseminate whatever lessons can be taken from our experience of engaging with new technologies. Intelligent engagement with emerging technologies presupposes systematic and reflexive learning.

Relative to these two essential conditions, institutional design and practice in the UK fall short. Crucially, in the UK, there is no institutional hub with the responsibility to gather together our intelligence about regulating emerging technologies (and about the use of technologies for governance purposes); we might have some intelligence or 'know-how', but we have no repository for it. Moreover, there is no clear understanding about who is responsible for making the initial engagement with an emerging technology; there is no clear allocation of responsibility for review; there is no body to audit our performance; there is no sense of whether we are getting better at regulating emerging technologies; and, unless things have gone very well or very badly, there is no sense of how they have gone and whether there is anything to be learnt from our regulatory experience. Indeed, it seems to be largely a matter of happenstance as to who addresses which technology and what regulatory issue; and there is absolutely no pattern or consistency in how such matters are addressed. Possibly, institutional design is more adequate elsewhere. If so, we should certainly learn from it. However, so long as we fail to learn from our own governance experience—whether governance of technologies or governance by technologies—we are unlikely to be positioned to learn from others.

There might be more than one adequate response to these shortcomings. For example, some might argue that a bespoke governance agency should be established for each new technology as it emerges—such as an agency for synthetic biology or for algorithms and AI, or that there should be sectoral governance, or that there should be some other design. Whichever approach we take, it is essential that it is clear who has the responsibility for foresight (in relation to emerging smart technologies), for a first assessment, for regulatory intervention, and for ex post audit. Crucially, it is also imperative that the importance of gathering and analysing our governance intelligence is appreciated and that it is clear whose responsibility this is. Because smart technologies raise cross-border and global issues, it is also crucial that appropriate arrangements are made for cooperation and coordination at local, regional, and international level.

Unfortunately, the circumstances for establishing new governance institutions of the right kind internationally are far from ideal. On the one hand, the self-serving national tendencies that are characteristic of international relations coupled with the disproportionate power and influence of some nation states militates against the effective operation of global agencies; and, on the other, global agencies need to be careful to avoid over-reaching (by impinging improperly on national sovereignty) lest this compromises their legitimacy.

This makes for a somewhat depressing read. Once upon a time, and even now in the case of some good citizens, we could at least say that the guiding spirit of international law and international relations was and is one of good intentions; but, nowadays, even that might be too generous. Nevertheless, at the national and regional levels, these pathologies of international governance are no excuse for failing to take a smart (and intelligence-led) approach within our own communities.

In relation to our preparedness for the governance of our technological futures, the Metaverse is an interesting test-case. For the sake of illustration, let us assume that the Metaverse is understood as referring to large-scale networked 3D virtual environments that give users an unprecedented sense of real-time immersion and presence. Now, if our institutions were fit for purpose, then it would be clear who has the responsibility to be forming an initial view about the development of the Metaverse. In part, this view would be informed by intelligence that draws on the scientific and technical experts. Just how considerable are the technical challenges involved in this project? Is it all hype? If not, when are we likely to see the Metaverse—is it on the near, mid, or distant horizon? Is it likely to be for both personal and business use?

Furthermore, the governance of the Metaverse should also be on the agenda. A smart approach to governance, whether entrusted to an agency that is dedicated to the Metaverse or that is of a more generic nature, should already have started to reflect on the governance questions that are likely to arise. For example, in addition to consumer protection issues, there will be questions about the massive amount of data that is collected from the headsets or other kit that is used to access the Metaverse; and, if we think that the protection of children who access online content is a big issue, it might prove to be nothing compared to questions about the use of the Metaverse by children. Moreover, there are likely to be important questions about unfair competition and restrictive practices, about ownership, control, and exchangeability of assets that are held within the Metaverse, about a multitude of intellectual property applications, about liability for bad conduct or harms caused by avatars, about the status of avatars or human proxies, and about what is inside the Metaverse and what is outside it, and so on. However, intriguing though these questions might be, we might wonder whether, for governance purposes, they are really any different to similar questions that have been raised already in relation to multi-party online games or virtual worlds such as Second Life, or the use of remote sensing technologies.

While these are all relevant lines of inquiry, some might be more pressing than others: but, the point is that we need to be ahead of the game, already systematically asking these questions. We also need to turn these questions round. Instead of viewing the Metaverse as a set of technologies, or as so many new spaces, to which law's governance needs to be applied—that is, instead of thinking about the Metaverse as, so to speak, 'out there' waiting to be subjected to governance or regulation—we need to be asking whether it is a resource that might facilitate governance. In other words, might the Metaverse itself be a tool that can be used to assist governance? As we have said, it is not entirely clear where a conversation of this kind might be held, or who should be parties to it, but this is the conversation to have if we are really to get ahead of the game.

Fit to govern using smart tools

Smart lawyers need to understand the landscape of law's governance and they need to be able to operate in a Law 3.0 paradigm. For example, they need to be thinking about how we might make use of the Metaverse for regulatory purposes and what we might learn about governance from the Metaverse. In other words, our lines of inquiry need to go beyond asking how best to govern consumer transactions, or protect privacy or IP interests, or the like, in the Metaverse. From a governance perspective, the Metaverse is more than a challenge, it might also be an opportunity. But, an opportunity for what precisely?

One thought is that the Metaverse might function as a kind of sandbox in which a variety of regulatory approaches—for example, approaches that involve different mixes of incentives and disincentives, or that involve different combinations of rules and technological tools—are tested. In this way, those responsible for law's governance might gain a better understanding about both the effectiveness of these mixes and their acceptability to users. Another thought is that the Metaverse presents an opportunity to learn much more about governance by technological management. At one level, the developers of the Metaverse have the advantage of being able to design the environment in such a way that any uses that might compromise the viability of the project are technologically managed. Moreover, there might also be opportunities to experiment with technological management in the governance of particular zones within the Metaverse. In these different ways, governance experiences within the Metaverse might improve governance outside the Metaverse.

If this seems somewhat fanciful, some of the remarks made by Tom Boellstorff (2008) in his ethnography of Second Life should give us pause. According to Boellstorff:

> Virtual worlds raise the possibility of a whole new degree of control over culture … An actual-world government could ban slot machine gambling, but a virtual-world government could, in theory, disable all random-number generating scripts in the virtual world, an act for which there is no true actual-world parallel … Virtual worlds are sites of culture constituted through computer languages, shaped by menus, commands, and windows all designed and modified by the virtual worlds' owners, administrators, and open-source contributors, raising possibilities for social engineering of which any actual-world ruler could only dream.
>
> *(231)*

In line with these remarks, already we see that, where there is inappropriate behaviour by avatars in the Metaverse, there can be a technological response (for example, we have already mentioned the case of Nina Jane Patel, where Meta created a personal boundary functionality for users of Horizon Venues).

With the thought that technological management and design might be applied to protect the platforms and infrastructures for online cyber and Meta communities, we have come a long way from law's traditional governance. Nevertheless, the question hinted at here is whether new technologies, particularly applied to technological management and design, might be the solution to the governance of the essential infrastructure for our human communities (just like the platform or grid in a virtual world), whether the members of human communities act or transact in offline places and spaces, in cyberspace, or in the virtual spaces of the Metaverse. The question is whether, if we cannot protect the global commons by a combination of rules and principles, might we do better if we were to use some of the tools that we now have at our disposal?

PART 7
Final reflections

39

THE RADICAL THREADS REVISITED

Introduction

In this introduction to law, four radical threads have been emphasised: viewing law as a particular mode of governance; appreciating the important role that law plays in relation to civilised human life; thinking outside the doctrinal box; and, always, placing law within the context of the development of new technologies and technological mind-sets. By way of a concluding summary, we can underline the key aspects of each of these threads and suggest a further thread.

The role of law in relation to civilized human life

A central thread of this introduction is to retrieve the idea that the mission of law is to address the governance requirements that need to be met for any viable group of humans. Lawyers might need to apologise for losing sight of this mission but they should not have to apologise for being part of a practice that has this mission. Quite simply, law is a necessary condition for civilised human communities; law is important for all civilised communities; but, it is especially important in our time of unprecedented technological development and reliance.

Why is our time special? It is special not only because humans have a dazzling array of new tools but because those tools can be applied for both great good but also extreme harm. In line with this reading, in *The Precipice*, Toby Ord (2020) suggests that we are in a unique period of human history, an era when there is an existential risk to the future of humanity that is created not only by natural phenomena (asteroid strikes,

DOI: 10.4324/9781003507802-46

volcanic eruptions, and so on) but also by our own human practices and technological innovation. This risk could materialise in the extinction of humans or in the unrecoverable collapse of civilisation. According to Ord (at 7):

> Understanding the risks requires delving into physics, biology, earth science and computer science; situating this in the larger story of humanity requires history and anthropology; discerning just how much is at stake requires moral philosophy and economics; and finding solutions requires international relations and political science.

In other words, we need to call on all our resources if we are to engage effectively with this kind of risk. And, yet, in his list of resources, Ord makes no mention of law, regulation, or governance (although, towards the end of his book, he does speak to legal initiatives that might be taken at the international level). This cannot be right.

If the perception is that law is not relevant to preventing the collapse of civilised human life, then this (both the perception and the practice) needs to be corrected as a matter of urgency. It needs to be understood by everyone—those who are about to study law, those who are already studying or practising law, and those who are not in law—that human communities need governance to engage with these risks; and that they might well need law and regulation to prevent the collapse of civilisation. Law and lawyers need to be central to maintaining civilised life in our increasingly technological world. We need to view the law in a radically different way and we need to be introduced to law in a radically different way.

The importance of technology

In the 1960s, Gordon Moore predicted that the number of transistors on microchips would double every two years (https://en.wikipedia.org/wiki/Moore%27s_law). Or, put simply, computing power would double every two years. The effect of doubling is often illustrated by imagining that we place one grain of rice on a first square of a chess board and then, doubling it, place two grains of rice on a second square, and so on. Before we have placed rice on half the squares, we are into millions of grains of rice. So, if we started doing this in 1946, when I was born, and then doubling the grains every two years, by now we would be well into the millions. Putting this another way, in 1946, there was a certain amount of main frame computing power in the world; it took up a lot of space and it was expensive. In 2025, in line with Moore's Law, the computing power of my smart phone exceeds the sum total of the computing power that existed at the time of my birth.

For lawyers, whether students, academics, or practitioners, the availability of computers has been transformative. However, in relation to law's governance generally, it is not only computers but a whole raft of emerging technologies that have created both challenges and opportunities. Accordingly, in this radical introduction, we need to understand that new technologies pose significant questions and challenges for legal rules and principles that originate in less technologically developed times but that they also offer new tools to assist with governance functions.

Law's governance of technology

In the burgeoning field of law and technology, everyone knows about 'Easterbrook and the "law of the horse"'. This story goes back to a conference in Chicago in the 1990s, a conference that brought together a group of early 'cyberlaw' enthusiasts. This conference, one of the first of its kind, is recalled, not for the innovative contributions of these cyberlawyers but for an unexpectedly conservative intervention made by Judge Frank Easterbrook (1996). Stated shortly, Easterbrook's point was that it was fine for lawyers to take an interest in computers, but he objected to the idea that this warranted recognition as a new area of law, 'cyberlaw'. Famously, Easterbrook objected that, if we had a new area of law for each new area of interest, we could end up with 'The Law of the Horse'. This, he claimed, would be 'shallow' and it would 'miss unifying principles' (207). Rather, the better approach, Easterbrook contended, was 'to take courses in property, torts, commercial transactions, and the like ... [For only] by putting the law of the horse in the context of broader rules about commercial endeavours could one really understand the *law* about horses' (208).

Nevertheless, the law of cyberspace was a horse that was destined to bolt. Easterbrook's doubts notwithstanding, courses and texts on 'cyberlaw', or 'Internet law', or 'the law of e-commerce', or the like, abound and few would deny that they have intellectual integrity and make pedagogic sense. Similarly, research centres that are dedicated to the study of cyberlaw or digital law (or law and technology more generally) have mushroomed and are seen as being in the vanguard of legal scholarship.

That said, was Easterbrook wrong? And, if so, why exactly was he wrong? In 1996, cyberlaw was still in its formative stages and there were a number of questions of law that were being tested out in the courts—for example, about the liability of parties for defamatory online content and about conflicts of laws matters concerning the applicable law and the jurisdiction of the courts. These cases were textbook examples of Law 1.0 and Easterbrook's objection to cyberlaw reflects this kind of mind-set. It was not too long, though, before bespoke laws for e-commerce, for internet content (and the liability of internet service providers or other intermediaries), for cybercrime, for online privacy, and so on were being put in place (conspicuously so in Europe). Such laws were quite distinct from the general principles of law that Easterbrook had in mind, and they were shaped by Law 2.0 regulatory-instrumentalist thinking. In short, Easterbrook's remarks seem to assume that the laws governing computers and cyberspace would be Law 1.0 when it rapidly became clear that the relevant laws were largely Law 2.0.

Viewing Easterbrook's intervention from a twenty-first century vantage point, it seems that he failed to grasp the extent of the technological disruption of the law. Not only did Easterbrook fail to anticipate the regulatory thinking of much of the incoming law of cyberspace, he failed to anticipate that the law might engage with cybertechnologies as both regulatory targets (technologies to be regulated) and regulatory tools (technologies to be used by regulators). In other words, Easterbrook did not foresee Law 2.0 on the near horizon, and he did not foresee the emergence of Law 3.0 on the mid horizon.

With the benefit of hindsight, it is easy to be wise. Nevertheless, Easterbrook was wrong; and, in retrospect, his mistake was not so much to default to a Law 1.0 coherentist mind-set but to underestimate the disruptive effects of technology on the law and, at the same time, to over-estimate the flexibility of the general principles. If we are to 'really understand the *law*', it is essential to step outside a Law 1.0 mind-set. Only then is it possible to recognise the extent of the disruption wrought by new technologies and, concomitantly, the range of regulatory modalities employed by law's governance.

In sum, the problem with Easterbrook's approach is that it is a denial of (or, in denial about) disruption. While this might be appropriate in the age of slow-moving horses, it is not at all appropriate in an age of fast-moving disruptive technologies. In such an age, we need to re-imagine the field of legal interest and the landscape of law's governance.

Governance by technology

One of the leading cyberlawyers at the time of the Chicago conference was Lawrence Lessig. In the years following the conference, Lessig underlined the way in which the coding of hardware and software can, by intent, limit the options available to those who use the technology (Lessig, 1999). The thought that code might be likened to a kind of law has been much debated but, once we frame our thinking in terms of governance, it is easy to see how a range of instruments (including law's rules as well as coding features) can shape human conduct. Moving beyond computing technologies, it becomes clear that developments in a range of technologies can be deployed to assist with law's governance—for example, the use of DNA profiling and CCTV in the criminal justice system, or the use of AI by legal decision-makers.

In some cases, humans will still be in or on these governance loops but we might entrust governance functions to the technology and take humans out of the loop. Moreover, Law 3.0 thinking also invites consideration of the use of technological management, such as the kind of digital rights management that was uppermost in Lessig's thinking, to do the governance work.

In sum, Easterbrook's thinking is what Lessig would characterise as 'East coast' (and, indeed, very traditional East coast) when computing and other technological power was pointing to a quite different 'West coast' style of governance. That is to say, the reason why 'cyberlaw' merits picking out is not so much because computers challenge Law 1.0 (as well as Law 2.0) types of governance but because it prefigures Law 3.0 (West coast) governance (Brownsword, 2005). If so, what future might there be for lawyers? Should we all become data scientists?

Is there a future for lawyers?

Back in the 1960s, no one buying goods or services would have asked whether a supplier would accept a cash payment; yet, today, with the rapid adoption of digital payments and cryptocurrencies, we can no longer take it as read that suppliers will accept cash. 'Will you accept cash?' is no longer a stupid question. In the same way, back in the 1960s, no one would have asked whether there was a future for those who aspired to make a career as a lawyer; yet, today, we can no longer take it as read that there will be work for lawyers. If AI tools are able to match human lawyers in undertaking document review but complete the task in less than a minute rather than more than an hour, who needs lawyers? If this is not a stupid question—and it surely is not a stupid question—then those who are contemplating a career in law need to consider how the impingement of new technologies on legal practice is likely to affect their prospects.

While we can be confident that legal practice will be transformed by the adoption of tools that assist human providers of legal services (see Chapter 37), and while there will be some lawyering functions that are performed by tools that replace humans, it is not so clear that humans will no longer be required. Thus, concluding their review of the impact of AI on the legal profession, Michael Legg and Felicity Bell (2020) identify three reasons that will contribute to the continuing involvement of humans in legal practice. First, the lawyer-client relationship is not purely commercial; it is also professional and fiduciary. Secondly, human lawyers can 'provide judgment, discretion, creativity, empathy and understanding to a client' (349). Thirdly, human 'lawyers, in their many roles, are essential to civil society, liberty and the rule of law; goals or conditions that humans value and seek to protect' (ibid). Implicitly, this prognosis rests on the assumption either that technology cannot match humans in these various respects or that, even if technology can match (or outperform) humans, humans prefer their lawyers to be fellow humans. In other words, so long as law's governance is essentially a human enterprise, there will be a need for lawyers; and lawyers will have an important role to play in the maintenance of civilised life within and between communities.

While this is reassuring, for those who are thinking outside the box of law's governance, there is the question of whether lawyers will have a future if the two spearheads of Law 3.0 thinking really take hold: that is, if determined efforts are made to take humans out of the loop of governance and if technological management is employed to channel conduct. To be sure, there might still be some advisory and transactional work left for lawyers but, if governance becomes more technological than legal, it will be those lawyers who can situate themselves in the bigger picture of governance and human values who will be able to make a contribution to the enterprise. In these circumstances, the human aspiration will be for good governance and the challenge for lawyers is to show that they can lead their communities in a way that respects the generic global pre-conditions for governance while also being attuned to local ideals.

These radical thoughts raise a further question: technological development and legal disruption will not end with Law 3.0, so what can we expect in Law 4.0?

Law 4.0?

In *Law, Technology and Society* (Brownsword, 2019), I contemplated the possibility that further developments in human genetics—on the one hand enabling us to manipulate genes more precisely and, on the other, helping us to understand just how particular genetic profiles account for us being the person that we are, acting and re-acting in the way that we do—might encourage a technocratic strategy that focuses on internal coding controls. If so, we would not so much find ourselves in technologically managed environments as be technologically managed through our genetic coding. However, I qualified this by saying that a more attractive option for regulators might be simply to take a much more managed approach to reproduction (compare Greely, 2016).

It might be, though, that biotechnology is not the driver for Law 4.0. Rather, it might be that there are further advances in, say, neurotechnologies and brain-computer interfaces that transform governance practices. More likely, perhaps, the key development will be in AI, enabling other technologies, such that humans decide that the entire legal and regulatory enterprise would be better entrusted to the machines. If it is acceptable to have robots staffing prisons, why not also robocops? And, if robocops are acceptable, why not also robojudges? And, if robojudges are acceptable, why not also roboregulators? Of course, there are huge functional leaps in these moves, but a community might be prepared to make them, especially if in other domains, notably health, we entrust life and death decisions and procedures to intelligent machines (compare Tegmark, 2017: 107). In Law 4.0, we might find that it is *Lex Machina* that rules.

But....but, might a community think about doing a technological U-turn? In Law 4.0, might we find that, as in Samuel Butler's *Erewhon* (1872), the machines have been destroyed? To Butler's Victorian readers, living through the transition from Law 1.0 to Law 2.0, it must have seemed quite extraordinary that the Erewhonians—concerned that their machines might develop some kind of 'consciousness', or capacity to reproduce, or agency, and fearful that machines might one day enslave humans—had decided that the machines must be destroyed. How, Butler's readers must have wondered, could such intelligent and technologically sophisticated people have gone backwards in this way? How, indeed? Perhaps Law 4.0, or subsequent waves of disruption, will shed some light on the mystery.

Thinking outside the box

As lawyers, we have a particular field of interest. Traditionally, this is the field of legal systems, the field of legislation, cases and constitutions, the field of lawyers and lawyering, and so on. It does not follow that we have no interests outside this field but, as lawyers, our field of interest is traditionally limited in the way just indicated. As Easterbrook might have said, law is for lawyers and computers are for computer scientists. Within our legal field, we also have a particular way of framing our questions and our responses, all of this being captured in what we have termed a Law 1.0 way of thinking like a lawyer.

Law 1.0 is our doctrinal box and Law 1.0 is the box that this radical introduction insists we must think outside. However, our introduction also demands that we think outside the box of our own community, so that we understand the preconditions for governance in any community of humans. Beyond this, it is also important that we think outside the box that focuses on human-to-human transactions and interactions. These transactions and interactions are now so heavily mediated by enabling technologies that we must look critically at the relationship between humans and their tools.

The doctrinal box of Law 1.0

Legal reasoning has been dominated by a Law 1.0 mind-set. If we break outside this box, so that we also reason in a Law 2.0 way, we can see the distinction between reasoning based on legal principles and reasoning based on policy in a new light as well as the distinction between the distinctive role of, on the one hand, judges and, on the other, politicians and lawmakers.

Moreover, thinking in a Law 2.0 regulatory way, we can identify the generic challenges that emerging technologies present to law's governance—challenges such as those of regulatory connection, effectiveness, and legitimacy. However, this is still a relatively limited box.

The crucial move is to think beyond the boxes of both Law 1.0 and Law 2.0 so that we engage more comprehensively with emerging technologies in a Law 3.0 way and, at the same time, understand how all three modes of thinking are represented in the landscape of law's governance. The point about a Law 3.0 mind-set is that it engages questions about the application of emerging technologies for governance purposes, a hugely significant feature of the modern governance landscape; and the point about a big picture view of the landscape, including Law 1.0, 2.0, and 3.0, is that we can understand the tensions between the different modes of legal thinking and the feedback between them.

Once we have both rules and principles and new tools being developed to guide conduct and to settle disputes, we can capture our extended field of interest by simply treating it as 'governance'. As traditional lawyers, we are interested only in the law, not at all in technology; but as lawyers of the present century, we have to be interested in both legal rules and principles as well as technologies that are deployed to support or even replace law's rules and functionaries. In sum, governance by rules in conjunction with governance by technologies becomes our field of interest.

The box of our own particular community (leading to the preconditions)

Another box that inhibits our engagement with law's governance is the one that restricts our thinking to our own community or to our own national legal system. Unless we think beyond the box of our own particular community, we cannot identify the values that are truly foundational for civilised human communities. These are the values that speak to the conditions for human existence and co-existence and for human agency. This is where we find the deepest interest of humans as human agents, regardless of their location on Earth or the particular values of their communities or their own individual preferences, priorities, and values. Once we are thinking beyond the limits of our own community box, we can gain a new appreciation of the legitimacy of law's governance, the force of precautionary reasoning, the line between the cosmopolitan and the community's own sovereignty, and what it is that is so unreasonable that no human could reasonably support such a position.

Humans and tools

Our traditional legal thinking and the concepts that give shape to law's governance are largely predicated on human-to-human relationships. In this context, our concepts have a particular meaning and significance. However, we now need to think outside this box so that we can understand the direction of travel in governance and the way that human-to-human concepts are being given new meaning and significance in technological contexts.

We can start by noting the difference between the traditional, albeit heavily contested, understanding of human 'autonomy' and the emerging notion of 'autonomous' technologies and then we can note how the idea of 'trust' and 'trustworthiness' is being transformed in technological governance.

The traditional understanding starts with the idea that a human acts autonomously where the acts in question are free from the control of other humans. Autonomous human action is independent and *self*-directed. However, conceptions of human autonomy are sharpened and shaped once we reflect on the capacity for *self*-direction that humans, free from the control of *others,* now have. One view is that humans act autonomously where they have developed the capacity to be guided by their long-term critical interests rather than their short-term inclinations; and another view is that it is the capacity to act in a way that gives consideration (morally) to the legitimate interests of others that is characteristic of human autonomy.

By contrast, the concept of autonomy when applied to technologies simply connotes independence from human control—not an independent human in control—and it does not speak at all to the development of the capacity for long-term prudential or moral self-direction. So, any reference to 'autonomous systems' should not be taken to signal that such systems are autonomous in the sense that humans might be autonomous. The more autonomous that a technology (such as an autonomous vehicle) becomes the less it resembles human autonomy, Accordingly, it would be foolish, and confused, to think that it would be a good idea to train machines to operate autonomously simply because we value autonomy in humans.

So, recalling the three imperatives that we outlined in Chapter 22, given that we should in no circumstances compromise the conditions that enable humans to develop their capacity for autonomous action and decision (whether conceived of as a prudential or a moral capacity), it is far from clear that autonomous technologies should be protected and supported. Indeed, the closer that weapons systems—or, for that matter, vehicles or vessels—get to being fully autonomous, the more that we should be concerned. In this context, to describe a technology as autonomous should be less a commendation than a caution. Indeed, far from feeling more comfortable about governance by technologies that are autonomous, once we have re-centred autonomy with humans, we are likely to feel both discomfort and concern about the operation of these technologies.

In the same breath that we speak about the development of so-called autonomous technologies and systems, we also hear much about trust in these technologies and trustworthy systems. Like autonomy, trust is a contested concept. The starting point is that trust is a relational concept: A trusts B with regard to some matter C. But, if A is a human, who or what is B; and, what is the particular C in relation to which A places trust in B? More importantly, is the trusting relationship between A and B moral or prudential in nature? If B is a fellow human, does A treat B as trustworthy in the (moral) sense that A judges that B will do the right thing (for the right reason), or is A making a prudential judgment about, say, the skill and expertise of B or the safety and risk presented by leaving C to B?

Then, if B is not a human but rather a robot, machine, or technology of some kind, how does A's trust in B relate to moral or prudential trust? For example, if those who support fully autonomous vehicles or other technologies that are out of human control, respond to the concerns of potential users by insisting that the technologies can be trusted, are they speaking to our moral and/or our prudential interests or neither? Is some new technical and regulatory concept of trust being set against the traditional human-centric paradigm?

In another context, following the global financial crisis in 2008, one response to the loss of trust and confidence in banks and other financial intermediaries was to devise decentralised systems that would take out human intermediaries and their institutions and place our trust in technologies for the transfer of digital assets (instead of fiat currency) and registration that would make use of the best cryptography. Such was the promise of blockchain (De Filippi and Wright, 2018), a promise that we might now think was somewhat inflated (Low and Mik, 2020).

Be that as it may, trust in technology—not even in blockchain—is not equivalent to trust in fellow humans. To trust a person to do the right thing (or indeed to do anything) is to rely on them without any security or insurance even though one has reservations about doing so and even though one is aware that there is a risk in doing so. In a context where humans are out of the loop, to trust a technology is to rely on it without any security or insurance because, viewed prudentially, this is a use that serves one's interests and is risk-free (or subject only to acceptable risks). Whereas, in the context of law's governance, to judge that a person is 'trustworthy' is to judge that a person will do the right thing even when they are disposed to (and have the opportunity to) do otherwise, in the context of governance by machines, trustworthiness is a proxy for reliability. In an insightful analysis, Christoph Kletzer (2021: 322) hits this nail on the head when he says:

> There are entirely different stakes at play in reliance and trust. Whilst reliance is a mundane and technical issue, trust is a morally laden issue that potentially concerns our very human essence. This makes it crucial to keep these two concepts neatly separated. Failing to do so leads to a

host of misunderstandings not only about trust and reliance itself but also about the relationship of technology and law.

So, on this analysis, parties who make use of AI or who commit their transactions to a blockchain, do not place their 'trust' in the technology; they merely rely on it; and, although we should not jump too quickly to this conclusion, we might infer that, by relying on the technology rather than their fellow human, they do not trust the latter (or regard the latter as trustworthy). Moreover, contrary to much of the conventional wisdom, it is not so much the difference between trust and trustworthiness that is critical but the difference between reliance based on trust (or trustworthiness), which involves a judgment as to the moral character of a human, and mere reliance on technology, which signifies only the use of a tool or, at most, a prudential judgment. This kind of judgment might be more or less reflective, more or less informed about the technology's fitness for purpose and its quality,more or less a matter of choice, but never morally judgmental.

In this context, when governance on both sides of the Channel aspires to instate an ecosystem of trust for the application of AI, we would do well to note that where governance itself relies on tools (such as AI or on design and architecture) to discourage or preclude particular acts, what this signals is *a lack of* trust in those who are governed. Those members of the club at Westways (Chapter 14) who regretted the loss of trust when CCTV was introduced had a point; and, if those who govern really want AI to be accepted in an ecosystem that evinces trust in the technology, then they might want to reflect on the signals given by their own governance practices.

Law as a particular mode of governance

We have already said that, thinking outside the box, we will come to characterise our field of interest as being that of the governance of humans and their communities. This enables us to focus on a regulatory environment that is a mix of rules and tools—or, better, a matrix spanning public, public/private, and private governance which allows for variable degrees of reliance on humans, rules, and tools—without having to justify our interest, as lawyers, in emerging technologies.

One of the apparent strengths of a more technological approach to governance is that its instruments will be more effective in achieving its regulatory objectives than would be the case with reliance only on rules. To this extent, a governance perspective chimes in with much of modern regulatory thinking which is pre-occupied with understanding more about what works, what does not work, and why. However, we must not restrict ourselves to questions of effectiveness, efficiency, and economy. To the contrary, we must treat the justifiability of our governance purposes and particular approaches as our most pressing concern. In our quest for good governance, it is legitimacy that comes first.

Good governance as legitimate governance

Within our human communities, we might equate good governance with a number of features—for example, with the integrity of those who have governance responsibilities, with governance in the interests of those who are governed, with transparency and inclusiveness, and with effectiveness, and so on (compare Addink, 2019). However, I suggest that our thinking about good governance should start with legitimate and justified (or, we might simply say, ethical) governance (Brownsword, 2023). The difficulty here, though, is that there are any number of arguable criteria of legitimacy; there are too many contested conceptions of justice, fairness, dignity, and so on; and, without an Archimedean reference point, we will end up with a plurality of views as to whether governance is good or not.

If there is no consensus within the group, and if we cannot find the key to good governance within each group or community of humans, we must look for it in the conditions that make human social existence possible in the first place. These are the pre-conditions that are essential if humans are to have any prospect of living in viable communities. These are conditions that relate to the sustainability of human life on planet Earth, to peaceful co-existence within and between communities, and to the opportunity for humans (individually and collectively) to develop and operationalise their agency. Accordingly, there needs to be some global stewardship of these conditions but also governance within each community—whether as we now think of the governance map, these are national, subnational, transnational, regional, or international communities—must above all do nothing to compromise these conditions. So much for the global stage for human communities.

Assuming that governance within each community is compatible with the maintenance of the essential conditions, it is for each community to identify its fundamental values and to reach its particular accommodations of the competing and conflicting preferences and priorities of its members. This all needs governance within the community and, subject to the requirement of compatibility with the essential conditions for viable human communities, it is for each community to adopt its preferred modality (or paradigm) of governance. In other words, our governance map might reveal a plurality of not only governance procedures and positions community by community but also of governance modalities. So, we have plurality but it is constructed on a platform of community-building possibility.

Translating this idea of good governance into practice, we might require all acts of governance to satisfy a 'triple licence': first, being compatible with the imperatives that relate to the possibility of governance; secondly, being compatible with the fundamental values of the community, and, thirdly, being acceptable to the members of the community.

A fifth thread: Looking forward not back

This leaves one more radical thought. In the common law world, where law has been made through cases, the direction of our Law 1.0 mind-set is backward-looking. Judges look back at the leading cases and precedents; they aim to treat today's cases in the same way that yesterday's equivalent cases were treated. Not only this, in a world that is relatively stable, the mission of Law 1.0 is largely to respond to wrongdoing by restoring the injured party to the position that they were in before the wrongdoing took place.

In the twenty-first century, when the majority of law's governing rules are made by politicians, often in pursuit of a particular regulatory policy, our Law 2.0 mind-set is not backward-looking. Rather, by setting targets, we are often looking forward. Unlike Law 1.0, where the question 'What do you hope the law will have achieved in the next five years?' has little resonance, in forward-looking Law 2.0, this is a meaningful question. As we move on to think in a Law 3.0 way, we need to become even more forward-looking. We need to be engaged in horizon-scanning so that when a new technology or application emerges, we are not caught cold. At the same time, we also need to be looking back to the intelligence that we have gathered in our attempts to govern new technologies.

Most importantly, though, we need to be anticipating an increasing reliance on technologies to undertake governance functions. We need to be looking ahead to a shift from governance by law and its rules to governance by technology. True, it is not only lawyers who need to be forward-looking in this way; and this is not science fiction. This is a question for everyone in the community, and, to repeat, it is a question where lawyers should be playing a leading role in helping communities understand the options that are open to them and how civilised governance can be sustained.

40

GOOD QUESTIONS AND GOOD GOVERNANCE

Introduction

No introductory talk would be complete without the audience having the opportunity to ask questions. For readers of this book, there might be many questions that they would like to ask but there is not the same opportunity. Nevertheless, the importance of reading and thinking in a critical spirit cannot be overstated and so let me encourage the process by posing a few questions—questions of the kind that, had they been put by members of an audience, we academics would welcome as 'good', or 'excellent', or even 'great' questions.

Good questions

First, someone might ask how I would capture the mission of law schools, academic lawyers, and everyone associated with law's governance. It will be evident that I would not say that the law school mission should centre on getting students 'to learn the law'; and, equally, I reject the idea that law school education should focus exclusively on training students to think like lawyers in a Law 1.0 sense. Rather, it will be clear that I would frame legal education in terms of understanding why human communities need governance, what law offers as a particular mode of governance, where the tensions are found in law's particular mode of governance, and how technology is now disrupting the legal enterprise. Beyond this, I would view legal and regulatory scholarship as well as legal practitioners as sharing an aspiration to contribute to the better governance of human communities. So, whether we are students, academics, or practitioners we should share the concern to

DOI: 10.4324/9781003507802-47

improve law's imperfect governance and contribute to the good governance of our communities.

Secondly, readers will note that the concept of law is contested and that some want to draw a sharp distinction between legal and moral reason (see Chapter 11). Be that as it may, we know that moral reason will show up on the radar of governance and the question is whether we need to differentiate between considerations of justice (Chapter 26), ethics (Chapter 27), and morals. In general, where we are questing after good governance, we do not need to differentiate between these three considerations. We can treat both justice and ethics as articulations of moral concern and we will want to audit governance relative to these criteria. That said, there might be some conversations in which we do want to narrow justice to a particular context (perhaps that of dispute resolution or algorithmic decision-making) or to a particular moral concern (for example, where governance has to make decisions about rationing or the distribution of scarce resources, or where unfair bias or discrimination is the issue); and, in the same way, there might be occasions where we want to confine ethics to particular kinds of question (for example, to questions of self-respect (compare Dworkin, 2010)). That said, we need to be careful not to diminish the importance of moral value by muddying the distinction between moral reason and prudential (self-serving) considerations, or by subordinating questions about (morally) legitimate governance to considerations of efficiency and effectiveness.

Thirdly, for readers who are familiar with Max Tegmark's work, it might be asked how my ideas of *Law* 1.0, 2.0, and 3.0 relate to his *Life* 1.0, 2.0, and 3.0 (Tegmark, 2017). According to Tegmark, we can conceive of life developing through three stages. In Life 1.0, the 'biological' stage, life forms (such as bacteria) simply evolve; in Life 2.0, the 'cultural' stage, which is where we humans find ourselves, biology still develops through evolution but humans are able to learn new skills and develop new tools and technologies; and, in Life 3.0, the 'technological' stage, biology is freed from its evolutionary shackles, life forms now being able, as Tegmark puts it, to design both their hardware and software. In this developmental story, humans instantiate Life 2.0 and the three conversations of Law 1.0, 2.0, and 3.0 all fall within this cultural stage. That said, both narratives highlight the increasing significance of technological development and the overall direction of travel, whether it is to making a life form the master of its own destiny or to increasing the effective control exercised by regulators.

Fourthly, it might be asked whether we can ever escape from 'thinking in a box'. It might be objected that, while I insist that we must break out of the box of Law 1.0 doctrinal thinking, I succeed only in replacing it with a much larger box of Law 3.0 and governance. Now, that is a question that looks like 'check' in a game of chess, but I do not think it is 'check-mate'. In response to the check, I need only say that the box of Law 3.0 and governance is a more productive way of opening our inquiries and framing our thinking; I am not arguing that we do not need some kind of box to organise our thinking. Whether or not there is a check-mate some moves later, I do not know; but it seems to me that, whether there is or not, the box that is Law 1.0 is not a good place to be.

Finally, there might be a question arising from my discussion of the challenges facing, and concomitantly the discontent with, law's governance in Part Five of the book. This discussion draws on another book that I recently published (Brownsword, 2023). When I was road-testing some of the main ideas, more than once, a comment that was made to me was that we need to see the bigger picture of law's governance. Of course, it will be no surprise that I agree with that. However, it was the nature of the bigger picture that was striking.

The thrust of the comment was that, given the bigger picture, we will find it hard to believe that, even if the kind of discontent that I discuss could be addressed, we could ever really be content with the law or with lawyers. What stands in the way of our being content, so the argument goes, is that what passes for law tends to consolidate and reinforce the interests of those who are propertied, privileged, and powerful; in unequal societies, law (aided and abetted by lawyers) ensures that the 'haves' come out ahead of the 'have nots'; and, in the name of the Rule of Law, powerful states colonise and exploit other peoples. So, once law's governance comes to town, it purports to tell us who are the good guys and who are the bad, but what it does not do is announce that it is those who bring law to town who are really the bad guys. Rather, what law does is to 'legitimise' or 'legitimate' prior exercises of force and ongoing exploitation. We need to demystify law's governance and, once we do that, we will see that the problem is not so much law's failure to address local discontent as its success in pulling the wool over the eyes of exploited populations.

In mitigation, let me say that, although readers might detect some elements of this sceptical bigger picture as a foil for the view of good governance that I was developing in the book, this systematic discontent was not my primary focus. My starting point was not that law's governance is necessarily bad and always a reason for discontent. Rather, the bigger picture that was in my mind when writing that previous book was one in which governance by technological means presents itself as an alternative to law's governance (but an alternative which might give humans reasons for discontent to a greater or lesser degree).

Now, much the same could be said about this present radical introduction to law. For those who want to bring into the foreground the picture of one group of humans relying on law's governance in order to exploit other humans, I take it that there might be some comfort to be found in the prospect of law's time coming to an end. On the other hand, if the humans who govern by technological means are as exploitative as those who have prospered under law's governance, then this is not a future to be welcomed. At all events, big pictures or small pictures, as I have declared, I see this introductory book as part of a common quest for better, non-exploitative, governance and I see lawyers as having a radically different, valued, and vanguard role to play in that quest.

LIST OF CASES

Airedale NHS Trust v Bland [1993] 1 All ER 821
Associated Provincial Picture Houses Ltd v Wednesbury Corporation ([1948] 1 KB 223
Attorney-General v Blake [2000] UKHL 45
Beshada v Johns-Manville Products Corp. 90 N.J. 191, 447 A.2d 539 (1982)
Blue v Ashley [2017] EWHC 1928 (Comm)
Bolam v Friern Hospital Management Committee [1957] 1 WLR 582
Bolitho v City and Hackney Health Authority [1997] UKHL 46
Burmah Oil Company Ltd v Lord Advocate [1965] AC 75
Carmarthenshire County Council v Lewis [1955] AC 549
Case of S. and Marper v The United Kingdom (2009) 48 EHRR 50
Dobbs v Jackson Women's Health Organization 597 US 215 (2022) (https://www.supremecourt.gov/opinions/21pdf/19-1392_6j37.pdf)
Donoghue v Stevenson [1932] AC 562
Federal Republic of Germany v European Parliament and Council of the European Union (the Tobacco Advertising case), Case C-376/98 (2000) ECR I-8419
Fisher v Bell [1961] 1 QB 394
Gillick v West Norfolk and Wisbech Area Health Authority [1985] 3 All ER 402
Greater Glasgow Health Board v Doogan [2014] UKSC 68
Grimmark v Sweden (2020) (https://hudoc.echr.coe.int/fre?i=001-201915)
Herne Bay Steam Boat Company v Hutton [1903] 2 KB 683
Ingram v Little [1961] 1 QB 31
Krell v Henry [1903] 2 KB 740
Montgomery v Lanarkshire Health Board [2015] UKSC 11
Moore v Regents of University of California 51 Cal. 3d 120, 793 P.2d 479, 271 Cal. Rptr. 146 (Cal. 1990)
ParkingEye Ltd v Beavis ([2015] UKSC 67
Phillips v Brooks [1919] 2 KB 243
R (on the application of AAA (Syria) and others) v Secretary of State for the Home Department [2023] UKSC 42

R (Miller) v Secretary of State for Exiting the European Union [2016] EWHC 2768 (Admin); on appeal, *R (Miller) v Secretary of State for Exiting the European Union* [2016] UKSC 5 (*Miller 1*)
R (Miller) v The Prime Minister; Cherry v Advocate General for Scotland [2019] UKSC 41 (*Miller 2*)
R (on the application of Nicklinson and another) v Ministry of Justice; R (on the application of AM) (AP) v The DPP [2014] UKSC 38
Re A (Children) [2000] 4 All ER 961
Re B, R v Cambridge Health Authority [1995] EWCA Civ 43).
Reference by the Lord Advocate of devolution issues under paragraph 34 of Schedule 6 to the Scotland Act 1998 [2022] UKSC 31
Reg. v. Ireland [1998] A.C. 147
Ruxley Electronics v Forsyth [1996] AC 344
Smith v Hughes [1960] 1 WLR 830
Strunk v Strunk 445 SW 2d 145 (Ky 1969)
Suisse Atlantique Societe d'Armement SA v NV Rotterdamsche Kolen Central [1967] 1 AC 361
Thaler v Comptroller General of Patents Trade Marks and Designs [2021] EWCA Civ 1374, [2023] UKSC 49
Uber BV and others v Aslam and others [2021] UKSC 5
United States v Salerno and Cafaro (1987) 481 US 739
Washington v Glucksburg (1997) 521 US 702
White v Jones [1995] 2 AC 207
Yearworth v North Bristol NHS Trust [2009] EWCA Civ 37

REFERENCES

Abbott, Ryan (2020): *The Reasonable Robot: Artificial Intelligence and the Law*, Cambridge, Cambridge University Press

Adams, John N. and Brownsword, Roger (2006): *Understanding Law*, London, Sweet and Maxwell

Addink, Henk (2019): *Good Governance*, Oxford, Oxford University Press

Alarie, Benjamin (2016): 'The Path of the Law: Toward Legal Singularity' (2016) 66 *University of Toronto Law Journal* 443

Ashcroft, Richard E. (2010): 'Could Human Rights Supersede Bioethics?' 10 *Human Rights Law Review* 639

Ashworth, Andrew and Zedner, Lucia (2014): *Preventive Justice*, Oxford, Oxford University Press

Atwood, Margaret (2023): *Burning Questions*, London, Vintage

Auerbach, Jerold S. (1976): *Unequal Justice*, Oxford, Oxford University Press

Ball, Matthew (2022): *The Metaverse—And How It Will Revolutionise Everything*, New York, W.W. Norton

Barlow, John Perry (1994): 'The Economy of Ideas: Selling Wine Without Bottles on the Global Net', available at https://www.wired.com/1994/03/economy-ideas/

Barton, Benjamin H. and Bibas, Stephanos (2017): *Justice Rebooted*, New York, Encounter Books

Beyleveld, Deryck and Brownsword, Roger (2001): *Human Dignity in Bioethics and Biolaw*, Oxford, Oxford University Press

Beyleveld, Deryck and Brownsword, Roger (2007): *Consent in the Law*, Oxford, Hart

Bimber, Bruce (1996): *The Politics of Expertise in Congress*, Albany, State University of New York Press

Bingham, Tom (2011): *The Rule of Law*, London, Penguin

Boellstorff, Tom (2008): *Coming of Age in Second Life*, Princeton, Princeton University Press

Borghi, Maurizio and Brownsword, Roger (eds) (2023): *Law, Regulation and Governance in the Information Society*, Abingdon, Routledge

Brownsword, Roger (2003): 'Bioethics Today, Bioethics Tomorrow: Stem Cell Research and the "Dignitarian Alliance"' 17 *University of Notre Dame Journal of Law, Ethics and Public Policy* 15

Brownsword, Roger (2005): 'Code, Control, and Choice: Why East is East and West is West' 25 *Legal Studies* 1
Brownsword, Roger (2008): *Rights, Regulation and the Technological Revolution*, Oxford, Oxford University Press
Brownsword, Roger (2012): 'Regulating Brain Imaging: Questions of Privacy and Informed Consent' in Sarah J.L. Edwards, Sarah Richmond, and Geraint Rees (eds), *I Know What You Are Thinking: Brain Imaging and Mental Privacy*, Oxford, Oxford University Press, 223
Brownsword, Roger (2017a): 'Law, Liberty and Technology' in R. Brownsword, E. Scotford, and K. Yeung (eds), *The Oxford Handbook of Law, Regulation and Technology*, Oxford, Oxford University Press, 41
Brownsword, Roger (2017b): 'From Erewhon to Alpha Go: For the Sake of Human Dignity Should We Destroy the Machines?' 9 *Law, Innovation and Technology* 117
Brownsword, Roger (2019): *Law, Technology and Society: Re-imagining the Regulatory Environment*, Abingdon, Routledge
Brownsword, Roger (2020): *Law 3.0*, Abingdon, Routledge
Brownsword, Roger (2022a): *Rethinking Law, Regulation and Technology*, Cheltenham, Elgar
Brownsword, Roger (2022b): *Technology, Governance and Respect for the Law: Pictures at an Exhibition*, Abingdon, Routledge
Brownsword, Roger (2023): *Technology, Humans, and Discontent with Law: The Quest for Good Governance*, Abingdon, Routledge
Brownsword, Roger, Cornish, W.R. and Llewelyn, Margaret (eds) (1998): *Law and Human Genetics*, Oxford, Hart
Brownsword, Roger and Goodwin, Morag (2012): *Law and the Technologies of the Twenty-First Century*, Cambridge, Cambridge University Press
Brownsword, Roger and Howells, Geraint (1999): 'When Surfers Start to Shop: Internet Commerce and Contract Law' 19 *Legal Studies* 287
Brownsword, Roger and Wale, Jeffrey (2018): 'Testing Times Ahead: Non-Invasive Prenatal Testing and the Kind of Community that We Want to Be' 81 *Modern Law Review* 646
Brownsword, Roger and Yeung, Karen (eds) (2008): *Regulating Technologies: Legal Futures, Regulatory Frames, and Technological Fixes*, Oxford, Hart
Bussani, Mauro, Cassese, Sabino and Infantino, Marta (eds) (2023): *Comparative Legal Metrics*, Leiden, Brill
Butler, Samuel (1872): *Erewhon*, Dover Thrift (2003)
Bygrave, Lee (2017): 'Hardwiring Privacy', in Roger Brownsword, Eloise Scotford, and Karen Yeung (eds), *The Oxford Handbook of Law, Regulation and Technology*, Oxford, Oxford University Press, 754
Caulfield, Tim and Brownsword, Roger (2006): 'Human Dignity: A Guide to Policy Making in the Biotechnology Era' 7 *Nature Reviews Genetics* 72
Chesterman, Simon (2021): *We, the Robots? Regulating Artificial Intelligence and the Limits of the Law*, Cambridge, Cambridge University Press
Cohen, Julie E. (2019): *Between Truth and Power*, Oxford, Oxford University Press
Collingridge, David (1982): *The Social Control of Technology*, New York, St Martin's Press
Craig, Paul P. (1997): 'Formal and Substantive Conceptions of the Rule of Law: An Analytical Framework' *Public Law* 467
Deakin, Simon and Markou, Christopher (eds) (2020): *Is Law Computable?* Oxford, Hart
De Filippi, Primavera and Wright, Aaron (2018): *Blockchain and the Law*, Cambridge, Mass., Harvard University Press

Department for Science, Innovation and Technology (2023): *A Pro-innovation Approach to AI Regulation* (CP 815)
Devlin, Patrick (1965): *The Enforcement of Morals*, Oxford, Oxford University Press
Dworkin, Ronald (2010): *Justice for Hedgehogs*, Cambridge Mass, Harvard University Press
Dyson, Lord (2018): *Justice: Continuity and Change*, Oxford, Hart
Easterbrook, Frank H. (1996): 'Cyberspace and the Law of the Horse' *University of Chicago Legal Forum* 207
Ehrlich, Eugen (2001) [originally 1913]: *Fundamental Principles of the Sociology of Law*, New Brunswick, Transaction Publishers
Ellickson, Robert C. (1994): *Order Without Law*, Cambridge, Mass, Harvard University Press
Ellison, Robin (2018): *Red Tape*, Cambridge, Cambridge University Press
Ellson, Andrew (2022): 'Legal Complaints Go Untouched for Years', *The Times*, July 30, 38
Eubanks, Virginia (2018): *Automating Inequality*, New York, St Martin's Press
Fairfield, Joshua A.T. (2021): *Runaway Technology*, Cambridge, Cambridge University Press
Fairfield, Joshua A.T. (2022): 'Tokenized: The Law of Non-Fungible Tokens and Unique Digital Property' 97 *Indiana Law Journal* 1261
Fenwick, Mark, Kaal, Wulf A. and Vermeulen, Erik P.M. (2020): 'Legal Education in the Blockchain Revolution', 20 *Vanderbilt Journal of Entertainment and Technology Law* 351
Finck, Michèle (2018): *Blockchain Regulation and Governance in Europe*, Cambridge, Cambridge University Press
Fisher, Max (2022): *The Chaos Machine: The Inside Story of How Social Media Rewired Our Minds and Our World*, London, Quercus
Franklin, Sarah (2019): 'Ethical Research—The Long and Bumpy Road from Shirked to Shared' 574 *Nature* 627
Freedman, Lawrence (2017): *The Future of War: A History*, London, Allen Lane
Fukuyama, Francis (2002): *Our Posthuman Future*, London, Profile Books
Fuller, Lon L. (1958): 'Positivism and Fidelity to Law—A Reply to Professor Hart' 71 *Harvard Law Review* 630
Fuller, Lon L. (1969): *The Morality of Law*, New Haven, Yale University Press
Gal, Michal and Elkin-Koren, Niva (2017): 'Algorithmic Contracts' 30 *Harvard Journal of Law and Technology* 309
Gash, Tom (2016): *Criminal: The Truth About Why People Do Bad Things*, London, Allen Lane
Gibb, Frances (2023): 'Killers Dragged to the Dock Won't All Come Quietly, Lord Chief Justice Warns' *The Times*, September 2, 32
Goddard, David (2022): *Making Laws that Work*, Oxford, Hart
Gov UK Press Release (2024): 'Wrongful Post Office Convictions to be Quashed through Landmark Legislation: 13 March 2024', available at https://www.gov.uk/government/news/wrongful-post-office-convictions-to-be-quashed-through-landmark-legislation-13-march-2024#:~:text=Press%20release-,Wrongful%20Post%20Office%20convictions%20to%20be%20quashed%20through%20landmark%20legislation,today%20%5BWednesday%2013%20March%5D
Graeber, David (2015): *The Utopia of Rules*, Brooklyn, Melville House
Grayling, A.C. (2022): *For the Good of the World*, London, Oneworld Publications
Greely, Henry T (2016): *The End of Sex and the Future of Human Reproduction*, Cambridge, MA, Harvard University Press

Griffith, J.A.G. (1977): *The Politics of the Judiciary*, London, Fontana
Haidt, Jonathan (2012): *The Righteous Mind*, New York, Vintage Books
Harcourt, Bernard E. (2007): *Against Prediction*, Chicago, University of Chicago Press
Hart, H.L.A. (1961): *The Concept of Law*, Oxford, Clarendon Press
Hart, H.L.A. (1963): *Law, Liberty and Morality*, Stanford, Stanford University Press
Hart, H.L.A. (1967): 'Social Solidarity and the Enforcement of Morality' 35 *University of Chicago* LR 1
Hartzog, Woodrow (2018): *Privacy's Blueprint*, Cambridge, MA, Harvard University Press
Henkin, Louis (1974): 'Privacy and Autonomy' 74 *Columbia Law Review* 1410
Hohfeld, Wesley Newcomb (1964): *Fundamental Legal Conceptions*, New Haven, Yale University Press
House of Commons, Science, Innovation and Technology Committee (2023): *The Governance of Artificial Intelligence: Interim Report, Ninth Report of Session 2022–23*, HC 1769
Hutchinson, Allan C. (2022): *Cryptocurrencies and the Regulatory Challenge*, Abingdon, Routledge
Jasanoff, Sheila (2007): *Designs on Nature*, Princeton, Princeton University Press
Jennings, W. Ivor (1964): *The Law and the Constitution*, London, University of London Press
Johnson, David R. and Post, David (1996): 'Law and Borders—The Rise of Law in Cyberspace' 48 *Stanford Law Review* 1367
Joseph, Wendy (2022): *Unlawful Killings*, London, Doubleday
Kass, Leon R. (2002): *Life, Liberty, and the Defense of Dignity*, San Francisco, Encounter Books
Katsh, Ethan and Rabinovich-Einy, Orna (2017): *Digital Justice*, Oxford, Oxford University Press
Kerr, Ian (2010): 'Digital Locks and the Automation of Virtue', in Michael Geist (ed), *From 'Radical Extremism' to 'Balanced Copyright': Canadian Copyright and the Digital Agenda*, Toronto, Irwin Law 247
Kletzer, Christoph (2021): 'Law, Disintermediation and the Future of Trust' in Larry A. DiMatteo, André Janssen, Pietro Ortolani, Francisco de Elizalde, Michel Cannarsa, and Mateja Durovic (eds), *The Cambridge Handbook of Lawyering in the Digital Age*, Cambridge, Cambridge University Press, 312
Latour, Bruno (2010): *The Making of Law*, Cambridge, Polity Press
Law Commission (2023): *Digital Assets: Final Report (Law Com No 412)* (HC 1486)
Legal Services Board and Solicitors' Regulation Authority (2022): *Social acceptability of technology in legal services*, London
Legg, Michael and Bell, Felicity (2020): *Artificial Intelligence and the Legal Profession*, Oxford, Hart
Lessig, Lawrence (1999): *Code and Other Laws of Cyberspace*, New York, Basic Books
Levin, Sam (2022): 'San Francisco Lawmakers Vote to Ban Killer Robots in Drastic U-turn', *The Guardian*, December 7, available at https://www.theguardian.com/us-news/2022/dec/06/san-francisco-lawmakers-ban-killer-robots-u-turn
Liu, Hin-Yan (2018): 'The Power Structure of Artificial Intelligence', 10 *Law, Innovation and Technology* 197
Llewellyn Karl, N (1940): 'The Normative, the Legal, and the Law-Jobs: The Problem of Juristic Method' 49 *Yale Law Journal* 1355

Low, Kelvin FK and Yeo, Ernie GS (2017): 'Bitcoins and Other Cryptocurrencies as Property?' 9 *Law, Innovation and Technology* 235

Low, Kelvin FK and Mik, Eliza (2020): 'Pause the Blockchain Legal Revolution' (2020) 69 *International Comparative Law Quarterly* 135

Macaulay, Stewart (1963): 'Non Contractual Relations in Business: A Preliminary Study' 28 *American Sociological Review* 55

Marr, Bernard (2023): 'Virtual Influencer Noonouri Lands Record Deal: Is She the Future of Music?' *Forbes*, September 5 available at https://www.forbes.com/sites/bernardmarr/2023/09/05/virtual-influencer-noonoouri-lands-record-deal-is-she-the-future-of-music/

Mattei, Ugo and Nader, Laura (2008): *Plunder: When the Rule of Law is Illegal*, Malden, MA, Blackwell

McBride, Nicholas J. (2022): *Letters to a Law Student*, 5th ed, Harlow, Pearson

Micklethwait, John and Wooldridge, Adrian (2014): *The Fourth Revolution*, London, Penguin

Micklitz, Hans W. (2023): 'AI Standards, EU Digital Policy Legislation and Stakeholder Participation' 12 *Journal of European Consumer and Market Law* 212

Mill, John S. (originally 1859): 'On Liberty' in J.S. Mill (ed), *Utilitarianism* (ed Mary Warnock), London, Fontana Press, 1962

Morozov, Evgeny (2013): *To Save Everything, Click Here*, London, Allen Lane

Newburn, Tim and Ward, Andrew (2022): *Orderly Britain*, London, Robinson

Noto la Diega, Guido (2023): *Internet of Things and the Law*, Abingdon, Routledge

O'Neil, Cathy (2016): *Weapons of Math Destruction*, London, Allen Lane

Ord, Toby (2020): *The Precipice*, London, Bloomsbury

Pavia, Will (2023): 'Injuries Confirm Paltrow hit skier from Behind, Trial Told' *The Times*, March 25, p. 5

Pearl, Tracy (2018): 'Compensation at the Crossroads: Autonomous Vehicles and Alternative Victim Compensation Schemes' 60 *William and Mary Law Review* 1827

Plomer, Aurora (2015): *Patents, Human Rights and Access to Science*, Cheltenham, Edward Elgar

Prosser, William L. (1960): 'Privacy' 48 *California Law Review* 383

Raz, Joseph (1977): 'The Rule of Law and its Virtues' 93 *Law Quarterly Review* 195

Reed, Chris and Murray, Andrew (2018): *Rethinking the Jurisprudence of Cyberspace*, Cheltenham, Edward Elgar

Reidenberg, Joel R. (2005): 'Technology and Internet Jurisdiction' 153 *University of Pennsylvania Law Review* 1951

Reynold, Frederic (2019): *High Principle, Low Politics, and the Emergence of the Supreme Court*, London, Wildy, Simmonds and Hill Publishing

Roberts, Simon (1979): *Order and Dispute*, London, Penguin

Rockström, Johan, et al (2009): 'Planetary Boundaries: Exploring the Safe Operating Space for Humanity' 14 *Ecology and Society* 32

Rodell, Fred (1936): 'Goodbye to Law Reviews' 23 *Virginia Law Review* 38

Rosa, Hartmut (2015): *Social Acceleration*, New York, Columbia University Press

Roth, Andrea (2016): 'Trial by Machine' 104 *Georgetown Law Journal* 1245

Rozenberg, Joshua (2020): *Enemies of the People? Bristol*, Bristol University Press

Russell, Stuart (2020): *Human Compatible*, London, Penguin

Sayre, Francis (1933): Public Welfare Offences', 33 *Columbia Law Review* 55

Scalia, Antonin (1989): 'Originalism: The Lesser Evil' 57 *U. Cin LR* 849

Schmidt, Harald and Schwartz, Jason L. (2016): 'The Mission of National Commissions: Mapping the Forms and Functions of Bioethics Advisory Bodies' 26 *Kennedy Institute Ethics Jnl* 431
Sedley, Stephen (2018): *Law and the Whirligig of Time*, Oxford, Hart
Senthillingam, Meera (2014): 'Shared Space, Where the Streets Have No Rules' September 22, available at https://edition.cnn.com/2014/09/22/living/shared-spaces/index.html
Sharma, Vivek (2022): 'Introducing a Personal Boundary for Horizon Worlds and Venues' February 4, available at https://about.fb.com/news/2022/02/personal-boundary-horizon/
Shearing, Clifford and Stenning, Phillip (1985): 'From the Panopticon to Disney World: The Development of Discipline' in A.N. Doob and E.L. Greenspan (eds), *Perspectives in Criminal Law: Essays in Honour of John Ll. J. Edwards*, Toronto, Canada Law Book, 335
Stock, Gregory (2003): *Redesigning Humans*, London, Profile Books
Sumption, Jonathan (2019): *Trials of the State*, London, Profile Books
Sumption, Jonathan (2021): *Law in a Time of Crisis*, London, Profile Books
Sun, Haochen (2022): *Technology and the Public Interest*, Cambridge, Cambridge University Press
Sunstein, Cass R. (2005): *Laws of Fear*, Cambridge, Cambridge University Press
Susskind, Jamie (2022): *The Digital Republic*, London, Bloomsbury
Susskind, Richard (2017): *Tomorrow's Lawyers*, Oxford, Oxford University Press
Tegmark, Max (2017): *Life 3.0*, London, Allen Lane
Thompson, E.P. (1975): *Whigs and Hunters: The Origin of the Black Act*, New York: Pantheon Books
Todd, Paul (2019): 'Electronic Bills of Lading, Blockchains and Smart Contracts' 27 *International Journal of Law and Information Technology* 339
Turner, Janice (2023): 'A Womb Must Not Become a Spare Part for Sale' *The Times*, August 26, 23
Tyler, Tom R. (2006): *Why People Obey the Law*, Princeton, Princeton University Press
Warnock, Mary (1993): 'Philosophy and Ethics' in C. Cookson, G. Nowak, and D. Thierbach (eds), *Genetic Engineering—The New Challenge*, Munich, European Patent Office, 67
Warren, Samuel D. and Brandeis, Louis D (1890): 'The Right to Privacy' 5 *Harvard Law Review* 193
Waterson, Jim (2022): '"Wagatha Christie" Trial: Vardy Ordered to Pay up to 1.5m of Rooney's Legal Fees' *The Guardian*, October 4 https://www.theguardian.com/uk-news/2022/oct/04/rebekah-vardy-to-pay-15m-in-legal-fees-after-losing-wagatha-christie-libel-trial
Weitzenboeck, Emily M. (2014): 'Hybrid Net: The Regulatory Framework of ICANN and the DNS' 22 *International Journal of Law and Information Technology* 49
Wilson, W.A. (1969): 'Questions of Fact and Degree' 32 *Modern Law Review* 361
Wittes, Benjamin and Blum, Gabriella (2015): *The Future of Violence*, New York, Basic Books
Wolff, Jonathan (2010): 'Five Types of Risky Situation' 2 *Law Innovation and Technology* 151
Wood, Philip R. (2017): *The Fall of the Priests and the Rise of the Lawyers*, Oxford, Hart
World Justice Project (2019): '*Rule of Law Index 2019*', available at https://worldjusticeproject.org/sites/default/files/documents/ROLI-2019-Reduced.pdf (last accessed March 20, 2021)

Yeung, Karen (2019): 'Why Worry about Decision-Making by Machine?' in Karen Yeung and Martin Lodge (eds), *Algorithmic Regulation*, Oxford, Oxford University Press, 21

Zirin, James D. (2016): *Supremely Partisan*, Lanham, Rowman and Littlefield

Zittrain, Jonathan (2008): *The Future of the Internet*, London, Penguin

Zuboff, Shoshana (2019): *The Age of Surveillance Capitalism*, London, Profile Books

INDEX

Taylor & Francis Group
an informa business

Taylor & Francis eBooks

www.taylorfrancis.com

A single destination for eBooks from Taylor & Francis with increased functionality and an improved user experience to meet the needs of our customers.

90,000+ eBooks of award-winning academic content in Humanities, Social Science, Science, Technology, Engineering, and Medical written by a global network of editors and authors.

TAYLOR & FRANCIS EBOOKS OFFERS:

A streamlined experience for our library customers

A single point of discovery for all of our eBook content

Improved search and discovery of content at both book and chapter level

REQUEST A FREE TRIAL

support@taylorfrancis.com

For Product Safety Concerns and Information please contact our EU representative GPSR@taylorandfrancis.com Taylor & Francis Verlag GmbH, Kaufingerstraße 24, 80331 München, Germany

Printed and bound by CPI Group (UK) Ltd, Croydon, CR0 4YY

16/06/2025

01901671-0001